Fasting: Unlocking Spiritual Power and Breakthrough

Volume 2

Personal Reflections

Sheldon Juell, Ph.D.

To Vanessa

May the Lord bring the spiritual
Power you need to live in daily breakthroughs.
May the Lord give you increasing victory in
your life

Blessings

Sheldon

Fasting: Unlocking Spiritual Power and Breakthrough, Volume 2, Personal Reflections

ISBN: 978-1-59755-387-2

Published by: Advantage Books ™
Longwood Florida, USA
www.advbookstore.com

Library of Congress Catalog Number: 2015942743

Cover Designed by: Calvin Wray
Juice Creative
www.juiceonline.ca

First Printing: February 2016
15 16 17 18 19 20 21 10 9 8 7 6 5 4 3 2
Printed in the United States of America

Acknowledgements

I, first of all, want to thank my Lord and Saviour Jesus Christ for His gracious gift of salvation that has been freely given to me, and the Holy Spirit who guided, directed and empowered me to complete this project. I never dreamed that I could start and complete a project of this magnitude, but I did by the grace of God. Second, to God's gift of love, my wife, Ivone who inspires, supports, and encourages me to go after my dreams, and to become the person that God intends for me to be. I love you very much.

I am grateful and sincerely appreciate the following men of God who took time out of their busy schedules to read *Fasting: Unlocking Spiritual Power and Breakthrough* and write an endorsement.

To my friend, Pastor and author, Dr. Barry Buzza, Northside Church, Coquitlam BC. Thank you for writing such an inspiring Foreword. You are truly a living example of Jesus Christ as you reveal the profound truths of the Word of God through your life and ministry.

To President Steve Falkiner, The Canadian Foursquare Church, may the Lord bless you and give you wisdom as you continue to give leadership, guidance, and direction to pastors and church leaders across Canada and throughout the world.

To Dr. Ken Deeks, Vice President for Academic Affairs. May the Lord bless you and give you wisdom as you continue to give academic leadership and direction to the faculty and in educating, equipping, and empowering the students to academic excellence at Pacific Life Bible College.

Foreword by Dr. Barry Buzza

It's Fall in British Columbia as I write this foreword to my friend, Dr. Sheldon Juell's, classic book on *Fasting: Unlocking Spiritual Power and Breakthrough.* I'm sitting in my living room, looking out at the front yards of my neighbor's and our homes. Our front lawn is carpet green and free of weeds, while our neighbor's lawn is littered with an unattractive mixture of crabgrass, clover, buttercups and dandelions. I'm happy with our lush grass and my neighbor is discouraged with his carpet of weeds.

Two weeks ago, as we were chatting outside, he asked me what my secret of success was. I didn't want to insult or discourage my friend. I really like him, but I had to tell the truth. I said that our healthy lawn was due to a combination of good fertilizer and regularly attacking weeds. Just by keeping my lawn well nourished, the good strong grass pushes out weeds that don't belong, but I still need to keep careful watch out for weeds and deal ruthlessly with them as soon as they appear.

In the formula I shared with my neighbor that day, is a life lesson that will help us keep our souls as healthy as my front lawn. The twofold secret of daily nourishment of our souls, plus regularly dealing with invasive predators, will keep our hearts pure and soft.

In each of our lives, there are enemies who want to see our souls get tangled up in destructive weeds. As Jesus illustrated in the third soil of his parable of the farmer who scattered seeds, those weeds, if not dealt with severely, will ultimate kill any fruitfulness we are meant to produce.

In Sheldon Juell's newest book, *Fasting: Unlocking Spiritual Power and Breakthrough*, I believe he has clearly introduced us to one of Jesus' most powerful weed killers and fertilizers. Maybe we could think of the Spiritual Fast as "Weed and Feed" for our souls.

As far back as the Bible story goes, we can see the battle that all of us face with this enemy called "the flesh". Adam and Eve were instructed by Jesus himself to not eat the fruit in middle of the garden. We can easily picture the conversation between the Angel of Light and Eve.

"Why don't you try it? It's the best tasting fruit in the entire Garden!"

"Well yes, it certainly does look delicious!"

It didn't seem like it took too much convincing for him to get Eve to pick the fruit and taste it.
And it was sumptuous! "Adam, you have to try it. You'll really like it!"

Even more quickly than Eve had succumbed, Adam dove in and joined her. The weeds of their flesh had easily taken root; they'd "*leaned to their own understanding*" and away from the way of God's Word. Before they knew what was happening, Adam's and Eve's souls were polluted with weeds of self-centeredness.

Story after story throughout the Bible record, we see in the lives of our Bible heroes, this same battle between the flesh and the spirit. Cain followed in his parents' footsteps, then Noah, Abraham, Jacob, Achan, Samson, Saul and David. Each of their lawns, from time to time, became infected with weeds.

Turn the page to the New Testament. Maybe daily walking with Jesus would help his followers keep healthy.

One of the stories that shocks us the most was set in a spiritually dynamic scene near the end of the earthly ministry of Jesus. It was Passover, April 30AD. On the very night that Jesus was to die for the sins of the world, he got up after dinner, disrobed and tied a towel around his waist. Then Jesus Christ, God himself, knelt down before each of his disciples and began to wash their feet. He was teaching by his example that the way to be great in the Kingdom of God is to be a servant.

I'm not sure how long it was after that, maybe minutes, that Jesus interrupted his disciples in the middle of an argument. Believe it or not, they were verbally jesting over the question, "Who is the greatest?"

Jesus was righteously disturbed. "Guys, don't you get it? *Among you it is supposed to be different. Those who are the greatest among you should take the lowest rank, and the leader should be like a servant.*"

What had happened? The same thing as happened to Adam and Eve. It's the same battle we have each faced over and over. The weeds of our flesh blow over our souls, and too often take root.

What are we to do? What kind of "Weed and Feed" do we need?

Jesus taught that unless a grain of wheat falls into the ground and dies it abides alone. Paul said that he had to die daily to himself. The weeds of self-centeredness have to die and our souls must be nourished.

There are many nourishing fertilizers with which we can feed our souls. Worship, Bible reading and study, meditation, Christian fellowship, communion ... The list goes on. But I believe one of the most powerful antidotes to infection of the flesh, and health promoting nutrients we can apply to our souls is the discipline of fasting.

Sheldon Juell's treatise on how to unlock spiritual power and breakthrough through fasting is the best I have ever read. This valuable book has been thoroughly researched through meticulous Bible study and historical examples. Everything we need to know about this priceless key to spiritual vitality is in these pages. When I first read *Fasting: Unlocking Spiritual Power and Breakthrough*, I was encouraged and stimulated in the discipline of fasting like never before.

If my neighbor would simply listen to my teaching and follow my example, when it comes to lawn care, he would have a lush green carpet of lawn by next summer. How much more important is it that we hear this expert teaching on fasting, and follow the example of spiritual leaders who have gone before! We would live in Spiritual Power and Breakthrough like Jesus has promised. "*This kind will only come out through fasting and prayer!*" I heartily recommend this book to you. Apply its lessons liberally to the lawn of your souls. You'll be glad you did.

Dr. Barry Buzza
Lead Pastor, Northside Church
Author of "Teach Us To Pray"
Coquitlam, BC Canada

Table of Contents

This book entitled *Personal Reflections* is the companion to *Fasting: Unlocking Spiritual Power and Breakthrough.* Therefore, you will need a copy of both books to complete this in-depth study on fasting. At the end of each fast, you will be asked to ponder personal life situations, respond to relevant questions, and then apply them to your personal life, family, church, and/or ministry. You will be asked to write a prayer that you will address to the Lord that reflects your new commitment and dedication to Him. Each fast also includes a section called *Journaling*, which can be used for spiritual and/or personal insights, areas of spiritual growth, and also writing down thoughts and insights from others who are involved with you in fasting. This can include your family, home group, church, or a corporate fast.

Chapter 1: Introduction to Personal Reflections

The purpose of this chapter is to describe the factors that can become a hindrance to Christians participating in fasting. Moreover, it presents the reasons why Christians, churches, church leaders, and congregations must implement fasting and prayer as a spiritual discipline as a necessary means of throwing off "everything that hinders and the sin that so easily entangles" (Heb. 12:1). Finally, the significance of both corporate and individual fasting as Jesus taught His disciples.

It was after Jesus had been fasting for forty days that the devil came to Him and asked "If you are the Son of God, tell these stones to become bread" (Mt. 4:3). Jesus' response is quite interesting, "It is written: 'Man does not live on bread alone, but on every word that comes from the mouth of God'" (Mt. 4:4). Jesus resisted the temptation by speaking the Word of God to the devil (cf. Deut. 8:3). His response demonstrated that life is not dependent upon bread or food, but being dependent upon God for all sustenance for living. Moreover, importance lies upon our obedience to the will of God and not upon satisfying our physical appetite with food and water. Jesus proved that His Father would take care of Him like He sustained the Israelites in the wilderness by providing food and clothing (cf. Deut. 8:3-5). Jesus provided the greatest example for us to follow by demonstrating the importance of depending upon God as the source of all life.[1]

> He humbled you, causing you to hunger and then feeding you with manna, which neither you nor your fathers had known, to teach you that man does not live on bread alone but on every word that comes from the mouth of the LORD. Your clothes did not wear out and your feet did not swell during these forty years. Know then in your heart that as a man disciplines his son, so the LORD your God disciplines you. . . . He gave you manna to eat in the wilderness, something your ancestors had never known, to humble and test you so that in the end it might go well with you (Deut. 8:3-5, 16).

The Hebrew noun for "manna" used above is מָן *mān*. The Book of Exodus states "It was white like coriander seed and tasted like wafers made with honey" (Ex. 16:31). "The manna was like coriander seed and looked like resin. The people went around gathering it, and then ground it in a hand mill or crushed it in a mortar. They cooked it in a pot or made it into loaves. And it tasted like something made with olive

---

[1] Thoralf Gilbrant, ed., *The Complete Biblical Library, Matthew* (Springfield, IL: World Library Press, Inc., WORDsearch CROSS e-book, 1988), 61-63.

oil. When the dew settled on the camp at night, the manna also came down" (Num. 11:7-9). Through sending manna every night, the Lord was teaching His people that they must look to Him for their daily provision, and to depend upon Him and His Word for their life and the daily and miraculous provision for their needs as stated in Deuteronomy 8:3, 16. Moses explains in Exodus 16 that Yahweh's miraculous provision was to become a daily part of their lives and it was prohibited to be kept or preserved for the following day. If it was, it would become full of maggots and begin to smell (Ex. 16:20). As the Israelites needed fresh manna daily for nourishment and strength so we need to spend time in the Word of God daily to give us spiritual nourishment and strength. Moses commanded the Israelites that only on the day before the Sabbath could they gather enough for two (2) days without any issues of maggots or smell.[2]

Manna was the staple food of the Israelites during their forty years of wandering in the wilderness. At first the Israelites did not know what it was and Moses needed to explain that the manna מָן *mān* was "the bread the LORD has given you to eat" (Ex. 16:15).[3] David, in the Psalms, refers to the manna as "the grain of heaven" וּדְגַן־שָׁמַיִם *ûdĕgan-šāmayim* (Ps. 78:24) and "the bread of angels" לֶחֶם אַבִּירִים *leḥem ʾabbîrîm* or literally the might ones (Ps. 78:25).[4]

> The translation "angel's food", while picturesque, is not accurate. The ASV "bread of the mighty" is preferable. There is no other instance of "angel" being used to translate *ʾabbîrîm*. "Mighty" or "strong" is more usual, and fits the parallel structure of the Psalm better. Possibly it could be "bread of God" using the word *ʾābîr* (q.v.) as a surrogate for deity (cf. Jn. 6:33). . . . If the Word of God is his creative instrument in bringing the cosmos into existence (Gen. 1:3ff.; Ps. 33:6, 9), then here too what God utters from his mouth is concretely realized. Man can only survive by depending on his saving creative Word.[5]

In Deuteronomy 8:3-5, Moses also states "that man does not live on bread alone but on every word that comes from the mouth of the LORD". It is interesting that the Hebrew noun for bread is לֶחֶם *lechem* and has figurative meanings throughout the Old Testament.

1. "The bread of heaven" refers to the manna which came down upon the Israelites in the wilderness (Ps. 105:40).
2. "the bread of adversity" refers to an overwhelming sense of affliction and sorrow that took away the appetite for any food (Ps. 80:5; Isa. 30:20).
3. "the bread of sorrow" is food obtained and enjoyed through much labor and grief (Ps. 127:2).
4. "the bread of affliction" (and the water of affliction) connotes coarse and scanty provisions given to prisoners who were to be treated with great cruelty (Deut. 16:3; 1 Kgs. 22:27).
5. "the bread of the governor" refers to his salary (Neh. 5:14).

---

[2] מָן *mān* "4620", In Thoralf Gilbrant, ed., *The Complete Biblical Library Hebrew-English Dictionary, Kaph-Mem* (Springfield, IL: World Library Press, Inc., WORDsearch CROSS e-book, 1998.).

[3] לֶחֶם *lechem* "4035", in Gilbrant, ed., *The Complete Biblical Library Hebrew-English Dictionary, Kaph-Mem.*

[4] מָן "1209" In R. Laird Harris, Gleason L. Archer Jr., and Bruce K. Waltke, eds. *Theological Wordbook of the Old Testament* (Chicago, IL: Moody Press, 1999), 511.

[5] מָן "1209" In Harris, Archer Jr., and Waltke, eds., *Theological Wordbook of the Old Testament*, 511-12.

6. “the bread of humans” means common food (Eze. 24:17).
7. “the bread of mourners” was the food eaten by people in mourning (Hos. 9:4).
8. “the bread of wickedness, of deceit, of violence, of idleness” is that which was acquired by fraud, robbery, oppression, or laziness and even refers to the wickedness, laziness and deceit in which some souls take delight (Pr. 4:17; 20:17; 31:27).
9. “bread pleasant when eaten in secret” means unlawful and sinful pleasures (Pr. 9:17).
10. “bread” or “bread and water” often denotes everything necessary to sustain life (Isa. 3:1; 33:16).[6]
11. “bread which strengthens man’s heart” refers to God as the source of physical, emotional, mental strength and energy (Ps. 104:14-15).[7]

The Israelite’s exodus from Egypt happened so quickly that they only brought unleavened bread dough since they had no time to make bread for their journey out of bondage at the hands of Pharaoh (Ex. 12:39). It should be noted that the two (2) loaves used for the wave offering were leavened bread.

> From wherever you live, bring two loaves made of two-tenths of an ephah of the finest flour, baked with yeast, as a wave offering of firstfruits to the LORD (Lev. 23:17).
>
> The Pentecost wave loaves were to be baked with leaven! So leaven cannot always be a principle of evil. The “bread of wickedness” (Pr. 4:17) or the “bread of deceit” (Pr. 20:17) is always obtained by wrong and results in bitterness of life. No better is the “bread of adversity” (Isa. 30:20), which spells times of persecution, or the “bread eaten in secret” (Pr. 9:17) with the seductress, for the act of adultery will poison a man’s whole life.[8]

As we have seen, God was teaching His people that as manna and bread were used to teach His people that He alone is the source of all life and trying to find anything that can only come from God is futile and temporal. It is only through the Word of God—as the manna and bread—that we can find ultimate satisfaction and survive, grow, and thrive in every area of our lives.

As we have studied, fasting is not something that was instituted in our modern day. It was established in ancient times and has been practiced by various religions and cultures for millenniums. Overall, fasting serves the metaphysical needs of chastening the soul, repentance, atonement, and redemption, physical, emotional, and mental health, which are the focus of religious and cultural fasting. Throughout the centuries, men and women of God have testified of the miracles that have occurred through fasting and prayer. For example, Esther, the widow (Lk. 2:36-37) and Christian leaders, such as: Martin Luther, John Calvin, Jonathan Edwards, Charles Finney, Andrew Murray, and many others.

The early church and the Early Church Fathers recognized fasting as a channel through which people could acquire spiritual power.

---

[6] לֶחֶם *lechem* “4035”, Gilbrant, ed., The Complete Biblical Library Hebrew-English Dictionary, Kaph-Mem.

[7] לֶחֶם *lechem* “1105”, In Harris, Archer Jr., and Waltke, eds, *Theological Wordbook of the Old Testament*, 477. Frank E. Gaebelein, ed., *The Expositor's Bible Commentary, Volume 5: Psalms, Proverbs, Ecclesiastes, Song of Songs* (Grand Rapids, MI: Zondervan Publishing House, 1991), WORD*search* CROSS e-book, 661. James Luther Mays, ed., *Harper’s Bible Commentary* (San Francisco, CA: Harper & Row, 1988), 480.

[8] לֶחֶם *lechem* “1105”, In Harris, Archer Jr., and Waltke, eds, *Theological Wordbook of the Old Testament*, 477.

> Fasting is calculated to bring a note of urgency and importunity into our praying, and to give force to our pleading in the court of heaven. The man who prays with fasting is giving heaven notice that he is truly in earnest; that he will not give up nor let God go without the blessing; that he does not intend to take "no" for an answer. Not only so, but he is expressing his earnestness in a divinely appointed way. He is using a means that God has chosen to make his voice to be heard on high.[9]

He also states that during the first few centuries, fasting was seen as a channel of spiritual power for the New Testament believers. However, over time spirituality declined, and the power and influence of the Holy Spirit became less of the life-giving force within the lives of the believers.

> As spirituality waned and worldliness flourished in the churches, the power and gifts of the Spirit were withdrawn. With the loss of that inward power, men could only cling to what they had left, its outward accompaniment. More and more emphasis was placed upon the outward act of fasting, though bereft of the inward spirit that alone could give it value. Asceticism became the mark of piety and spirituality.[10]

Paul's prediction about "having a form of godliness but denying its power" (2 Tim. 3:5) was being fulfilled. The spiritual erosion that had begun in the first century church is still an issue in believers today. But when we consider what the Word of God declares in regards to fasting and prayer, we can see that together these two spiritual disciplines are powerful channels to affect the power of God within the person's life. It is this fire of God that produces the fruit of the Holy Spirit (Gal. 5:22-23) and also the fruit of righteousness and spiritual power that conquers the lust of the flesh and the enemy's deception. It is as Paul states concerning the reciprocal action that occurs between our sinful nature which strives for control and the Spirit who leads us.

> And this is my prayer: that your love may abound more and more in knowledge and depth of insight, so that you may be able to discern what is best and may be pure and blameless until the day of Christ, filled with the fruit of righteousness that comes through Jesus Christ—to the glory and praise of God (Phil. 1:9-11).

> For the sinful nature desires what is contrary to the Spirit, and the Spirit what is contrary to the sinful nature. They are in conflict with each other, so that you do not do what you want. But if you are led by the Spirit, you are not under law (Gal. 5:17-18).

It is through fasting and prayer that we submit ourselves to Jesus Christ and experience spiritual conquest and personal revival that comes through the Holy Spirit. Likewise, fasting subdues our sinful nature and to the extent that our sin nature is subdued to that extent the Holy Spirit intensifies his transforming work within our lives. Moreover, the Holy Spirit (1) brings a sense of yielding ourselves to the Lord; (2) renews spiritual vision and our faith in the Lord; (3) inspires us with the resolve to follow and obey God's will for our lives. When we add this all up, fasting and prayer results in a spiritual

---

[9] Arthur Wallis, *God's Chosen Fast: A Spiritual and Practical Guide to Fasting* (Fort Washington, PA: CLC Publications, 1968), 42.

[10] Wallis, *God's Chosen Fast*, 11.

weapon like none other that destroys spiritual strongholds and unlocks the power of God in your life, your family, and your church. Arthur Wallis states,

> In giving us the privilege of fasting as well as praying, God has added a powerful weapon to our spiritual armory. In her folly and ignorance the Church has largely looked upon it as obsolete. She has thrown it down in some dark corner to rust, and there it has lain forgotten for centuries. An hour of impending crisis for the Church and the world demands its recovery.[11]

We need to come to the place where we believe that the spiritual discipline of fasting is not rooted in proving to God our seriousness, our resolve to resist temptation and the schemes of the enemy, and/or seeking God only to answer our prayers. Even though these represent Christian virtues and benefits of fasting, our inspiration can only be the result of our hunger for more of the Lord, a hunger for living a godly life, and a hunger to

> "Love the Lord your God with all your heart and with all your soul and with all your mind". This is the first and greatest commandment. And the second is like it: "Love your neighbor as yourself". All the Law and the Prophets hang on these two commandments (Mt. 22:37-40; 2 Chr. 7:14; Zech. 7:5).

We can see throughout the Word of God, the church fathers, historical records, and church leaders today who offer valuable insight into the relevance of the spiritual discipline of fasting in the lives of Christians today. Yet many Christians struggle with the relevance of fasting in today's society. Have we come to the place where we have allowed the deception of the enemy to dictate our spiritual lives? Are we so out of tune with the Holy Spirit that we can no longer distinguish between the voice of God and the enemy? As we approach the return of the Lord Jesus Christ, the attacks, deception, and schemes of the enemy are going to increase and we need to be so in tune with the Lord that we know Him when He calls. Many Christians today struggle and live in bondage to the enemy and need strength to stand against his schemes. Jesus states that His sheep know His voice and follow Him,

> The watchman opens the gate for him, and the sheep listen to his voice. He calls his own sheep by name and leads them out. When he has brought out all his own, he goes on ahead of them, and his sheep follow him because they know his voice. But they will never follow a stranger; in fact, they will run away from him because they do not recognize a stranger's voice". Jesus used this figure of speech, but they did not understand what he was telling them. Therefore Jesus said again, "I tell you the truth, I am the gate for the sheep. All who ever came before me were thieves and robbers, but the sheep did not listen to them" (Jn. 10:3-8).

The Wilderness Trap

As the Israelites departed from their lengthy Egyptian bondage (400 years, Gen. 15:13), they needed to choose which route they would take in their conquest of Canaan. They choose the longer southern route, by the Red Sea, since it led to freedom and was inhabited by their kinsmen and avoided the direct

---

[11] Wallis, *God's Chosen Fast*, 43.

northern route, through Philistine territory, on their way to the Promised Land. The Israelites were not strong enough yet and developed enough for life outside of bondage to confront enemy strongholds, military forces, and highly developed people groups.[12]

Before we delve into the trap and cycle of defeat the Israelites encountered in the wilderness, it is important to state possible reasons why they did not immediately enter and conquer the Promised Land.

1. Egypt still ruled southern Palestine where the Israelites would encounter opposition if their conquest came from the desert.
2. They had been in Egyptian bondage for many generations and were not physically, mentally, emotionally strong. They did not have the military courage, resolve, resilience, and training to conquer highly civilized military forces of the inhabitants of Canaan. They also lacked the courage, resolve, and resilience to conquer an enemy.
3. They were nomads traveling and living in the wilderness, their flocks, herds of animals, and lack of military training facilities and weapons made it impossible to sustain a prolonged siege on enemy territory.
4. The Israelites needed wilderness and military training under the leadership of Moses and Joshua to become an effective military force.
5. They needed develop and maintain necessary physical resources and a supply of basic needs to sustain them through a lengthy and unrelenting military confrontation.
6. The Israelites were not ready to enter the Promised Land because of their bad choices and lived in a perpetual state of defeatism.[13]

The success of the Israelite conquest was dependent upon growing physically, emotionally, mentally, and spiritually. Since they had spent the last 400 years in Egyptian bondage they needed a strong leader like Moses and Joshua, life situations, and the school of hard knocks to develop courage, resolve, and self-denial to unite them as the people of God.

> Their strenuous life developed physical strength and endurance, courage and skill in warfare. It impressed upon them the necessity and advantages of combined action, and facilitated the work of Moses in moulding the incipient nation. Their constant feeling of hunger and fear of attack deepened their sense of dependence upon divine power. Their simple religious life, which apparently centred in Kadesh, enabled Moses to impress upon them his own sense of Jehovah's constant presence and care for his people. On the other hand, as their judge and prophet, he was able definitely to illustrate those simple ethical principles, which appear from the first to have been the cornerstones of Israel's faith and civilization. Thus, in divine Providence, quietly out in the solitude and privation of the wilderness, under the leadership of one of the world's great prophets, a nation, ambitious, strong of limb and loyal to its tribal God and leader, was being prepared for the destiny which awaited it.[14]

Like the Israelites, do you feel like you are trapped in a revolving door that year after year you move from being trapped, living in bondage and/or defeat, repentance, seeking help, and then sensing some

---

[12] Charles Foster Kent, *The Heroes and Crises of Early Hebrew History: From the Creation to the Death of Moses*, The Historical Bible (New York: Charles Scribner's Sons, 1908), 214.

[13] Kent, *The Heroes and Crises of Early Hebrew History*, 214-15.

[14] Kent, *The Heroes and Crises of Early Hebrew History*, 216.

level of freedom only to fall back into the same trap? Are you taking the long route to your Promised Land or are you on the short direct route? Do you feel that you are falling into the same problem like your father or your mother? This is the same cycle of defeat that the Israelites lived in for forty years in the wilderness and throughout their history. They delayed entering the Promised Land because they made bad choices. To break free from this cycle of defeat, we need to either confront the areas in our lives where we have made bad choices, before we start our time of fasting, or these areas will inevitably surface during fasting. These bad choices include, setting up of idols (anything that takes the place of God in our lives), murmuring and complaining, not obeying and trusting God with our lives and provision, believing that He will not fulfill His promises, or not following God wholeheartedly (Num. 32:11). The choice is yours. We cannot continue to do things the same way and expect different results. The Word of God describes this cycle of defeat as generational curses.

> You shall not make for yourself an image in the form of anything in heaven above or on the earth beneath or in the waters below. You shall not bow down to them or worship them; for I, the LORD your God, am a jealous God, punishing the children for the sin of the parents to the third and fourth generation of those who hate me, but showing love to a thousand generations of those who love me and keep my commandments (Ex. 20:4-6).

Pastor John Hagee, in his book *Life's Challenges, Your Opportunities*, states

> When the same bad habits control you and those you love from generation to generation, you are mired in the pits of an inherited problem that can only be resolved by the supernatural deliverance of the Holy Spirit.
>
> Don't become ensnared in your problem! It's time to break your down-spiral pattern. It is time to take the steps out of your bondage and prepare yourself to receive your promise.
>
> You can choose to take another lap around Mt. Sinai, extending your time in the problem, or you can determine that you are no longer going to tolerate a problem-ridden life. The children of Israel were faced with two choices: wander aimlessly in the wilderness for years, or go directly to their provision. We are faced with the same choices; in which direction re you going? Are you going to stay in your problem, or are you going to walk into your provision?
>
> Remember, the Israelites had many reasons to rejoice. Pharaoh, the man who was worshiped as an earthly god, was drowned along with his mighty army, and the Jews were delivered from bondage. Remember this truth . . . . When we walk out of Egypt (bondage), through the Red Sea (water baptism), and enter the wilderness (problem), we will be faced with making right choices until we reach our provision (promised land).[15]

Moreover, the reason why people cannot break free from their problems is because they make excuses thinking that the problem(s) will somehow go away, like the sacred custom of the "scapegoat" on the Day of Atonement.

> Aaron is to offer the bull for his own sin offering to make atonement for himself and his household. Then he is to take the two goats and present them before the LORD at the entrance to the tent of meeting. He is to cast lots for the two goats—one lot for the LORD and the other for the

[15] John Hagee, *Life's Challenges, Your Opportunities* (Lake Mary, FL: Charisma House, 2009), 61-62.

> scapegoat. Aaron shall bring the goat whose lot falls to the LORD and sacrifice it for a sin offering. But the goat chosen by lot as the scapegoat shall be presented alive before the LORD to be used for making atonement by sending it into the wilderness as a scapegoat (Lev. 16:6-10).

On the Day of Atonement, the high priest would choose two goats; one would be sacrificed on the altar and the other would be become the scapegoat, שָׂעִיר *sā'îr* or "goat of removal" that the high priest would lay his hands upon the head of the goat transferring the sins, rebellion, agonies and anxieties of the Israelites and then the goat would be led away into the wilderness, illustrating the removal of their sins and rebellion.[16] Many Christians have adopted a type of pathological pattern to explain their behaviour while trapped in their problem. This is referred to as *excusiology*.[17]

> You are not trapped in your problem because you are a bad person; you are trapped because you refuse to change and you continually fail to walk away from bad behavior. You would rather make excuses instead of right choices. . . . People who stay trapped in their problems make excuses a ceremonial ritual, and when analyzing this habitual behavior one can discover a pathological pattern that keeps God's children from receiving their promise. They are deceived into thinking that making excuses will somehow carry their problems away. Nothing could be further away from the truth.[18]

Excusiology includes three (3) areas of pathology:

1. *Denial*. This is simply a rejection of the reality that you have a problem(s);
2. *Refusing responsibility*. This is where the blame and/or guilt is transferred onto someone else. A good example of this is seen above and what can be referred to as "scapegoatism";
3. *But syndrome*. This is simply "I did it, but . . ." It is admitting that we were involved in the problem(s) but, we blame someone or something else.[19]

These pathologies are a trap the enemy uses to delay us from finding freedom and the fulfillment and/or promises of God for our lives. If we truly desire to be free and take hold of all the Lord has for us, we need to confess that we have a problem, and take responsibility for our part of the problem. Like the Israelites, when you are faced with an obstacle, temptation, difficult decision, or struggles do you choose to take another lap around Mt. Sinai disobeying the Word of God and murmuring and complaining? Even though the Israelites witnessed many miracles performed by the Lord, such as, Moses and the burning bush (Ex. 3), the 10 plagues of Egypt (Ex. 7-11), the parting of the Red Sea (Ex. 14, 15), and the Ten Commandments (Ex. 20; Deut. 5), they still chose to take many laps in the wilderness before entering the Promised Land. Like them, do you feel as though you are bound for the Promised Land, yet feel as

---

16 שָׂעִיר *sā'îr* "7988", In Gilbrant, ed., *The Complete Biblical Library Hebrew-English Dictionary, Sin-Taw* (Springfield, IL: World Library Press, Inc., 1998), WORD*search* CROSS e-book. "Scapegoat", In Chad Brand et al., eds., *Holman Illustrated Bible Dictionary* (Nashville, TN: Holman Bible Publishers, 2003), 1450.

17 Glenn Van Ekeren, *Speakers Sourcebook II* (New York: Prentice Hall Press, 2002), 148.

18 Hagee, *Life's Challenges, Your Opportunities*, 62-63.

19 Hagee, *Life's Challenges, Your Opportunities*, 64-65.

though you are trapped in your current problem with what seems to be no way of escape? You will never enter the Promised Land (receive the fullness of the Father's promise and provision) until you leave Egypt (bondage).

To break the wilderness trap of *excusiology*, the following are necessary steps to enter into the Promised Land of the Lord's promise and provision:[20]

1. Accept the Problem. When problems arise, and they certainly will, the tendency is to ignore, deny, or avoid the problem. This type of response only causes the problem to further trap us into a downward spiral of defeat. Resolving problems in our lives, we must, first of all, acknowledge and then accept the problem. The Word of God does not call us to surrender to the problem; we must speak the faith of God into the problem. Whether the problem is a sickness, disease, a financial situation, family situation, emotional distress, or emotional and/or psychological in nature, the pathway to the provision lies in accepting the problem and then speaking the Word of God into our problem.

2. Take Responsibility for Your Behaviour. The pathway from the problem to the provision requires taking responsibility and accepting the consequences for our actions. For example, Adam blamed both God and Eve, "The woman you put here with me—she gave me some fruit from the tree, and I ate it", and Eve blamed the serpent "The serpent deceived me, and I ate" (Gen. 3:12-13). When we ignore, deny, avoid or do not take responsibility for the problem we become "trapped in the wilderness and live a life of absolute misery, attempting to avoid the very problem whose solution holds the key to your success. . . . The person who accepts responsibility for his or her problem is the person who will overcome it".[21] We need to ask ourselves, how long do I want to remain in the wilderness trap?

3. Admit Your Faults. It is never easy to admit our faults or that we were wrong. It may take everything we have to speak these words of freedom, but until you do, we will remain in the cycle of defeat and continue to take another lap through the wilderness. It requires profound spiritual and moral resilience to admit our faults. However, we need to be honest with ourselves and know the difference, especially in the case of some form of abusive, that the abuse that we have suffered is not our fault.

4. Forgive. There are many benefits to forgiveness. However, the primary misunderstood fact about forgiveness is that it is NOT for the benefit of the person who lied to you, hurt you, offended you, rejected you, mistreated you, or caused you pain or discomfort. Forgiveness is first and foremost for *your* benefit. Therefore, we should be eager to forgive those who have offended us in as Jesus stated in the Sermon on the Mount, "For if you forgive other people when they sin against you, your heavenly Father will also forgive you. But if you do not forgive others their sins, your Father will not forgive your sins" (Mt. 6:14-15).

   Forgiveness is the key that unlocks the door of resentment and the handcuffs of hatred. Forgiveness is a supernatural power that breaks the chains of bitterness, bringing joy that is unspeakable and full of glory. Forgiveness is not softhearted foolishness. It's the first step to ending the spiritual and emotional problem you find yourself in right now. . . . Forgiveness is not weakness; it takes great strength to forgive. Forgiveness is the first step toward happiness, toward

[20] The following outline has been modified from Hagee, *Life's Challenges, Your Opportunities*, 67-89.

[21] Hagee, *Life's Challenges, Your Opportunities*, 69, 71.

hope, and toward healing. Forgiveness is a huge step out of the problem and into the provision of God.[22]

If you find that it is difficult to forgive someone such as your spouse, your mother, your father, a sibling, relative, co-worker, other believers in Jesus Christ, yourself, or even God or . . . . . . you have believed the lie from the father of lies. "You belong to your father, the devil, and you want to carry out your father's desires. He was a murderer from the beginning, not holding to the truth, for there is no truth in him. When he lies, he speaks his native language, for he is a liar and the father of lies" (Jn. 8:44).

We continually need to remind ourselves not to listen and believe the lies of the enemy who says that you don't need to forgive. You see, the enemy is very crafty, scheming, and will use any area of our weaknesses to his advantage. If you listen and obey him that, "unforgiving spirit is a weapon of control over people, and that, my friend, is the sin of witchcraft. Unforgiveness is a form of bondage that thrives on hate and resentment"[23] (cf. 1 Sam. 15:23). However, if we look to Jesus, His grace is sufficient and His power is made perfect in our weakness.

> "My grace is sufficient for you, for my power is made perfect in weakness". Therefore I will boast all the more gladly about my weaknesses, so that Christ's power may rest on me. That is why, for Christ's sake, I delight in weaknesses, in insults, in hardships, in persecutions, in difficulties. For when I am weak, then I am strong (2 Cor. 12:9-10).

If we truly desire to find peace, healing, and a sense of well-being in mind, body, and spirit, then we must believe that forgiving others, ourselves, and God and the ramifications of forgiveness is a vital part of living the life that Jesus lived. Mark Twain said it well, "Forgiveness is the fragrance that the violet sheds on the heel that has crushed it".[24] Norman Vincent Peale once said, "The secret of life isn't what happens to you, but what you do with what happens to you".[25]

When challenges in life happen, and they will, we must, first of all, change our perception of the situation. We must ask ourselves, "What is the purpose?", "What can I learn?" and then seek to discover an opportunity within the challenge. Second, we must respond with the appropriate action based upon this new perception, and not become or remain a victim of this life challenge. We need to decide whether we will allow past problems to trap us from attaining the Lord's provisions, or we can respond with forgiveness and freeing ourselves from the anger, hatred, bitterness, resentment that the enemy uses against us.

It is through forgiving others, ourselves, and God that we can find peace of mind, happiness, and the fruit of the Holy Spirit. "Forgiveness is the manifestation of your promise! It's the place to find

---

[22] Hagee, *Life's Challenges, Your Opportunities*, 79.

[23] Hagee, *Life's Challenges, Your Opportunities*, 81.

[24] Mark Twain, http://www.brainyquote.com/quotes/quotes/m/marktwain109919.html#5fyZq92Umbv8tI4d.99. Accessed on November 14, 2014.

[25] Norman Vincent Peale, <http://personalexcellence.co/blog/101-most-inspiring-quotes-part-3>. Accessed on November 14, 2014.

health and well-being. Forgiveness benefits your eternal soul. It's the beginning of the end of the problem and the first step into your Promised Land".[26]

5. Control Your Tongue.

> When we put bits into the mouths of horses to make them obey us, we can turn the whole animal. Or take ships as an example. Although they are so large and are driven by strong winds, they are steered by a very small rudder wherever the pilot wants to go. Likewise, the tongue is a small part of the body, but it makes great boasts. Consider what a great forest is set on fire by a small spark. The tongue also is a fire, a world of evil among the parts of the body. It corrupts the whole body, sets the whole course of one's life on fire, and is itself set on fire by hell. . . . With the tongue we praise our Lord and Father, and with it we curse human beings, who have been made in God's likeness. Out of the same mouth come praise and cursing. My brothers and sisters, this should not be. (Jas. 3:3-6, 9-10).

"The tongue has the power of life and death, and those who love it will eat its fruit" (Pr. 18:21).

Life or death, it's your choice. This verse refers to three (3) types of people. The focus of the Book of Proverbs is to encourage people to make right choices that lead to life, which include the spoken word.[27]

a. The Wise. This type of person uses words that bring instruction, correction, healing, restoration, encouragement, and strengthen others with patience. This type of person is walking on the path that leads to life. "Preach the word; be prepared in season and out of season; correct, rebuke and encourage—with great patience and careful instruction" (2 Tim. 4:2; cf. Pr. 12:18; 15:1, 4, 28; 25:11f.).

b. The Foolish. This type of person does not understand the principle that life and death is in the power of the tongue and often inflicts pain upon others with their words (Pr. 12:18). This type of person is walking on the path that leads to death.

c. The Fool. This type of person understands the power that words can have upon others, and purposely distorts these words without respect to how they will affect others bringing harm and condemnation. This type of person is walking on the path that leads to death (cf. Pr. 10:11f., 18; 12:20; 26:20-28; 29:5).

Moreover, there are four (4) types of tongues that are revealed in the Book of Proverbs:

a. The Controlled Tongue. This refers to those who think before they speak. They have a close relationship with the lord and wait for the opportune time to speak and give wise advice (Pr. 10:19; 11:12-13; 12:16; 13:3; 15:1, 4, 28; 16:23; 17:14, 27-28; 21:23; 24:26).

---

[26] Hagee, *Life's Challenges, Your Opportunities*, 84.

[27] "Proverbs 18:21", In Gilbrant, *The Complete Biblical Library, Proverbs-Song of Songs* (Springfield, IL: World Library Press, Inc., 1996), WORD*search* CROSS e-book.

b. The Caring Tongue. This refers to those who speak the truth in love and seek to encourage (Pr. 10:32; 12:18, 25; 15:23; 16:24; 25:15; 27:9).

c. The Conniving Tongue. This refers to speech that is filled with wrong motives, gossip, slander, backbiting, and twist the truth for selfish gain (Pr. 6:12-14; 8:13; 15:4; 16:28; 18:8; 25:18; 26:20-28).

d. The Careless Tongue. This refers to speech filled with lies, curses, quick-tempered words, which can lead to rebellion and destruction (Pr. 10:18, 32; 11:9; 12:16, 18; 17:9, 14, 19; 20:19; 25:23).

Other verses that refer to our speech include: (Pr. 10:11, 20, 31; 12:6, 17-19; 13:2; 14:3; 19:5, 28; 25:11; 27:2, 5, 14, 17; 29:9).[28]

6. Enter the Promised Land. The Israelites due to their bad choices lived in a perpetual state of defeatism. They continually murmured, complained, failed to trust in the Lord even though He had done such marvellous signs, wonders, and miracles. It was only after the "whole generation" of those who were twenty years of age and older who had "done evil" in the sight of the Lord had died, that they were allowed to enter the Promised Land.

> The LORD's anger was aroused that day and he swore this oath: 'Because they have not followed me wholeheartedly, not one of those who were twenty years old or more when they came up out of Egypt will see the land I promised on oath to Abraham, Isaac and Jacob—not one except Caleb son of Jephunneh the Kenizzite and Joshua son of Nun, for they followed the LORD wholeheartedly'. The LORD's anger burned against Israel and he made them wander in the wilderness forty years, until the whole generation of those who had done evil in his sight was gone (Num. 32:10-13).

If we truly desire to enter the Promised Land of freedom, promise, and provision, we, first of all, must stop making excuses for our behaviour and make right choices. It is this kind of *excusiology*, pity-party like behaviour that poisons our entire being, robs us from believing in ourselves, and is a hindrance to spiritual growth. Walking in freedom, promise, and provision begins when we learn to accept the reality that we have a problem, take responsibility for our part of the problem, and cry out to the Lord in humility and repentance. It is time to walk in freedom, which only comes through Jesus Christ and knowing His plan and purpose for our life as the prophet Jeremiah says,

> This is what the LORD says: "When seventy years are completed for Babylon, I will come to you and fulfill my good promise to bring you back to this place. For I know the plans I have for you," declares the LORD, "plans to prosper you and not to harm you, plans to give you hope and a future. Then you will call on me and come and pray to me, and I will listen to you. You will seek me and find me when you seek me with all your heart. I will be found by you," declares the LORD, "and will bring you back from captivity. I will gather you from all the nations and places where I have banished you," declares the LORD, "and will bring you back to the place from which I carried you into exile" (Jer. 29:10-14).

---

[28] Keith Williams, ed. *Chronological Life Application Study Bible* (Carol Stream, IL: Tyndale House Publishers, Inc., 2012), 840.

In the Book of Proverbs, we can see a strategy for effective living.

1. It begins with the wisdom of God. This is expressing our respect and appreciation for who God is on a daily basis; a holy reverence and awe towards God and His creation.
2. It requires moral application. It involves trusting in God and His Word and allowing His Word to speak to us personally. This is then lived out in willing obedience.
3. It requires practical application. It is one thing to believe in the Word of God, but we are called to live out God's direction on a daily basis.
4. It results in experiencing what God does with our obedience.[29]

Factors That Inhibit Christians from Fasting

Do you know His voice? Are you following Him? If not, who are you following? In the midst of the chaos of life can you hear His voice calling you? Maybe you can identify with one or more of the following factors that inhibit Christians from fasting:[30] The first is ignorance. Many Christians are ignorant of biblical exhortations to practice fasting and its subsequent benefits.

> my people are destroyed from lack of knowledge. Because you have rejected knowledge, I also reject you as my priests; because you have ignored the law of your God, I also will ignore your children (Hos. 4:6).

Second, is selfishness. In the day in which we live, convenience and temporary pleasures have a tendency to take our focus off of seeking the Lord and His will for our lives.

> Since, then, you have been raised with Christ, set your hearts on things above, where Christ is seated at the right hand of God. Set your minds on things above, not on earthly things. For you died, and your life is now hidden with Christ in God (Col. 3:1-3).

> Therefore, I urge you, brothers, in view of God's mercy, to offer your bodies as living sacrifices, holy and pleasing to God—this is your spiritual act of worship (Rom. 12:1).

Third, is indifference. We need to not only see our own personal and spiritual needs, but also value and necessity of submitting ourselves to the spiritual discipline of fasting.

> I have not departed from the commands of his lips; I have treasured the words of his mouth more than my daily bread (Job 23:12).

Fourth, is a lack of self-control. We must appropriate self-control as a fruit of the Spirit as we deny ourselves and take up His cross and follow Him.

---

[29] Williams, ed. *Chronological Life Application Study Bible*, 636.

[30] The following is an excerpt from Gordon Cove, *Revival Now! Through Prayer and Fasting*, <http://rockofroseville.com/files/2009/09/Fasting.pdf>. Accessed on November 15, 2013. For a more detailed discussion on this section, please refer to Elmer L. Towns, *Fasting for Spiritual Breakthrough Study Guide*, <http://digitalcommons.liberty.edu/towns_books/17>. Accessed on November 15, 2013. Bill Bright, <http://www.unityinchrist.com/prayer/fasting.htm>. Accessed on November 15, 2013.

> So I say, live by the Spirit, and you will not gratify the desires of the sinful nature. For the sinful nature desires what is contrary to the Spirit, and the Spirit what is contrary to the sinful nature. They are in conflict with each other, so that you do not do what you want. But if you are led by the Spirit, you are not under law. But the fruit of the Spirit is love, joy, peace, patience, kindness, goodness, faithfulness, gentleness and self-control. Against such things there is no law (Gal. 5:16-18, 22-23).

> Then Jesus said to his disciples, "If anyone would come after me, he must as himself and take up his cross and follow me. For whoever wants to save his life will lose it, but whoever loses his life for me will find it. What good will it be for a man if he gains the whole world, yet forfeits his soul? Or what can a man give in exchange for his soul? For the Son of Man is going to come in his Father's glory with his angels, and then he will reward each person according to what he has done. I tell you the truth, some who are standing here will not taste death before they see the Son of Man coming in his kingdom" (Mt. 16:24-28).

Fifth, is misguided priorities. Anytime we place someone or something as a higher priority than the Lord in our lives it becomes an idol. We must strive towards seeing the Kingdom of God established in our lives and the world in which we live.

> But seek first his kingdom and his righteousness, and all these things will be given to you as well (Mt. 6:33).

> For the kingdom of God is not a matter of eating and drinking, but of righteousness, peace and joy in the Holy Spirit, because anyone who serves Christ in this way is pleasing to God and approved by men (Rom. 14:17-18).

Sixth, is delusional Christianity. Delusion is defined as

> . . . something that is falsely or delusively believed or propagated; a persistent false psychotic belief regarding the self or persons or objects outside the self that is maintained despite indisputable evidence to the contrary; something that is believed to be true or real but that is actually false or unreal. Delusion implies an inability to distinguish between what is real and what only seems to be real, often as the result of a disordered state of mind.[31]

In the day in which we live, what is right is often seen as being wrong and what is wrong is often seen as being right or what is referred to as inverted spiritual values. The same ideology can be seen in relation to ethics, morals, and/or belief system. Someone once defined FEAR as **F**alse **E**vidence **A**ppearing **R**eal. Therefore, when a person perceives something to be real when it's not it creates a sense of fear and doubt and often leaves them questioning reality.

In reference to Christianity and living a Christ-like life, delusional Christianity is when the truth in the Word of God is perceived as being false and subsequently the fullest extent of God's truth is not lived out within a person life. For example, through the crucifixion, death, and resurrection, the blood of Jesus restores the broken relationship that had existed between God and mankind. However, if our reality is that

---

[31] "delusion", In Frederick C. Mish, ed. *Merriam-Webster's Collegiate Dictionary* (Springfield, MA: Merriam-Webster, Inc., 2003).

we believe this to be false then we will never be able to receive the forgiveness of sins that Jesus provided for us and subsequently forgive others (cf. Mt. 26:28; Eph. 1:7-8; Heb. 9:22). Our salvation will become a legalistic effort to try to work for our salvation, which we will never accomplish. We must remember that the Word of God is our reality and we are called to live out the precepts of the Word of God and living contrary and not accepting these precepts we are living a delusional Christianity. We are the disciples of Jesus Christ and called to live according our new nature.

> So I say, live by the Spirit, and you will not gratify the desires of the sinful nature. For the sinful nature desires what is contrary to the Spirit, and the Spirit what is contrary to the sinful nature. They are in conflict with each other, so that you do not do what you want. But if you are led by the Spirit, you are not under law. But the fruit of the Spirit is love, joy, peace, patience, kindness, goodness, faithfulness, gentleness and self-control. Against such things there is no law (Gal. 5:16-18, 22-23).

> Rather, as servants of God we commend ourselves in every way: in great endurance; in troubles, hardships and distresses; in beatings, imprisonments and riots; in hard work, sleepless nights and hunger; in purity, understanding, patience and kindness; in the Holy Spirit and in sincere love; in truthful speech and in the power of God; with weapons of righteousness in the right hand and in the left; through glory and dishonor, bad report and good report; genuine, yet regarded as impostors; known, yet regarded as unknown; dying, and yet we live on; beaten, and yet not killed; sorrowful, yet always rejoicing; poor, yet making many rich; having nothing, and yet possessing everything (2 Cor. 6:4-10).

> I have labored and toiled and have often gone without sleep; I have known hunger and thirst and have often gone without food; I have been cold and naked. Besides everything else, I face daily the pressure of my concern for all the churches (2 Cor. 11:27-28).

Seventh, it's being Christ-like. We are called to follow Jesus and live like He lived. It's about walking as Jesus walked and living like Jesus lived. When we do not live like Jesus it can inhibit our walk with Him—it's all or nothing. A famous author once said, "The life that He lived qualified Him for the death that He died. The death that He died qualifies us to live the life that He lived" (unknown).

> I know your deeds, that you are neither cold nor hot. I wish you were either one or the other! So, because you are lukewarm—neither hot nor cold—I am about to spit you out of my mouth (Rev. 3:15-16).

> Join with others in following my example, brothers, and take note of those who live according to the pattern we gave you. For, as I have often told you before and now say again even with tears, many live as enemies of the cross of Christ. Their destiny is destruction, their god is their stomach, and their glory is in their shame. Their mind is on earthly things (Phil. 3:17-19).

> For such people are not serving our Lord Christ, but their own appetites. By smooth talk and flattery they deceive the minds of naive people (Rom. 16:18).

> Then Jesus said to his disciples, "If anyone would come after me, he must deny himself and take up his cross and follow me. For whoever wants to save his life will lose it, but whoever loses his

> life for me will find it. What good will it be for a man if he gains the whole world, yet forfeits his soul? Or what can a man give in exchange for his soul?" (Mt. 16:24-26).

Can you relate to any of these factors? If you can, what is holding you back from living a life of freedom in Jesus Christ? Jesus has called you and me as His disciples to live in abundance, so what are we doing living a life where we are barely making ends meet. This abundance can be seen in the most read Psalm of Psalms and probably the most read and spoken context in all of Scripture. Psalms 23 illustrates the Hand of the Lord upon our life in the most wonderful way.

> The LORD is my shepherd, I shall not be in want. He makes me lie down in green pastures, he leads me beside quiet waters, he restores my soul. He guides me in paths of righteousness for his name's sake. Even though I walk through the valley of the shadow of death, I will fear no evil, for you are with me; your rod and your staff, they comfort me. You prepare a table before me in the presence of my enemies. You anoint my head with oil; my cup overflows. Surely goodness and love will follow me all the days of my life, and I will dwell in the house of the LORD forever (Ps. 23:1-6).

The following promises can be appropriated into our lives as we walk in communion with the Lord.

1. He promises that we will never be in want—His provisions are ours forever.
2. He promises newness of life, peacefulness, restoration of our soul (mind, will, and emotions), guidance to live a godly life, and protection and freedom from fear and evil as He walks beside us.
3. He promises to comfort us as we encounter the challenges and struggles in life.
4. He promises to bring hope, healing, freedom, and solutions to these challenges and struggles.
5. He promises that during perilous times He will comfort, provide a feast, and divinely protect us against our enemies as He did with David.
6. He promises to anoint us and bring times of refreshing and abundant blessing that overflows through our lives and into the lives of others.
7. He promises that His goodness and love will always be with us and we will enjoy everlasting communion with Him forever.

It is time that we break free from those things that keep us in bondage and strive forward and take hold of everything that is ours through our Lord. In Him, we lack nothing.

> Not that I have already obtained all this, or have already been made perfect, but I press on to take hold of that for which Christ Jesus took hold of me. Brothers, I do not consider myself yet to have taken hold of it. But one thing I do: Forgetting what is behind and straining toward what is ahead, I press on toward the goal to win the prize for which God has called me heavenward in Christ Jesus (Phil. 3:12-14).

Why Should Christians Fast

Now that we have discussed those things that inhibit Christians from fasting, we now turn to the reasons why Christians, churches, and church leaders need to implement fasting and prayer into their lives. If you identify with one or more of these reasons, you are in need of unlocking spiritual power and breakthrough in your life.

On an individual level:

1. Fasting brings us humbly before the Lord (Ps. 35:13; Ezra 8:21).
2. Fasting can facilitate a healthier nutritional lifestyle (Dan. 1:8-17).
3. Fasting can bring the physical and emotional healing and the fortitude to live victorious over sinful and destructive behaviours (1 Sam. 1:5-11, 18-20; 28:16-20; 1 Kgs. 19:1-9; Dan. 6:18-24).
4. Fasting is a powerful spiritual warfare weapon and Satan will do whatever it takes to keep believers from understanding the spiritual power and breakthrough that is ours through hearing the truth found in the Word of God (Est. 4:9-17).
5. Fasting reveals our inner spiritual condition and brings us to a place of repentance, brokenness where the Holy Spirit can bring necessary transformation.
6. Fasting heightens personal revival and spiritual resolve.
7. Fasting heightens our understanding of the Word of God.
8. Fasting heightens and deepens our relationship with the Lord.
9. Fasting transforms our prayer life into a richer and more meaningful personal experience.
10. Fasting can restore those who "have forsaken your first love" (Rev. 2:4).
11. Fasting is a primary means of restoration.
12. Fasting can bring necessary solutions to the challenging issues of our lives.
13. Fasting can bring freedom to those who feel entangled in striving for financial and social pursuits and sense a loss in their effective witness for Jesus Christ.[32]

On a corporate level:

1. Fasting heightens the need for revival within our churches, community, city, nation, and the need for evangelization.
2. Fasting heightens our awareness of being men and women of godly character and integrity.
3. Fasting heightens our awareness of the humanitarian needs of the world.
4. Fasting heightens our awareness of demonic activities, the declining influence of our Christian witness, and the need for protection from the enemy.[33]

We are on the brink of the return of the Lord and more than ever, as disciples of Jesus Christ, we must be prepared for the ever-increasing attacks of the enemy who will unleash his greatest warfare against the people of God. We must be prepared like the Word of God outlines for us, that the foundation is Jesus Christ and living a life of repentance. We can no longer live in denial of hiding sin, and allow unconfessed sin to rule and reign in our lives, since it will hinder our prayers from being answered and living in abundance and victory. The Lord is calling His church to fast and pray like never before.

---

[32] For further discussion, please see <http://www.unityinchrist.com/prayer/fasting.htm>. Accessed on November 15, 2013.

[33] Mark A. Copeland, *Fasting: A Special Study*, 1992-2007, In Rick Meyers, e-Sword, Version 10.2.1, 2000-2012, <http://www.e-sword.net>. Should Christians "Fast" Today? <http://www.bible.ca/d-fasting.htm>. Accessed on November 15, 2013.

It is essential that before you begin to fast that you prepare yourself and your heart to fast. The following is a guide to help you prepare for your chosen fast:

1. Ask God to help you make a comprehensive list of your sins.
2. Confess every sin that the Holy Spirit calls to your remembrance and accept God's forgiveness (1 Jn. 1:9).
3. Seek forgiveness from all whom you have offended, and forgive all who have hurt you (Mk. 11:25; Lk. 11:4; 17:3, 4).
4. Make restitution as the Holy Spirit leads you.
5. Ask God to fill you with His Holy Spirit according to His command in Ephesians 5:18 and His promise in 1 John 5:14, 15.
6. Surrender your life fully to Jesus Christ as your Lord and Master; refuse to obey your worldly nature (Rom. 12:1-2).
7. Meditate on the attributes of God, His love, sovereignty, power, wisdom, faithfulness, grace, compassion, and others (Ps. 48:9-10; 103:1-8, 11-13).
8. Begin your time of fasting and prayer with an expectant heart (Heb. 11:6).
9. Do not underestimate spiritual opposition. Satan sometimes intensifies the natural battle between body and spirit (Gal. 5:16-17).[34]

Fasting: Individually and Corporately

A concern today is for the church to fast. There are five reasons why churches should become involved in corporate fasting. First of all, Jesus exhorted His disciples and the Body of Christ to fast. It is quite significant that Jesus spoke about fasting as being distinctly separate from prayer, yet they are often linked together in Scripture.

However, there are examples when prayer is not mentioned with fasting, such as in the Book of Esther and also when the prophets and teachers in the church of Antioch were "worshiping the Lord and fasting", not praying (Acts 13:1-2). Jesus declared, "But the time will come when the bridegroom will be taken from them, and on that day they will fast" (Mk. 2:20). Jesus knew that the church would be attacked in every direction from the enemy and exhorted His church to fast (Mt. 16:18). Therefore, Jesus urged His disciples and His body to fast both corporately and individually. When we as believers fast corporately, four things happen:

1. It is easier to fast as a church or group because we can encourage one another.
2. We become united as the body of Christ.
3. We become a powerful weapon against the attacks of the enemy.
4. A corporate anointing is released within the church and among the members.

In reference to individual or private fasting, A. W. Pink wrote,

> From the very nature of the case we should never let our minds dwell on the act of fasting, as though we had therein discharged a duty. Fasting is not to be undertaken for the mere sake of

---

[34] Bill Bright, "Why Should Christians Fast", <http://www.cru.org/training-and-growth/devotional-life/personal-guide-to-fasting/02-why-you-should-fast.htm>. Accessed on November 15, 2013. Should Christians "Fast" Today? <http://www.bible.ca/d-fasting.htm>. Accessed on November 15, 2013.

> fasting. It is not as the doing of penance that we are ever to abstain from food, neither is it as though the abstaining were a process of holiness; still less must we regard it as in any wise a meritorious performance. Private fasting must issue from an urge within and not because it is imposed from without. Private fasting should be spontaneous, the result of our being under a great stress of spirit, and the simple act itself be entirely lost sight of in the engrossing fervour which prompted it. There had been little or no practical difficulties on the subject of fasting if these simple rules had been understood and observed.[35]

It is also quite significant that Jesus in the Sermon on the Mount (Mt. 6:1-18), exhorts His disciples to give, to pray, and to fast. He states "when you give to the needy" (vv. 2, 3), also, "when you pray" (vv. 5, 6, 7), and "when you fast" (vv. 16, 17). Jesus does not exhort His disciples "**if**" you give, pray, fast, but "**when**" you give, pray, fast. Jesus expected His disciples to regularly practice these three spiritual disciplines.

Second, fasting produces faith which must be released through our spoken word. Our source of faith is the Word of God, but we must speak the Word of God with our mouths. Fasting increases our faith as we read, meditate, saturate our minds, and speak the Word of God into our problem.

> That if you confess with your mouth, "Jesus is Lord", and believe in your heart that God raised him from the dead, you will be saved. For it is with your heart that you believe and are justified, and it is with your mouth that you confess and are saved (Rom. 10:9-10).

Third, fasting, along with prayer, is the spiritual vehicle through which revival comes (Joel 2:28). In this context, the prophet Joel states, "Blow the trumpet in Zion, declare a holy fast, call a sacred assembly" (2:15) and later he states "And afterward" (2:28). Fasting was a prerequisite to the coming revival.

> And afterward, I will pour out my Spirit on all people. Your sons and daughters will prophesy, your old men will dream dreams, your young men will see visions. Even on my servants, both men and women, I will pour out my Spirit in those days. I will show wonders in the heavens and on the earth, blood and fire and billows of smoke. The sun will be turned to darkness and the moon to blood before the coming of the great and dreadful day of the LORD. And everyone who calls on the name of the LORD will be saved; for on Mount Zion and in Jerusalem there will be deliverance, as the LORD has said, among the survivors whom the LORD calls (Joel 2:28-32).

Not "**if**" but "**when**" we begin to fast as a church, the Lord promises to send a revival. However, we must be careful that we do not fast for selfish motives because God cannot be manipulated into fulfilling our desires (cf. Isa. 58).

Fourth, fasting positions us to know God's perfect will.

> Therefore, I urge you, brothers, in view of God's mercy, to offer your bodies as living sacrifices, holy and pleasing to God—this is your spiritual act of worship. Do not conform any longer to the

---

[35] "Fasting", In A. W. Pink, *An Exposition of the Sermon on the Mount*, Rick Meyers, e-Sword, Version 10.2.1, 2000-2012, <http://www.e-sword.net>. Chapter 26.

> pattern of this world, but be transformed by the renewing of your mind. Then you will be able to test and approve what God's will is—his good, pleasing and perfect will (Rom. 12:1-2).

Paul urges the Romans to present their bodies to the Lord as a living sacrifice. One way we can do this is through fasting. We present our bodies, denying ourselves of food and pleasure so that we can use this time to draw closer to the Lord. Paul also states that through meditating on the Word of God daily our mind will be renewed. It is through fasting that we create a spiritual hunger for more of God. The more fasting is absent in our spiritual lives, the more we have become content and comfortable with the way we live our lives independent of Jesus Christ. It is as we truly draw closer to the Lord that we "will be able to test and approve what God's will is—his good, pleasing and perfect will". It is also through the process of fasting that our mind is renewed, disciplined, and a desire is created within us to not only know His perfect will for our lives, but to live out and experience all that He desires for us.[36]

Fifth, fasting precedes victory, but many of us live in defeat, when victory is only a short distance away achieved through fasting. However, with fasting comes a price and many of us are afraid of change, afraid of leaving our area of comfort, afraid of tasting the sweetness of victory that the Lord has already provided for us through Jesus Christ. If the people of God would only take seriously the disciplines of fasting and prayer, we would have the spiritual weapons to defeat the strongest enemy, live in victory, and experience the abundant life that the Lord provided for us through the cross, death, resurrection, and the eternal life that is ours through Jesus Christ (Jn. 10:10; Eph. 3:20). Victory is already ours and through fasting we appropriate that victory into your life, ministry, and everything the Lord has called you to do.

---

[36] John Piper, *A Hunger for God: Desiring God Through Fasting and Prayer* (Wheaton, IL: Crossway Books, 1997), 14, 87.

Chapter 2: Preparatory and Concluding Logistics to Fasting

The purpose of this chapter is to present preparatory and concluding logistics to fasting. It also discusses the nature of fasting and that we should expect transformation of our physical, emotional, and spiritual lives since through fasting our entire being is detoxed from those things that hinder us from reaching the heights of what the Lord has for us. It is imperative that those who have medical conditions should consult a physician before beginning to fast. This chapter also discusses how discouragement can set in and become an obstacle to the Lord's purpose from being accomplished in our lives. It is through fasting that we draw close to the Lord and we should expect and believe that the Lord will bring a fresh new move of the Holy Spirit in our lives.

Preparatory Logistics to Fasting

Remember, fasting is about focusing on Jesus, not about abstaining from food. It is imperative that you begin and conduct your fast properly since it will determine the extent of your success in your fast. There are a number of suggested steps that can guide you in fasting.[37] First of all, set a specific purpose for fasting. The *Personal Reflections* for each fast that follow will help give you the foundation on which to conduct your fast.

Second, prepare yourself spiritually as you begin your fast. The foundation to fasting is asking the Holy Spirit to reveal the motives of your heart. The Word of God says

> If I had cherished sin in my heart, the Lord would not have listened; but God has surely listened and heard my voice in prayer. Praise be to God, who has not rejected my prayer or withheld his love from me! (Ps. 66:18-20).

Therefore, any unconfessed sin and/or areas in our lives that are not pleasing to the Lord can nullify our fast and hinder our prayers from being answered. Ask the Holy Spirit to reveal obvious sin, but also those that are "cherished sin in my heart" and confess every sin that the Holy Spirit brings to your remembrance. Other types of sin(s) could include, forsaking your first love, worldly-mindedness, self-centeredness, spiritual indifference—not sharing your faith in Jesus Christ, a divisive spirit, and a lack of spending time with the Lord in His Word and prayer. Likewise, the prophet Isaiah says,

> These people come near to me with their mouth and honor me with their lips, but their hearts are far from me. Their worship of me is made up only of rules taught by men (Isa. 29:13).
>
> But your iniquities have separated you from your God; your sins have hidden his face from you, so that he will not hear (Isa. 59:2).
>
> If we claim to be without sin, we deceive ourselves and the truth is not in us. If we confess our sins, he is faithful and just and will forgive us our sins and purify us from all unrighteousness. If we claim we have not sinned, we make him out to be a liar and his word has no place in our lives (1 Jn. 1:8-10).

---

[37] Bill Bright, <http://www.unityinchrist.com/prayer/fasting.htm>. Accessed on November 15, 2013.

As you prepare to fast, draw close to the Lord through prayer and worship and allow Him to reveal to you the purpose of the fast. The key to spiritual preparation in fasting is an intimacy with the Lord.

Third, prepare yourself physically as you begin your fast. Some helpful suggestions include: (1) take time to plan, being unprepared can result in giving into temptation; (2) begin by eating smaller meals so that your body is not shocked by a sudden lack of food and/or water. Also eat only raw foods, especially vegetables can be quite helpful; (3) avoid foods that are high in fat and contain high amounts of sugar; (4) a drastic change in your eating habits may distract you from giving your complete attention to the Lord in prayer.

Fourth, ask the Lord for guidance and direction in regards to the type and length of fast. Is the Lord asking you to do a partial or restricted fast, regular, private, personal, public, rotational, or complete fast? Is the Lord asking you to fast one day, three days, seven days, twenty-one days, or forty days? Make sure to ask for the guidance of the Holy Spirit to enrich your fast. Fasting usually includes water, but some fasts exclude water. Fifth, gradually reduce physical activity, exercise, and take time to rest and relax. Since you are limiting your nutrition to some degree, it is advisable to limit activity. Your body is detoxing or cleansing itself and therefore you may experience some changes, such as: stomach aches, vomiting, diarrhea, nausea, bad breath, and smelly perspiration. These changes depend upon the type and length of the fast.

Sixth, schedule time to seek the Lord either privately or in a group depending upon the fast. The more you focus your time upon developing a more intimate relationship with the Lord through worship, prayer, and reading and meditating on the Word of God the more effective your prayer and meaningful your fast will be. Set aside every morning before you begin your daily routine being conscious that you are fasting and watchful of what spiritual insights the Lord may reveal. Placing the Lord first in your life everyday will help you to prioritize your day as Scripture says, "But seek first his kingdom and his righteousness, and all these things will be given to you as well" (Mt. 6:33). This will help you to create a habit of placing the Lord first each day even after you have concluded your fast.

Remember that the Lord knows our hearts and He cannot be manipulated into fulfilling our request just because we go through the motions of fasting. Create a list of people to pray for, such as: your family, your pastor, your church, your community, and your nation. Take time to pray for revival, a spiritual harvest and the fulfillment of the Great Commission (Mt. 28:18-20). If you feel that you have prayed for everything under the sun wait quietly before Him and allow Him to gently speak to you. Moreover, turn to your favourite passage of Scripture, the Lord's Prayer, Psalms 23, and confess the Word of God over your life, family, church, community, and nation.

Consult A Physician

Before you begin your fast, it is advised that you consult your physician or a healthcare professional that is knowledgeable in regards to fasting. Moreover, keep in mind that many physicians, healthcare professionals, dieticians and others including family, friends, and even pastors may react negatively to you fasting. They may have heard horror stories, or their lack of understanding may create unnecessary fear, and discourage you from fasting. It would be advisable if you are planning an extended fast to have a complete physical done by your physician to make sure that you are in good health. This could lead to the discovery of a physical problem where you may need to postpone your fast until your health becomes 100%.

It is advisable that some people with health concerns, questions about your health and desire to fast should never fast without the supervision of their physician or healthcare professional. Even though you may have a health or medical condition, it should not become an obstacle that hinders you from fasting. Everyone can participate in some type of fast, even if it is partial or excludes some types of food. However, some people should not fast without medical supervision. If you cannot live without a certain type of food, such as: coke, french fries, coffee, chocolate, bread, you are a good candidate to fast. Some of these include, but is not limited to:

1. Those who are physically emaciated (e.g., anorexic, underweight).
2. Those who have medical conditions, such as: heart problems, chronic illness, take prescriptions.
3. Those who are anemic.
4. Diabetics.
5. Women who are pregnant or nursing.
6. Those who have doubts and/or concerns.[38]

For those who have a medical condition and cannot choose a fast that involves food, there are other possibilities available for you. Some of these include, fasting from a particular daily routine such as specific foods or beverages (coffee, coke), your favourite TV show, television in general, abstaining from using a computer or other technology or anything else. It is important to remember that the importance lies in the spirit of the fast and not in the details. Moreover, remember, fasting should never bring harm to your body or experience pain. If this happens consults your physician immediately before continuing your fast.

Do you have a medical condition that should be respected as you consider the spiritual discipline of fasting? If so, what is this medical condition? ____________________. It would be advisable to contact your doctor prior to engaging in fasting and follow their advice.[39]

Anticipate Transformation

One of the greatest results that we can have during fasting is that our body is literally eliminating toxins. When this happens you will experience some discomforts, such as: headaches and/or withdrawals, being irritable, lack of patience, loss of energy, diarrhea, and hunger pains of course. If you drink caffeinated beverages (e.g., coffee), it would be best to gradually decrease your consumption before you begin your fast. This will reduce headaches, withdrawals, and irritability. Use your time to listen to praise and worship music, reading Scripture, pray, and meditating on the Word of God. Limit as many

---

[38] Bill Bright, <http://www.unityinchrist.com/prayer/fasting.htm>. Accessed on November 15, 2013.

[39] "Abstinence", In James Hastings, ed., *Dictionary of the Apostolic Church* (New York: Charles Scribner's Sons, 1918).

distractions as possible and keep your heart and mind focused on the Lord. Expect the Lord to do great and wondrous things in your life and through your life.[40]

Predictable Discouragement

Many people while fasting become easily discouraged since they do not see the results that they desire when they believe that they should start to see results. Do not be preoccupied with the results since the Lord will bring the results in His timing, not yours. Many people do not see immediate results while fasting and this is okay, wait patiently on the Lord and He will bring the answers in His time. If you find yourself seeking results, take a moment to check your motives for fasting. If you deviate from your fast, don't worry or quit, just return to your fast where you left off. It is not necessary to start all over again. The Lord will give you the grace and strength to finish your fast.

> But he said to me, "My grace is sufficient for you, for my power is made perfect in weakness". Therefore I will boast all the more gladly about my weaknesses, so that Christ's power may rest on me. That is why, for Christ's sake, I delight in weaknesses, in insults, in hardships, in persecutions, in difficulties. For when I am weak, then I am strong (2 Cor. 12:9-10).

Anticipate Victory

In everything that we do we should always expect results, believing that He "rewards those who earnestly seek him".

> And without faith it is impossible to please God, because anyone who comes to him must believe that he exists and that he rewards those who earnestly seek him (Heb. 11:6).

We should expect no different when we fast. If we earnestly seek the Lord, humble ourselves in repentance, commit ourselves in worship, and dedicate ourselves to seeking the Lord through His Word then the Lord will bless those who seek Him wholeheartedly and experience and be refreshed physically, emotionally, and spiritually. It is through fasting that the Lord will meet each person where they are at in their life and experience the Lord in a fresh new way. We are all created "fearfully and wonderfully" and the Lord will meet us according to our needs.[41]

> For you created my inmost being; you knit me together in my mother's womb. I praise you because I am fearfully and wonderfully made; your works are wonderful, I know that full well (Ps. 139:13-14).

Expect the Lord to do great and wondrous things in and through your life as a result of following God's chosen fast (Isa. 58).

---

[40] Bill Bright, <http://www.unityinchrist.com/prayer/fasting.htm>. Accessed on November 15, 2013. See also <http://www.faithcycleministry.org/content/fasting-10>. Accessed on December 10, 2013.

[41] Bill Bright, <http://www.unityinchrist.com/prayer/fasting.htm>. Accessed on November 15, 2013.

Concluding Logistics to Fasting

When the established time set by the Lord and yourself has come to an end, it is quite important that as careful as you were to begin your fast that you end your fast in a proper manner. The benefits can be far reaching both spiritual and physical even after your fast has concluded. However, to avoid similar sickness as a result of fasting, do not be too hasty in eating solid foods or eating too quickly since this may cause diarrhea, vomiting, stomach ache, to name a few. Begin by eating soup, especially with vegetables and water based fresh fruits like watermelon and cantaloupe or other types of non-solid food since solid food can have detrimental effects upon your stomach and digestive system. Even short fasts of three to seven days require reasonable precautions. As your body—stomach and digestive system accepts these nourishing foods—gradually progress to solid food such as raw fruits and vegetables and so on. It would be wise to progress with knowledgeable precaution to avoid physical adverse reactions. It would be a great idea to study the physical effects of returning to eating too quickly.

Chapter 3: The Fasts of the Pentateuch, Historical Books, and Psalms

The purpose of this chapter is to present the fasts of biblical characters and the context in which the fasting occurs. It also highlights fasting as being not only practiced corporately, but also by individuals. Each fast concludes by reflecting and responding to questions relevant to each fast.

The Moses Fast

Please read the following Scripture references and then respond to the questions that follow.

> Remember this and never forget how you provoked the Lord your God to anger in the desert. From the day you left Egypt until you arrived here, you have been rebellious against the Lord. At Horeb you aroused the Lord's wrath so that he was angry enough to destroy you. When I went up on the mountain to receive the tablets of stone, the tablets of the covenant that the Lord had made with you, I stayed on the mountain forty days and forty nights; I ate no bread and drank no water. The Lord gave me two stone tablets inscribed by the finger of God. On them were all the commandments the Lord proclaimed to you on the mountain out of the fire, on the day of the assembly. At the end of the forty days and forty nights, the Lord gave me the two stone tablets, the tablets of the covenant. Then the Lord told me, "Go down from here at once, because your people whom you brought out of Egypt have become corrupt. They have turned away quickly from what I commanded them and have made a cast idol for themselves". And the Lord said to me, "I have seen this people, and they are a stiff-necked people indeed! Let me alone, so that I may destroy them and blot out their name from under heaven. And I will make you into a nation stronger and more numerous than they". So I turned and went down from the mountain while it was ablaze with fire. And the two tablets of the covenant were in my hands. When I looked, I saw that you had sinned against the Lord your God; you had made for yourselves an idol cast in the shape of a calf. You had turned aside quickly from the way that the Lord had commanded you. So I took the two tablets and threw them out of my hands, breaking them to pieces before your eyes. Then once again I fell prostrate before the Lord for forty days and forty nights; I ate no bread and drank no water, because of all the sin you had committed, doing what was evil in the Lord's sight and so provoking him to anger. I feared the anger and wrath of the Lord, for he was angry enough with you to destroy you. But again the Lord listened to me. And the Lord was angry enough with Aaron to destroy him, but at that time I prayed for Aaron too. Also I took that sinful thing of yours, the calf you had made, and burned it in the fire. Then I crushed it and ground it to powder as fine as dust and threw the dust into a stream that flowed down the mountain. You also made the Lord angry at Taberah, at Massah and at Kibroth Hattaavah. And when the Lord sent you out from Kadesh Barnea, he said, "Go up and take possession of the land I have given you". But you rebelled against the command of the Lord your God. You did not trust him or obey him. You have been rebellious against the Lord ever since I have known you. I lay prostrate before the Lord those forty days and forty nights because the Lord had said he would destroy you. I prayed to the Lord and said, "O Sovereign Lord, do not destroy your people, your own inheritance that you redeemed by your great power and brought out of Egypt with a mighty hand. Remember your servants Abraham, Isaac and Jacob. Overlook the stubbornness of this people, their wickedness and their sin. Otherwise, the country from which you brought us will say, 'Because the Lord was not able to take them into the land he had promised them, and because he hated them, he brought them out to put them to death in the desert'. But they are your people, your inheritance that you brought out by your great power and your outstretched arm" (Deut. 9:7-29).

As seen above, the Moses Fast involves two different purposes for fasting. The purpose of the first forty day fast was to receive divine direction which was given by God in the form of the Ten Commandments. The purpose of the second forty day fast is similar to the Disciple's Fast whose purpose was to find freedom from compulsive and/or obsessive behaviours, bad habits, cravings that are controlling you, or sins that are harassing or troubling you and hindering you from living a life of freedom. Therefore, two specific purposes are included in the Moses Fast: (1) divine direction; (2) freedom from besetting sins.

The following questions are a guide to help you receive divine direction or achieve freedom from besetting sins. They will also assist you in applying the Moses Fast to your personal life. It is vital that you pray and ask the Holy Spirit to give you the guidance and direction, wisdom, and the best course of action as you complete the Moses Fast. After completing the questions, find the appropriate prayer whether for divine direction or freedom from besetting sins.

1. What lessons can we learn from the Moses Fast?

____

____

2. Which lesson has had the greatest impact on your life? Explain.

____

____

3. How is the Moses Fast relevant today?

____

____

4. Which of the two purposes: (1) divine direction; (2) freedom from besetting sins in the Moses Fast will be your focus? Why?

____

____

5. What is your purpose in the Moses Fast? Be specific. I am fasting to:

____

6. How can fasting increase your desire to be completely set free from besetting sin?

7. What spiritual power and breakthrough do you desire to unlock through the Moses Fast?

8. If you experienced this spiritual breakthrough, how would your life be different? How would your relationships (family, friends, church) be different or affected by this spiritual breakthrough? Be specific.

9. How can your faith be increased and/or strengthened through the Moses Fast? How will you be benefited by having your faith increased and/or strengthened?

10. What other benefits, whether physical, emotional, relational, psychological, and spiritual do you desire to achieve during the Moses Fast?

11. What might you discover about yourself during the Moses Fast?

12. What steps can you take to guard yourself against relapsing into your former lifestyle associated with besetting sins?

13. How could the Moses Fast change your life?

14. What steps would you take to bring out these changes in your life? Who should be involved and to what extent?

15. What length of time (days) and hours each day will you commit to during the Moses Fast? When do you plan to begin and end your fast?

Prayer

Fasting is one of the spiritual disciplines that the Lord has established for you to achieve the spiritual power and breakthrough not only within your life but also in the lives of those whom are close to your heart. I acknowledge that I have become too comfortable in my current state of living and I sense you Holy Spirit calling me to confront the issues that I have been avoiding and find the freedom to live solely for Jesus Christ. Help me through the Moses Fast to break free from the bondages that have been controlling my life for too long. Therefore, prayerfully consider and write a prayer that you will address to the Lord that reflects a new commitment and dedication to Him.

The Moses Fast Journal

As you progress through this fast, write down any insights the Lord speaks to you, spiritual growth, and personal thoughts to further reflect upon in your walk with the Lord.

The Jewish Fast

Please read the following Scripture references and then respond to the questions that follow.

> This is to be a lasting ordinance for you: On the tenth day of the seventh month you must deny yourselves and not do any work—whether native-born or an alien living among you—because on this day atonement will be made for you, to cleanse you. Then, before the LORD, you will be clean from all your sins. It is a sabbath of rest, and you must deny yourselves; it is a lasting ordinance (Lev. 16:29-31).

> The tenth day of this seventh month is the Day of Atonement. Hold a sacred assembly and deny yourselves, and present an offering made to the LORD by fire. Do no work on that day, because it is the Day of Atonement, when atonement is made for you before the LORD your God. Anyone who does not deny himself on that day must be cut off from his people. I will destroy from among his people anyone who does any work on that day. You shall do no work at all. This is to be a lasting ordinance for the generations to come, wherever you live. It is a sabbath of rest for you, and you must deny yourselves. From the evening of the ninth day of the month until the following evening you are to observe your sabbath (Lev. 23:27-32).

> Then all the Israelites, the whole army, went up to Bethel, and there they sat weeping before the Lord. They fasted that day until evening and presented burnt offerings and fellowship offerings to the Lord (Jdg. 20:26).

> Then David and all the men with him took hold of their clothes and tore them. They mourned and wept and fasted till evening for Saul and his son Jonathan, and for the army of the Lord and for the nation of Israel, because they had fallen by the sword (2 Sam. 1:12).

The purpose of the Jewish Fast is seen in abstaining from eating food and pleasures like using oil and/or lotion to prevent dry skin, abstaining from any form of hygiene, or denying oneself from thinking "more highly than you ought" (Rom. 12:3). In the contexts above (Lev. 16:29-31; 23:27-32), Moses uses the Hebrew verb עָנָה *ʿānāh* for "deny yourselves" five times meaning "to answer" or "to be afflicted". This Hebrew verb connotes "to break the spirit of the one afflicted" and "being emotionally humbled". In Leviticus 16:29-31 and 23:27-32, the NIV notes that "fast" could be used in each case instead of "deny yourselves" (i.e., "must fast", "and fast", "anyone who does not fast"). The Lord uses affliction to motivate His people to repent of their disobedience, rebellion, and wickedness. God allowed His people to wander in the wilderness for forty years to humble Israel and likewise the Babylonian captivity (Deut. 8:2f.; Isa. 64:12; Zech. 10:2).

If we truly believe that God is sovereign in everything, then during times of suffering and affliction, we can be thankful knowing that God has a purpose for our affliction (Ps. 88:7; 90:15; 119:75; Lam. 3:33; cf. 1 Kgs. 11:39; Ps. 107:17; 132:1; Nah. 1:12). Scripture speaks of humbling ourselves voluntarily through repentance and fasting instead of God humbling those who are proud, evil, wicked, and arrogant,

> For whoever exalts himself will be humbled, and whoever humbles himself will be exalted (Mt. 23:12; Lk. 14:11; 18:14).

The LORD sustains the humble but casts the wicked to the ground (Ps. 147:6).

I will punish the world for its evil, the wicked for their sins. I will put an end to the arrogance of the haughty and will humble the pride of the ruthless (Isa. 13:11).

God opposes the proud but gives grace to the humble (Jas. 4:6).

The Lord commanded in the Mosaic Law an exclusive fast on the Day of Atonement that was "to be a lasting ordinance" (Lev. 16:29, 31). It is also mentioned as a voluntary discipline (Lev. 23:27, 32; Num. 29:7; Ps. 35:13; Isa. 58:3, 5, 10).[42]

The purpose of the Jewish Fast is not upon one's external appearance but the internal attitude of the heart. Please read the following Scripture references and Genesis 24 and then respond to the questions that follow. The following questions are a guide to help you abstain from food and pleasures and find freedom from thinking "more highly than you ought". They will also assist you in applying the Jewish Fast to your personal life. It is vital that you pray and ask the Holy Spirit to give you the guidance and direction, wisdom, and the best course of action as you complete the Jewish Fast.

1. What lessons can we learn from the Jewish Fast?

____

____

2. Which lesson has had the greatest impact on your life? Explain.

____

____

3. How is the Jewish Fast relevant today?

____

____

4. What is your purpose in the Jewish Fast? Be as specific. I am fasting to:

____

[42] עָנָה ʿānāh "6257", In Gilbrant, ed., *The Complete Biblical Library Hebrew-English Dictionary, Nun-Ayin* (Springfield, IL: World Library Press, Inc., 1998), WORD*search* CROSS e-book. עָנָה ʿānâ, "1650" In Harris, Archer Jr., and Waltke, eds, *Theological Wordbook of the Old Testament*, 679-680.

5. How can fasting increase your desire to be focused on the internal attitude of your heart?

6. What steps can you take to guard yourself against thinking "of yourself more highly than you ought, but rather think of yourself with sober judgment" (Rom. 12:3)?

7. What spiritual power and breakthrough do you desire to unlock through the Jewish Fast?

8. If you experienced this spiritual breakthrough, how would your life be different? How would your relationships (family, friends, church) be different or affected by this spiritual breakthrough? Be specific.

9. How can your faith be increased and/or strengthened through the Jewish Fast? How will you be benefited by having your faith increased and/or strengthened?

10. What other benefits, whether physical, emotional, relational, psychological, and spiritual do you desire to achieve during the Jewish Fast?

11. What might you discover about yourself during the Jewish Fast?

12. What specific things could you abstain from that brings attention to yourself?

13. How could the Jewish Fast change your life?

14. What steps would you take to bring out these changes in your life? Who should be involved and to what extent?

15. What length of time (days) and hours each day will you commit to during the Jewish Fast? When do you plan to begin and end your fast?

Prayer

Fasting is one of the spiritual disciplines that the Lord has established for you to achieve the spiritual power and breakthrough not only within your life but also in the lives of those whom are close to your heart. I acknowledge that I have become too comfortable in my current state of living and I sense you Holy Spirit calling me to confront the issues that I have been avoiding and find the freedom to live solely for Jesus Christ. Help me through the Jewish Fast to break free from the bondages that have been controlling my life for too long. Therefore, prayerfully consider and write a prayer that you will address to the Lord that reflects a new commitment and dedication to Him.

The Jewish Fast Journal

As you progress through this fast, write down any insights the Lord speaks to you, spiritual growth, and personal thoughts to further reflect upon in your walk with the Lord.

The Hannah Fast

Please read the following Scripture references and then respond to the questions that follow.

> But to Hannah he gave a double portion because he loved her, and the Lord had closed her womb. And because the Lord had closed her womb, her rival kept provoking her in order to irritate her. This went on year after year. Whenever Hannah went up to the house of the Lord, her rival provoked her till she wept and would not eat. Elkanah her husband would say to her, "Hannah, why are you weeping? Why don't you eat? Why are you downhearted? Don't I mean more to you than ten sons?" Once when they had finished eating and drinking in Shiloh, Hannah stood up. Now Eli the priest was sitting on a chair by the doorpost of the Lord's temple. In bitterness of soul Hannah wept much and prayed to the Lord. And she made a vow, saying, "O Lord Almighty, if you will only look upon your servant's misery and remember me, and not forget your servant but give her a son, then I will give him to the Lord for all the days of his life, and no razor will ever be used on his head". . . . She said, "May your servant find favor in your eyes". Then she went her way and ate something, and her face was no longer downcast. Early the next morning they arose and worshiped before the Lord and then went back to their home at Ramah. Elkanah lay with Hannah his wife, and the Lord remembered her. So in the course of time Hannah conceived and gave birth to a son. She named him Samuel, saying, "Because I asked the Lord for him" (1 Sam. 1:5-11, 18-20).

The Hannah Fast is a fast to receive healing. This is a great example as the Lord opened up Hannah's womb so that she could conceive. In Hannah's case, because of being greatly distressed she became barren and "Whenever Hannah went up to the house of the Lord, her rival provoked her till she wept and would not eat" (1 Sam. 1:7). It is a matter of common sense that when a person experiences a deep level of distress that they often lose their appetite. The purpose of the Hannah Fast is upon pouring out one's soul or emptying one's soul before the Lord—giving everything to the Lord.[43]

The following questions are a guide to help you receive your promised healing and find freedom from disease and live in health, wholeness, and soundness. They will also assist you in applying the Hannah Fast to your personal life. It is vital that you pray and ask the Holy Spirit to give you the guidance and direction, wisdom, and the best course of action as you complete the Hannah Fast.

1. What lessons can we learn from the Hannah Fast?

___

___

2. Which lesson has had the greatest impact on your life? Explain.

___

___

[43] Frank E. Gaebelein, ed., *The Expositor's Bible Commentary, Volume 3: Deuteronomy, Joshua, Judges, Ruth, 1 & 2 Samuel* (Grand Rapids, MI: Zondervan Publishing House, 1992), WORD*search* CROSS e-book, 571.

3. How is the Hannah Fast relevant today?

4. What is your purpose in the Hannah Fast? Be specific. I am fasting to:

5. What spiritual power and breakthrough do you desire to unlock through the Hannah Fast?

6. If you experienced this spiritual breakthrough, how would your life be different? How would your relationships (family, friends, church) be different or affected by this spiritual breakthrough? Be specific.

7. How can your faith be increased and/or strengthened through the Hannah Fast? How will you be benefited by having your faith increased and/or strengthened?

8. What other benefits, whether physical, emotional, relational, psychological, and spiritual do you desire to achieve during the Hannah Fast?

9. What might you discover about yourself during the Hannah Fast?

10. Is there something that you earnestly desire like Hannah that you feel that you need to surrender or pour out your soul to the Lord? Briefly explain.

11. If the Lord answered the cry of your soul: How would you respond to the Lord? What would it mean to you?

12. Do you have a personal concern that causes you mental and/or emotional anguish? Briefly explain.

13. How could the Hannah Fast change your life?

14. What steps would you take to bring out these changes in your life? Who should be involved and to what extent?

15. What length of time (days) and hours each day will you commit to during the Hannah Fast? When do you plan to begin and end your fast?

Prayer

Fasting is one of the spiritual disciplines that the Lord has established for you to achieve the spiritual power and breakthrough not only within your life but also in the lives of those whom are close to your heart. I acknowledge that I have become too comfortable in my current state of living and I sense you Holy Spirit calling me to confront the issues that I have been avoiding and find the freedom to live solely for Jesus Christ. Help me through the Hannah Fast to break free from the bondages that have been controlling my life for too long. Therefore, prayerfully consider and write a prayer that you will address to the Lord that reflects a new commitment and dedication to Him.

The Hannah Fast Journal

As you progress through this fast, write down any insights the Lord speaks to you, spiritual growth, and personal thoughts to further reflect upon in your walk with the Lord.

The King Saul Fast

Please read the following Scripture references and then respond to the questions that follow.

> Samuel said, "Why do you consult me, now that the Lord has turned away from you and become your enemy? The Lord has done what he predicted through me. The Lord has torn the kingdom out of your hands and given it to one of your neighbors—to David. Because you did not obey the Lord or carry out his fierce wrath against the Amalekites, the Lord has done this to you today. The Lord will hand over both Israel and you to the Philistines, and tomorrow you and your sons will be with me. The Lord will also hand over the army of Israel to the Philistines". Immediately Saul fell full length on the ground, filled with fear because of Samuel's words. His strength was gone, for he had eaten nothing all that day and night (1 Sam. 28:16-20).

The focus of the King Saul Fast like the Hannah Fast concerns fasting due to emotional distress. One of the lessons that we can learn is that King Saul's disobedience and rebellion against God resulted in serious consequences—losing everything and death. Second, we need to be careful when we sense a strong and unrelenting emotion of feeling rising from within, or coming upon us. In King Saul's situation, this uncontrollable emotion drove him to contact the witch of Endor, which the Law of Moses stated,

> When you enter the land the LORD your God is giving you, do not learn to imitate the detestable ways of the nations there. Let no one be found among you who sacrifices his son or daughter in the fire, who practices divination or sorcery, interprets omens, engages in witchcraft, or casts spells, or who is a medium or spiritist or who consults the dead. Anyone who does these things is detestable to the LORD, and because of these detestable practices the LORD your God will drive out those nations before you. You must be blameless before the LORD your God (Deut. 18:9-13).

Third, we can learn from Samuel's interaction with King Saul is that we cannot become stuck in past disappointments, broken dreams. Samuel became stuck in excessive mourning over his disappointment with King Saul. There's a problem when we only focus upon broken relationships and broken dreams. The enemy had used Samuel's excessive mourning as an attempt to stop him from laying hold of the future king of Israel—King David. This is seen as the Lord speaks to Samuel,

> The LORD said to Samuel, "How long will you mourn for Saul, since I have rejected him as king over Israel? Fill your horn with oil and be on your way; I am sending you to Jesse of Bethlehem. I have chosen one of his sons to be king" (1 Sam. 16:1).

When we become stuck in our past, we become blind to seeing our future, the abundance, the new beginnings that the Lord has in store for us. This divine "How long" is a prophetic rebuke—a wakeup call for Samuel to move on with his life and to be the Lord's instrument in the fulfillment of the history of Israel. The Lord then tells Samuel, "Fill your horn with oil" meaning to have a fresh new attitude on life and then "be on your way" meaning to move on with his life, leave the past behind and allow the Lord to guide and direct him to the new beginnings that He had prepared for him. If we cannot let go of our past, we will never be on our way to the new beginnings that the Lord has prepared for us.[44] When we are stuck

---

[44] Gaebelein, ed., *The Expositor's Bible Commentary, Volume 3*, 682.

in the past, we are not able to enjoy the present everyday life we could be living and subsequently our future. In essence, when we remain stuck in our past hurts, disappointments, broken dreams, broken relationships, we are losing both our present and our future.

The following questions are a guide to help you find freedom from emotional distress and become unstuck from your past and "be on your way" to a bright future with the Lord. They will also assist you in applying the King Saul Fast to your personal life. It is vital that you pray and ask the Holy Spirit to give you the guidance and direction, wisdom, and the best course of action as you complete the King Saul Fast.

1. What lessons can we learn from the King Saul Fast?

____

____

2. Which lesson has had the greatest impact on your life? Explain.

____

____

3. How is the King Saul Fast relevant today?

____

____

4. What is your purpose in the King Saul Fast? Be specific. I am fasting to:

____

____

5. What spiritual power and breakthrough do you desire to unlock through the King Saul Fast?

____

____

____

____

6. If you experienced this spiritual breakthrough, how would your life be different? How would your relationships (family, friends, church) be different or affected by this spiritual breakthrough? Be specific.

____

____

7. How can your faith be increased and/or strengthened through the King Saul Fast? How will you be benefited by having your faith increased and/or strengthened?

____

____

8. What other benefits, whether physical, emotional, relational, psychological, and spiritual do you desire to achieve during the King Saul Fast?

____

____

9. What might you discover about yourself during the King Saul Fast?

____

____

10. How could the King Saul Fast change your life?

____

____

11. What steps would you take to bring out these changes in your life? Who should be involved and to what extent?

____

____

____

12. Take a moment to ask the Lord if you are walking in disobedience and rebellion with the Lord. If so, how have you disobeyed or have rebelled against the Lord?

____

____

13. How has this disobedience and rebellion affected you? How should you respond?

____

____

14. What steps can you take to guard yourself from becoming emotionally distressed like Samuel (1 Sam. 28:16-20)?

____

____

15. Do you find yourself in a state of excessive mourning or grief over someone or something that has happened in your past and you feel stuck and hindered from moving forward and laying hold of the abundance the Lord has prepared for you? If so, what areas to you feel stuck? How can the King Saul Fast help you?

____

____

16. What length of time (days) and hours each day will you commit to during the King Saul Fast? When do you plan to begin and end your fast?

____

____

Prayer

The following prayer was given to me by a close friend who was woken up in the middle of the night and directed by the Lord to go to their Facebook page where they found the following prayer and declaration and then went back to sleep. They were not sure who had written them, but when they woke up in the morning and checked their Facebook page, the prayer and declaration had been removed. However, before they went back to sleep they saved them on their computer and then sent them to me and a few others.

I believe that an angel wrote this prayer and declaration on their Facebook page because both of us and others needed to hear this message of hope. For some time they had been going through a difficult time and like myself had been stuck in past hurts, disappointments, broken dreams, and broken relationships. Pray the following believing the Lord is moving you into new beginnings and new opportunities and then declare the Lord's abundant blessings upon your life.

> Now to him who is able to do immeasurably more than all we ask or imagine, according to his power that is at work within us, to him be glory in the church and in Christ Jesus throughout all generations, for ever and ever! Amen (Eph. 3:20-21).

> Heavenly Father, It's time for me to forget the past, forget the mistakes, and focus on what you are doing in my life today. I know you are doing a new thing. You are placing the right people in my life and removing the wrong ones. You are closing old doors and preparing me for new opportunities. The pruning process can be uncomfortable and painful, but I know it's for my good. I trust you. In Jesus' name.

> I declare unexpected blessings are coming my way. I will move forward from barely making it to having more than enough. God will open up supernatural doors for me. He will speak to the right people about me. I will see Ephesians 3:20, exceedingly, abundantly, above-and-beyond favor and increase in this life. This is my declaration.

What God has stated in His Word cannot be added to or subtracted from and that the Word of God is a "closed book" and that every word spoken and written belongs to you in Jesus Christ.

> I warn everyone who hears the words of the prophecy of this book: If anyone adds anything to them, God will add to him the plagues described in this book. And if anyone takes words away from this book of prophecy, God will take away from him his share in the tree of life and in the holy city, which are described in this book (Rev. 22:18-19).

Fasting is one of the spiritual disciplines that the Lord has established for you to achieve the spiritual power and breakthrough not only within your life but also in the lives of those whom are close to your heart. I acknowledge that I have become too comfortable in my current state of living and I sense you Holy Spirit calling me to confront the issues that I have been avoiding and find the freedom to live solely for Jesus Christ. Help me through the King Saul Fast to break free from the bondages that have been controlling my life for too long. Therefore, prayerfully consider and write a prayer that you will address to the Lord that reflects a new commitment and dedication to Him.

____

____

The King Saul Fast Journal

As you progress through this fast, write down any insights the Lord speaks to you, spiritual growth, and personal thoughts to further reflect upon in your walk with the Lord.

The Egyptian Servant Fast

Please read the following Scripture reference and then respond to the questions that follow.

> They found an Egyptian in a field and brought him to David. They gave him water to drink and food to eat—part of a cake of pressed figs and two cakes of raisins. He ate and was revived, for he had not eaten any food or drunk any water for three days and three nights (1 Sam. 30:11-12).

The focus of the Egyptian Servant Fast is threefold: (1) we should never mistreat ourselves and others since we are all God's creation; (2) we should not indulge in the pleasures of life at the expense of others; (3) we should take care of those who poor and needy, the sick and abandoned (cf. Lk. 10:25-37).

The following questions are a guide to help you expand your understanding of all people being created in the image of God and the freedom that comes through treating others with respect and dignity. They will also assist you in applying the Egyptian Servant Fast to your personal life. It is vital that you pray and ask the Holy Spirit to give you the guidance and direction, wisdom, and the best course of action as you complete the Egyptian Servant Fast.

1. What lessons can we learn from the Egyptian Servant Fast?

____

____

2. Which lesson has had the greatest impact on your life? Explain.

____

____

3. How is the Egyptian Servant Fast relevant today?

____

____

4. What is your purpose in the Egyptian Servant Fast? Be specific. I am fasting to:

____

____

____

5. What spiritual power and breakthrough do you desire to unlock through the Egyptian Servant Fast?

____

____

6. If you experienced this spiritual breakthrough, how would your life be different? How would your relationships (family, friends, church) be different or affected by this spiritual breakthrough? Be specific.

____

____

7. How can your faith be increased and/or strengthened through the Egyptian Servant Fast? How will you be benefited by having your faith increased and/or strengthened?

____

____

8. What other benefits, whether physical, emotional, relational, psychological, and spiritual do you desire to achieve during the Egyptian Servant Fast?

____

____

9. What might you discover about yourself during the Egyptian Servant Fast?

____

____

10. How could the Egyptian Servant Fast change your life?

____

____

____

11. What steps would you take to bring out these changes in your life? Who should be involved and to what extent?

____

____

12. Is there someone who you have mistreated and/or ridiculed? If so, how does the principle of sowing and reaping apply? How has this principle affected you personally?

____

____

13. Have you ever indulged in the pleasures of life at the expense of others? If so, ask the Lord to show you and then explain.

____

____

14. What can you do to help those who poor and needy, sick and abandoned? (cf. Lk. 10:25-37).

____

____

15. What length of time (days) and hours each day will you commit to during the Egyptian Servant Fast? When do you plan to begin and end your fast?

____

____

Prayer

Fasting is one of the spiritual disciplines that the Lord has established for you to achieve the spiritual power and breakthrough not only within your life but also in the lives of those whom are close to your heart. I acknowledge that I have become too comfortable in my current state of living and I sense you Holy Spirit calling me to confront the issues that I have been avoiding and find the freedom to live solely for Jesus Christ. Help me through the Egyptian Servant Fast to break free from the bondages that have been controlling my life for too long. Therefore, prayerfully consider and write a prayer that you will address to the Lord that reflects a new commitment and dedication to Him.

The Egyptian Servant Fast Journal

As you progress through this fast, write down any insights the Lord speaks to you, spiritual growth, and personal thoughts to further reflect upon in your walk with the Lord.

Chapter 4: The Fasts of the Pentateuch, Historical Books, and Psalms Continued

This chapter is a continuation of Chapter 3 on the fasts of the Pentateuch, Historical Books, and Psalms and the context in which the fasting occurs. This chapter begins by reflecting and responding to questions on fasting from the Old Testament. Each fast concludes by reflecting and responding to questions relevant to each fast.

Personal Reflections from the Old Testament

In the Old Testament, the foundation for fasting was commanded by Moses on the Day of Atonement to be observed "for the generations to come, wherever you live" (Lev. 23:26-32). Included in this fast was a strict warning for those who failed to observe, or observed for selfish reasons. It also provides the Old Testament foundation from ancient cultures, and the use of sackcloth and ashes in fasting.

Fasting occurs in the entire canon of Scripture and is frequently practiced along with mourning, lamentation or penitence, special occasions and calendrical days, and sackcloth and ashes. At times, it also functions apotropaically—as a preventative measure—prior to engaging in dangerous activity, such as a journey or battle. It parallels the practice of prayer; the two are often conjoined. At various points in history, societal conditions have brought the church to fast and pray to bring about necessary nationwide spiritual and political transformation.[45]

1. Briefly describe the practice of fasting in the Old Testament?

___

___

2. How does your understanding of fasting in the Old Testament practice influence you to practice the spiritual discipline of fasting today?

___

___

3. What conditions in society today might motivate you to fast?

___

[45] "Fast", In John D. Barry and Lazarus Wentz, eds., *Lexham Bible Dictionary* (Bellingham, WA: Logos Bible Software, 2012). "Fast, Fasting", In David Noel Freedman, ed., *The Anchor Yale Bible Dictionary*, Vol. 2 (New York: Doubleday, 1992), 773. Edward Burnett Tylor, *Primitive Culture*, Vol. 2 (Boston, MA: Estes and Lauriat, 1871), 410.

4. What conditions in the church today might motivate you to fast?

5. What conditions in the church today might motivate you to fast for revival?

6. What political conditions in society today might motivate you to fast?

Prayer

Heavenly Father, I recognize that I have not been faithful in practicing the spiritual discipline of fasting as I should and I need Your help to create a pattern of fasting on a regular basis. Help me to be a person like your servant David who was "a man after my own heart" (Acts 13:22) and a person who hungers and thirsts for You (Mt. 5:6). Therefore, prayerfully consider and write a prayer that you will address to the Lord that reflects a new commitment and dedication to Him.

Personal Reflections from the Old Testament Journal

Write down any insights the Lord speaks to you regarding spiritual growth and personal thoughts to further reflect upon in your walk with the Lord.

The Uriah Fast

Please read the following Scripture reference and then respond to the questions that follow.

> Uriah said to David, "The ark and Israel and Judah are staying in tents, and my master Joab and my lord's men are camped in the open fields. How could I go to my house to eat and drink and lie with my wife? As surely as you live, I will not do such a thing!" Then David said to him, "Stay here one more day, and tomorrow I will send you back". So Uriah remained in Jerusalem that day and the next. At David's invitation, he ate and drank with him, and David made him drunk. But in the evening Uriah went out to sleep on his mat among his master's servants; he did not go home. In the morning David wrote a letter to Joab and sent it with Uriah. In it he wrote, "Put Uriah in the front line where the fighting is fiercest. Then withdraw from him so he will be struck down and die". So while Joab had the city under siege, he put Uriah at a place where he knew the strongest defenders were. When the men of the city came out and fought against Joab, some of the men in David's army fell; moreover, Uriah the Hittite died (2 Sam. 11:11-17).

Uriah rejected David's suggestions to go to his home and "eat and drink" since how could he enjoy the comforts of his home and marital intimacies while his comrades in battle were denied these luxuries. His sense of allegiance to his comrades remained intact even while being tempted by King David with food and marital intimacy.[46] The focus of the Uriah Fast is upon not yielding to temptation. Like Uriah, we all face temptation to sensuality even though our thoughts and focus is upon living a Christlike character. We must constantly be aware of the fact that the devil looks for those who are idle and then tempts them through subtle sins. Once we yield to temptation it will lead us deeper into the cycle of sin to hide it.[47] Scripture has a lot to say concerning idleness, for example,

> Do not let anyone who delights in false humility and the worship of angels disqualify you for the prize. Such a person goes into great detail about what he has seen, and his unspiritual mind puffs him up with idle notions. He has lost connection with the Head, from whom the whole body, supported and held together by its ligaments and sinews, grows as God causes it to grow (Col. 2:18-19).

> In the name of the Lord Jesus Christ, we command you, brothers, to keep away from every brother who is idle and does not live according to the teaching you received from us. For you yourselves know how you ought to follow our example. We were not idle when we were with you, nor did we eat anyone's food without paying for it. On the contrary, we worked night and day, laboring and toiling so that we would not be a burden to any of you. We did this, not because we do not have the right to such help, but in order to make ourselves a model for you to follow (2 Th. 3:6-9).

> Besides, they get into the habit of being idle and going about from house to house. And not only do they become idlers, but also gossips and busybodies, saying things they ought not to. So I counsel younger widows to marry, to have children, to manage their homes and to give the enemy

---

[46] John F. Walvoord and Roy B. Zuck, eds., *The Bible Knowledge Commentary: An Exposition of the Scriptures*, Vol. 1 (Wheaton, IL: Victor Books, 1985), 467.

[47] Keith Brooks, *Summarized Bible: Complete Summary of the Old Testament* (Bellingham, WA: Logos Bible Software, 2009), 66.

no opportunity for slander. Some have in fact already turned away to follow Satan (1 Tim. 5:13-15).

The following questions are a guide to help you resist temptation and find freedom from destructive subtle sins. They will also assist you in applying the Uriah Fast to your personal life. It is vital that you pray and ask the Holy Spirit to give you the guidance and direction, wisdom, and the best course of action as you complete the Uriah Fast.

1. What lessons can we learn from the Uriah Fast?

____

____

2. Which lesson has had the greatest impact on your life? Explain.

____

____

3. How is the Uriah Fast relevant today?

____

____

4. What is your purpose in the Uriah Fast? Be specific. I am fasting to:

____

____

5. What spiritual power and breakthrough do you desire to unlock through the Uriah Fast?

____

____

____

____

6. If you experienced this spiritual breakthrough, how would your life be different? How would your relationships (family, friends, church) be different or affected by this spiritual breakthrough? Be specific.

____

____

7. How can your faith be increased and/or strengthened through the Uriah Fast? How will you be benefited by having your faith increased and/or strengthened?

____

____

8. What other benefits, whether physical, emotional, relational, psychological, and spiritual do you desire to achieve during the Uriah Fast?

____

____

9. What might you discover about yourself during the Uriah Fast?

____

____

10. How could the Uriah Fast change your life?

____

____

11. What steps would you take to bring out these changes in your life? Who should be involved and to what extent?

____

____

____

12. What temptation(s) do you struggle with internally and find it difficult to resist temptation?

____

____

13. Briefly describe why a person who committed adultery and/or sexual immorality was to be stoned to death while a person who committed murder had a much lesser punishment.

____

____

14. How does giving into these temptations affect your life and your family life?

____

____

15. What steps can you take to guard yourself from yielding to temptation?

____

____

16. What length of time (days) and hours each day will you commit to during the Uriah Fast? When do you plan to begin and end your fast?

____

____

Prayer

Fasting is one of the spiritual disciplines that the Lord has established for you to achieve the spiritual power and breakthrough not only within your life but also in the lives of those whom are close to your heart. I acknowledge that I have become too comfortable in my current state of living and I sense you Holy Spirit calling me to confront the issues that I have been avoiding and find the freedom to live solely for Jesus Christ. Help me through the Uriah Fast to break free from the bondages that have been controlling my life for too long. Therefore, prayerfully consider and write a prayer that you will address to the Lord that reflects a new commitment and dedication to Him.

The Uriah Fast Journal

As you progress through this fast, write down any insights the Lord speaks to you, spiritual growth, and personal thoughts to further reflect upon in your walk with the Lord.

The Man of God Fast

Please read the following Scripture references and then respond to the questions that follow.

> But the man of God answered the king, "Even if you were to give me half your possessions, I would not go with you, nor would I eat bread or drink water here. For I was commanded by the word of the Lord: 'You must not eat bread or drink water or return by the way you came'". So he took another road and did not return by the way he had come to Bethel (1 Kgs. 13:8-10).

The purpose of the Man of God Fast is threefold: (1) to break off or become cautious of counsel or advice that can lead you away from the Lord or follow advice that is a lie or deception; (2) to recognize and break any idols (person or object) that has been established in your life; (3) to break all yokes that have been placed upon you.

The lesson that we can learn from the Man of God Fast is that the Lord had given the prophet strict orders to abstain from eating and drinking during his mission (1 Kgs. 13:9). However, since he listened and obeyed the message of another person whose message was contrary to the Lord's message, he faced the consequences of his disobedience. We must remember that there are perils awaiting us when we trust the word of another over the Word of God. In the end,

> Jeroboam did not change his evil ways, but once more appointed priests for the high places from all sorts of people. Anyone who wanted to become a priest he consecrated for the high places. This was the sin of the house of Jeroboam that led to its downfall and to its destruction from the face of the earth. . . . I tore the kingdom away from the house of David and gave it to you, but you have not been like my servant David, who kept my commands and followed me with all his heart, doing only what was right in my eyes. You have done more evil than all who lived before you. You have made for yourself other gods, idols made of metal; you have provoked me to anger and thrust me behind your back (1 Kgs. 13:33-34; 14:8-9).

Jeroboam's pride, arrogance, and stubbornness had many consequences. His sin was that he did not keep the Lord's commands like David and committed more "more evil than all who lived before you". His son Abijah becomes sick, and the Prophet Ahijah announces doom for Jeroboam and all his offspring (14:1-20).

> Because of this, I am going to bring disaster on the house of Jeroboam. I will cut off from Jeroboam every last male in Israel—slave or free. I will burn up the house of Jeroboam as one burns dung, until it is all gone. Dogs will eat those belonging to Jeroboam who die in the city, and the birds of the air will feed on those who die in the country. The Lord has spoken! As for you, go back home. When you set foot in your city, the boy will die. All Israel will mourn for him and bury him. He is the only one belonging to Jeroboam who will be buried, because he is the only one in the house of Jeroboam in whom the Lord, the God of Israel, has found anything good (1 Kgs. 14:10-13).

Likewise, the Southern Kingdom of Judah apostatizes under King Rehoboam and the Lord punishes them through an Egyptian invasion that plunders the gold of Solomon's temple (1 Kgs. 14:21-31; 1 Kgs. 5-6). The following questions are a guide to help you recognize messages that are contrary to the Word of

God and break idols and every yoke and find freedom from every form of bondage. They will also assist you in applying the Man of God Fast to your personal life. It is vital that you pray and ask the Holy Spirit to give you the guidance and direction, wisdom, and the best course of action as you complete the Man of God Fast.

1. What lessons can we learn from the Man of God Fast?

____

____

2. Which lesson has had the greatest impact on your life? Explain.

____

____

3. How is the Man of God Fast relevant today?

____

____

4. What is your purpose in the Man of God Fast? Be specific. I am fasting to:

____

____

5. What spiritual power and breakthrough do you desire to unlock through the Man of God Fast?

____

____

6. If you experienced this spiritual breakthrough, how would your life be different? How would your relationships (family, friends, church) be different or affected by this spiritual breakthrough? Be specific.

____

____

7. How can your faith be increased and/or strengthened through the Man of God Fast? How will you be benefited by having your faith increased and/or strengthened?

8. What other benefits, whether physical, emotional, relational, psychological, and spiritual do you desire to achieve during the Man of God Fast?

9. What might you discover about yourself during the Man of God Fast?

10. How could the Man of God Fast change your life?

11. What steps would you take to bring out these changes in your life? Who should be involved and to what extent?

12. Do you feel that you have followed the counsel or advice of someone who you know in your heart that you should not have followed and you need to break off or become more cautious with your relationship with them? Explain. What do you feel needs to happen?

13. Is there someone or something that you cannot live without? Have you set up an idol in our heart which has been reserved for the Lord?

---

14. Have you in the past or present had fellowship with someone or something that is not from God? Explain. What steps can you take to avoid this from happening again?

---

15. Do you sometimes naïvely believe what people say without asking for clarification and later feel guilty? Briefly explain. What steps can you take to avoid this from happening again?

---

16. Do you have people in your life who exaggerate the truth sometimes or speak things that are partially true and partially false? Explain how this affects you. What should you do so that this does not happen again?

---

17. Do you feel that there is a heaviness upon your shoulders that is weighing you down? What is this yoke? How did attached itself to you? This yoke or bondage needs to be removed and destroyed.

> In that day their burden will be lifted from your shoulders, their yoke from your neck; the yoke will be broken because you have grown so fat (Isa. 10:27).

The adjective used for "fat" שָׁמֵן *šāmēn* does not refer to obesity but well-being and prosperity to the point that a person has turned away from Yahweh who had given them prosperity. They had become so well-fed and healthy that they no longer needed God to sustain them.[48]

---

[48] שָׁמֵן *šāmēn*, "2410", In Harris, Archer Jr., and Waltke, eds, *Theological Wordbook of the Old Testament*, 938.

18. What length of time (days) and hours each day will you commit to during the Man of God Fast? When do you plan to begin and end your fast?

Prayer

Fasting is one of the spiritual disciplines that the Lord has established for you to achieve the spiritual power and breakthrough not only within your life but also in the lives of those whom are close to your heart. I acknowledge that I have become too comfortable in my current state of living and I sense you Holy Spirit calling me to confront the issues that I have been avoiding and find the freedom to live solely for Jesus Christ. Help me through the Man of God Fast to break free from the bondages that have been controlling my life for too long. Therefore, prayerfully consider and write a prayer that you will address to the Lord that reflects a new commitment and dedication to Him.

The Man of God Fast Journal

As you progress through this fast, write down any insights the Lord speaks to you, spiritual growth, and personal thoughts to further reflect upon in your walk with the Lord.

The Jehoshaphat Fast

Please read the following Scripture reference and then respond to the questions that follow.

> After this, the Moabites and Ammonites with some of the Meunites came to wage war against Jehoshaphat. Some people came and told Jehoshaphat, "A vast army is coming against you from Edom, from the other side of the Dead Sea. It is already in Hazezon Tamar" (that is, En Gedi). Alarmed, Jehoshaphat resolved to inquire of the Lord, and he proclaimed a fast for all Judah. The people of Judah came together to seek help from the Lord; indeed, they came from every town in Judah to seek him (2 Chr. 20:1-4).

The purpose of the Jehoshaphat Fast is to break every yoke in our life and to bring divine direction. Jehoshaphat fasted at the time of the invasion of the confederated armies of the Canaanites and Syrians (2 Chr. 20:3). The following questions are a guide to help you enter into the presence of the Lord, maintain an attitude of confessing sin and find freedom through knowing the voice of God and responding to divine direction. They will also assist you in applying the Jehoshaphat Fast to your personal life. It is vital that you pray and ask the Holy Spirit to give you the guidance and direction, wisdom, and the best course of action as you complete the Jehoshaphat Fast.

1. What lessons can we learn from the Jehoshaphat Fast?

___

___

2. Which lesson has had the greatest impact on your life? Explain.

___

___

3. How is the Jehoshaphat Fast relevant today?

___

___

4. What is your purpose in the Jehoshaphat Fast? Be specific. I am fasting to:

___

___

___

5. What spiritual power and breakthrough do you desire to unlock through the Jehoshaphat Fast?

____

____

6. If you experienced this spiritual breakthrough, how would your life be different? How would your relationships (family, friends, church) be different or affected by this spiritual breakthrough? Be specific.

____

____

7. How can your faith be increased and/or strengthened through the Jehoshaphat Fast? How will you be benefited by having your faith increased and/or strengthened?

____

____

8. What other benefits, whether physical, emotional, relational, psychological, and spiritual do you desire to achieve during the Jehoshaphat Fast?

____

____

9. What might you discover about yourself during the Jehoshaphat Fast?

____

____

10. How could the Jehoshaphat Fast change your life?

____

____

____

11. What steps would you take to bring out these changes in your life? Who should be involved and to what extent?

____

____

12. Even though Jehoshaphat "proclaimed a fast for all Judah" (v. 3), the results were not favourable. Have you sought the Lord through fasting and prayer yet it seemed as though your purpose for fasting did not bring favourable results? What can you learn from this experience? Briefly explain the purpose for the fast and the results.

____

____

13. What is your greatest personal concern causing you mental and/or emotional anguish?

____

____

14. How might the Jehoshaphat Fast help you cope with this difficulty?

____

____

15. What length of time (days) and hours each day will you commit to during the Jehoshaphat Fast? When do you plan to begin and end your fast?

____

____

Prayer

Fasting is one of the spiritual disciplines that the Lord has established for you to achieve the spiritual power and breakthrough not only within your life but also in the lives of those whom are close to your heart. I acknowledge that I have become too comfortable in my current state of living and I sense you Holy Spirit calling me to confront the issues that I have been avoiding and find the freedom to live solely for Jesus Christ. Help me through the Jehoshaphat Fast to break free from the bondages that have been

controlling my life for too long. Therefore, prayerfully consider and write a prayer that you will address to the Lord that reflects a new commitment and dedication to Him.

The Jehoshaphat Fast Journal

As you progress through this fast, write down any insights the Lord speaks to you, spiritual growth, and personal thoughts to further reflect upon in your walk with the Lord.

The Nehemiah Fast

Please read the following Scripture references and then respond to the questions that follow.

> When I heard these things, I sat down and wept. For some days I mourned and fasted and prayed before the God of heaven. Then I said: "O Lord, God of heaven, the great and awesome God, who keeps his covenant of love with those who love him and obey his commands, let your ear be attentive and your eyes open to hear the prayer your servant is praying before you day and night for your servants, the people of Israel. I confess the sins we Israelites, including myself and my father's house, have committed against you. We have acted very wickedly toward you. We have not obeyed the commands, decrees and laws you gave your servant Moses (Neh. 1:4-7).

> On the twenty-fourth day of the same month, the Israelites gathered together, fasting and wearing sackcloth and having dust on their heads. Those of Israelite descent had separated themselves from all foreigners. They stood in their places and confessed their sins and the wickedness of their fathers. They stood where they were and read from the Book of the Law of the Lord their God for a quarter of the day, and spent another quarter in confession and in worshiping the Lord their God (Neh. 9:1-3).

The Nehemiah Fast focuses upon helping to meet the humanitarian needs of his fellow Jews. However, Nehemiah's specific purpose for fasting was to provide his people and the ancestral city of Jerusalem with protection and more importantly to repent of their disobedience and rebellion by corrupting God's holy seed through the intermarriage with the surrounding idolatrous nations. The Nehemiah Fast helps us to take an honest look at the state of the church in relation to those in our surrounding community that need a helping hand. It also encourages us as we reflect upon how the Lord has helped us in our time of distress, and then to help others in their time of distress. It helps us to count our own blessings and His mercy that has been shown towards us, which should leave us with a grateful heart.[49]

The following questions are a guide to help you live a life of obedience, reflect on the Lord helping you in your distress and then helping others and your community in their distress. Through the Nehemiah Fast you can find the freedom to count our blessings on a daily basis and live each daily with a grateful heart because of the Lord's mercy shown towards us. They will also assist you in applying the Nehemiah Fast to your personal life. It is vital that you pray and ask the Holy Spirit to give you the guidance and direction, wisdom, and the best course of action as you complete the Nehemiah Fast.

1. What lessons can we learn from the Nehemiah Fast?

____

____

____

[49] Brooks, *Summarized* Bible, 96-97.

2. Which lesson has had the greatest impact on your life? Explain.

3. How is the Nehemiah Fast relevant today?

4. What is your purpose in the Nehemiah Fast? Be specific. I am fasting to:

5. What spiritual power and breakthrough do you desire to unlock through the Nehemiah Fast?

6. If you experienced this spiritual breakthrough, how would your life be different? How would your relationships (family, friends, church) be different or affected by this spiritual breakthrough? Be specific.

7. How can your faith be increased and/or strengthened through the Nehemiah Fast? How will you be benefited by having your faith increased and/or strengthened?

8. What other benefits, whether physical, emotional, relational, psychological, and spiritual do you desire to achieve during the Nehemiah Fast?

9. What might you discover about yourself during the Nehemiah Fast?

10. How could the Nehemiah Fast change your life?

11. What steps would you take to bring out these changes in your life? Who should be involved and to what extent?

12. Take a moment to search your heart to see if you are walking in disobedience and rebellion with the Lord. If so, in what ways how have you disobeyed or have rebelled against the Lord?

13. What length of time (days) and hours each day will you commit to during the Nehemiah Fast? When do you plan to begin and end your fast?

Prayer

Fasting is one of the spiritual disciplines that the Lord has established for you to achieve the spiritual power and breakthrough not only within your life but also in the lives of those whom are close to your heart. I acknowledge that I have become too comfortable in my current state of living and I sense you Holy Spirit calling me to confront the issues that I have been avoiding and find the freedom to live solely for Jesus Christ. Help me through the Nehemiah Fast to break free from the bondages that have been

controlling my life for too long. Therefore, prayerfully consider and write a prayer that you will address to the Lord that reflects a new commitment and dedication to Him.

The Nehemiah Fast Journal

As you progress through this fast, write down any insights the Lord speaks to you, spiritual growth, and personal thoughts to further reflect upon in your walk with the Lord.

The Davidic Fast

Please read the following Scripture references and then respond to the questions that follow.

> Yet when they were ill, I put on sackcloth and humbled myself with fasting. When my prayers returned to me unanswered, I went about mourning as though for my friend or brother. I bowed my head in grief as though weeping for my mother (Ps. 35:13-14).

> When I weep and fast, I must endure scorn; when I put on sackcloth, people make sport of me (Ps. 69:10-11).

> My knees give way from fasting; my body is thin and gaunt. I am an object of scorn to my accusers; when they see me, they shake their heads (Ps. 109:24-25).

The prophet Isaiah spoke about righteous men and their behaviours as being like filthy rags. However, these righteous acts does not guarantee that we will not malicious enemies, which David needed to continually confront and ask the Lord for protection, deliverance, and safety.

> All of us have become like one who is unclean, and all our righteous acts are like filthy rags; we all shrivel up like a leaf, and like the wind our sins sweep us away (Isa. 64:6).

Our place of refuge is always with our righteous God who is just in His judgment at all times. David learned that when God is our friend, does it really matter who are enemies are since He promises to protect His children. David was seen as a type of Christ that the world rejected, showed no gratitude (Jn. 10:32), and who was insulted like no other person (Mt. 26:60). If we are falsely charged, like David, let us remember that the prophets were also persecuted as well as the Lord Himself. When David was on the run from Saul, he sought the Lord and fasted. We must remember that we will all experience times in our lives where we will need to call out to God for refuge.[50]

> The LORD is my rock, my fortress and my deliverer; my God is my rock, in whom I take refuge, my shield and the horn of my salvation. He is my stronghold, my refuge and my savior—from violent men you save me (2 Sam. 22:2-3).

> The LORD is my rock, my fortress and my deliverer; my God is my rock, in whom I take refuge. He is my shield and the horn of my salvation, my stronghold (Ps. 18:2).

> The LORD is good, a refuge in times of trouble. He cares for those who trust in him (Nah. 1:7).

It may seem as though God does not answer our prayers or that the enemy is closing is on every side. However, we must always remember that "he will never leave you nor forsake you" (Deut. 31:6, 8; Jos. 1:5; 1 Chr. 28:20; Heb. 13:5). Moreover, when we are hard pressed on every side and do not know where to turn, we must also remember that the only thing that remains is to place our lives in the Hand of God. By doing this we may neither become discontent nor drown with despair. The life of David is a great

---

[50] Brooks, *Summarized Bible*, 118.

example for us when "people insult you, persecute you and falsely say all kinds of evil against you because of me" (Mt. 5:11), when they are spiteful and malicious, we can rest in the fact that the Lord will avenge us. Our future will become as bright as the promises of God.[51]

The following questions are a guide to help you live a life under the protection of the Lord and when it seems like you are surrounded by our enemy, you can find rest in the Arms of God. Through the Davidic Fast you can find freedom as you abide in the Lord. They will also assist you in applying the Davidic Fast to your personal life. It is vital that you pray and ask the Holy Spirit to give you the guidance and direction, wisdom, and the best course of action as you complete the Davidic Fast.

1. What lessons can we learn from the Davidic Fast?

____

____

2. Which lesson has had the greatest impact on your life? Explain.

____

____

3. How is the Davidic Fast relevant today?

____

____

4. What is your purpose in the Davidic Fast? Be specific. I am fasting to:

____

____

5. What spiritual power and breakthrough do you desire to unlock through the Davidic Fast?

____

____

____

[51] Brooks, *Summarized* Bible, 66, 118, 125, 134.

6. If you experienced this spiritual breakthrough, how would your life be different? How would your relationships (family, friends, church) be different or affected by this spiritual breakthrough? Be specific.

____

____

7. How can your faith be increased and/or strengthened through the Davidic Fast? How will you be benefited by having your faith increased and/or strengthened?

____

____

8. What other benefits, whether physical, emotional, relational, psychological, and spiritual do you desire to achieve during the Davidic Fast?

____

____

9. What might you discover about yourself during the Davidic Fast?

____

____

10. How could the Davidic Fast change your life?

____

____

11. What steps would you take to bring out these changes in your life? Who should be involved and to what extent?

____

____

____

12. Do you feel sometimes that, like David, people hate or persecute you without a cause? If yes, briefly explain (Ps. 35; cf. Mt. 5:10-12).

____

____

13. Like David (Ps. 35), have you lost hope in God to deliver you from those to plot and scheme against you without cause? Explain

____

____

14. Do you need to appeal to the Lord for mercy, justice, grace and/or to forgive them?

____

____

15. David was known to fast at the death of Saul and Jonathan, the murder of Abner, and the sickness and death of his first-born son with Bathsheba. What does this say about David? How can this be an example for us to follow?

____

____

16. What length of time (days) and hours each day will you commit to during the Davidic Fast? When do you plan to begin and end your fast?

____

____

Prayer

Fasting is one of the spiritual disciplines that the Lord has established for you to achieve the spiritual power and breakthrough not only within your life but also in the lives of those whom are close to your heart. I acknowledge that I have become too comfortable in my current state of living and I sense you Holy Spirit calling me to confront the issues that I have been avoiding and find the freedom to live solely for Jesus Christ. Help me through the Davidic Fast to break free from the bondages that have been

controlling my life for too long. Therefore, prayerfully consider and write a prayer that you will address to the Lord that reflects a new commitment and dedication to Him.

The Davidic Fast Journal

As you progress through this fast, write down any insights the Lord speaks to you, spiritual growth, and personal thoughts to further reflect upon in your walk with the Lord.

Summary Questions to the Fasts of the Pentateuch, Historical Books, and Psalms

1. What are the primary themes throughout the Fasts of the Pentateuch, Historical Books, and Psalms? Name them in order of prominence.

2. What does this show you regarding the types of sins that have affected God's people throughout history?

3. To what degree are these sins or wickedness still prevalent within your personal life, family, community, city, and/or nation?

4. What are the primary lessons that we can learn from the Fasts of the Pentateuch, Historical Books, and Psalms?

5. How does your understanding of true fasting, as described in the Pentateuch, Historical Books, and Psalms, change the way in which you perceive and respond to our community and culture?

6. Which fast was the *most* meaningful to you? Why?

7. Which fast was the *least* meaningful to you? Why?

8. What steps do you need to take to live a life of abundance and freedom from the "sin that so easily entangles"?

> Therefore, since we are surrounded by such a great cloud of witnesses, let us throw off everything that hinders and the sin that so easily entangles, and let us run with perseverance the race marked out for us. Let us fix our eyes on Jesus, the author and perfecter of our faith, who for the joy set before him endured the cross, scorning its shame, and sat down at the right hand of the throne of God. Consider him who endured such opposition from sinful men, so that you will not grow weary and lose heart (Heb. 12:1-3).

The Fasts of the Pentateuch, Historical Books, and Psalms Journal

Take some time to reflect on these fasts. What are some of the common themes that were the most relevant to you? How can finding victory in these areas transform your life?

Chapter 5: The Fasts of Isaiah 58

The purpose of this chapter is to present some of the fasts that are included in Isaiah 58 and the context in which the fasting occurs. The next chapter will present the remainder of the fasts of Isaiah 58. Each fast concludes by reflecting and responding to questions relevant to each fast.

Even though this Isaiahic oracle was probably intended for the post-exilic community, it contains many features common to the eighth century prophets. Isaiah emphasizes social righteousness and is connected to Zechariah 7, where the prophet stresses a harmony that is indicative of earlier prophets and also with the teaching of Jesus in the Sermon on the Mount (Mt. 5-7). Isaiah concludes his prophetic word by summoning his audience to comprehend the reality of sin. Isaiah begins by describing a superficial righteousness (Isa. 58:1-3a), which disguises the hypocritical personal, societal, and corrupt lifestyle of the people (Isa. 58:3b-7). Isaiah calls the people to a spiritual reformation that breaks "the yoke of oppression" and only then does the Lord promise to hear, answer their prayers, sustain them, and bring "the joy of the Lord" and "feast on the inheritance of your father Jacob (Isa. 58:8-14).[52]

The Disciple's Fast

Please read the following scripture references and then respond to the questions that follow.

> Therefore, since we are surrounded by such a great cloud of witnesses, let us throw off everything that hinders and the sin that so easily entangles, and let us run with perseverance the race marked out for us (Heb. 12:1).
>
> When they came to the crowd, a man approached Jesus and knelt before him. "Lord, have mercy on my son", he said. "He has seizures and is suffering greatly. He often falls into the fire or into the water. I brought him to your disciples, but they could not heal him". "You unbelieving and perverse generation", Jesus replied, "how long shall I stay with you? How long shall I put up with you? Bring the boy here to me". Jesus rebuked the demon, and it came out of the boy, and he was healed at that moment. Then the disciples came to Jesus in private and asked, "Why couldn't we drive it out?" He replied, "Because you have so little faith. Truly I tell you, if you have faith as small as a mustard seed, you can say to this mountain, 'Move from here to there', and it will move. Nothing will be impossible for you. But this kind does not go out except by prayer and fasting" (Mt. 17:14-21).
>
> When they came to the other disciples, they saw a large crowd around them and the teachers of the law arguing with them. As soon as all the people saw Jesus, they were overwhelmed with wonder and ran to greet him. "What are you arguing with them about?" he asked. A man in the crowd answered, "Teacher, I brought you my son, who is possessed by a spirit that has robbed him of speech. Whenever it seizes him, it throws him to the ground. He foams at the mouth, gnashes his teeth and becomes rigid. I asked your disciples to drive out the spirit, but they could not". "O unbelieving generation", Jesus replied, "how long shall I stay with you? How long shall I put up with you? Bring the boy to me". So they brought him. When the spirit saw Jesus, it

---

[52] Lawrence O. Richards, *The Bible Reader's Companion*, electronic ed (Wheaton, IL: Victor Books, 1991), 442. Frank E. Gaebelein , ed., *The Expositor's Bible Commentary, Volume 6: Isaiah, Jeremiah, Lamentations, Ezekiel* (Grand Rapids, MI: Zondervan Publishing House, 1986), WORD*search* CROSS e-book, 321.

immediately threw the boy into a convulsion. He fell to the ground and rolled around, foaming at the mouth. Jesus asked the boy's father, "How long has he been like this?" "From childhood", he answered. "It has often thrown him into fire or water to kill him. But if you can do anything, take pity on us and help us". "'If you can't?" said Jesus. "Everything is possible for him who believes". Immediately the boy's father exclaimed, "I do believe; help me overcome my unbelief!" When Jesus saw that a crowd was running to the scene, he rebuked the evil spirit. "You deaf and mute spirit", he said, "I command you, come out of him and never enter him again". The spirit shrieked, convulsed him violently and came out. The boy looked so much like a corpse that many said, "He's dead". But Jesus took him by the hand and lifted him to his feet, and he stood up. After Jesus had gone indoors, his disciples asked him privately, "Why couldn't we drive it out?" He replied, "This kind can come out only by prayer" (Mk. 9:14-29).

The next day, when they came down from the mountain, a large crowd met him. A man in the crowd called out, "Teacher, I beg you to look at my son, for he is my only child. A spirit seizes him and he suddenly screams; it throws him into convulsions so that he foams at the mouth. It scarcely ever leaves him and is destroying him. I begged your disciples to drive it out, but they could not". "O unbelieving and perverse generation", Jesus replied, "how long shall I stay with you and put up with you? Bring your son here". Even while the boy was coming, the demon threw him to the ground in a convulsion. But Jesus rebuked the evil spirit, healed the boy and gave him back to his father. And they were all amazed at the greatness of God (Lk. 9:37-43).

The purpose of the Disciple's Fast is to "loose the bands of wickedness" in your life (Isa. 58:6). The disciple's fast begins with making a life-freeing choice to be delivered from bondage and/or addictions to sin. The writer of Hebrews identifies the problem of besetting sins that many of us struggle with.

The following questions are a guide to help you "loose the bands of wickedness" in your life and find freedom from bondage and/or addictions, and overcoming besetting sins. A besetting sin is a type of bondage that a person has been unsuccessful in their attempts to being set free from that sin. They will also assist you in applying the Disciple's Fast to your personal life. It is vital that you pray and ask the Holy Spirit to give you the guidance and direction, wisdom, and the best course of action as you complete the Disciple's Fast.[53]

1. What lessons can we learn from the Disciple's Fast?

____

____

2. Which lesson has had the greatest impact on your life? Explain.

____

____

[53] For further study, please refer to Elmer L. Towns, *Fasting for Spiritual Breakthrough Study Guide*, <http://digitalcommons.liberty.edu/towns_books/17>. Accessed on November 15, 2013.

3. How is the Disciple's Fast relevant today?

____

____

4. What is your purpose in the Disciple's Fast? Be specific. I am fasting to:

____

____

5. What spiritual power and breakthrough do you desire to unlock through the Disciple's Fast?

____

____

6. If you experienced this spiritual breakthrough, how would your life be different? How would your relationships (family, friends, church) be different or affected by this spiritual breakthrough? Be specific.

____

____

7. How can your faith be increased and/or strengthened through the Disciple's Fast? How will you be benefited by having your faith increased and/or strengthened?

____

____

8. What other benefits, whether physical, emotional, relational, psychological, and spiritual do you desire to achieve during the Disciple's Fast?

____

____

9. What might you discover about yourself during the Disciple's Fast?

____

10. How could the Disciple's Fast change your life?

11. What steps would you take to bring out these changes in your life? Who should be involved and to what extent?

12. Define "besetting sins" in your own words. State your own "besetting sins".

13. How can fasting increase your desire to be completely free from besetting sins?

14. How are these "besetting sins" affecting you, your family, and those closest to you?

15. State the areas in your life in which you constantly struggle to find freedom from bondage and addictions to "besetting sins"?

16. How can Satan use "besetting sins" as a stronghold in our lives?

17. What length of time (days) and hours each day will you commit to during the Disciple's Fast? When do you plan to begin and end your fast?

Prayer

Fasting is one of the spiritual disciplines that the Lord has established for you to achieve the spiritual power and breakthrough not only within your life but also in the lives of those whom are close to your heart. I acknowledge that I have become too comfortable in my current state of living and I sense you Holy Spirit calling me to confront the issues that I have been avoiding and find the freedom to live solely for Jesus Christ. Help me through the Disciple's Fast to break free from the bondages that have been controlling my life for too long. Therefore, prayerfully consider and write a prayer that you will address to the Lord that reflects a new commitment and dedication to Him.

The Disciple's Fast Journal

As you progress through this fast, write down any insights the Lord speaks to you, spiritual growth, and personal thoughts to further reflect upon in your walk with the Lord.

The Ezra Fast

Please read the following Scripture references and then respond to the questions that follow.

> There, by the Ahava Canal, I proclaimed a fast, so that we might humble ourselves before our God and ask him for a safe journey for us and our children, with all our possessions. I was ashamed to ask the king for soldiers and horsemen to protect us from enemies on the road, because we had told the king, "The gracious hand of our God is on everyone who looks to him, but his great anger is against all who forsake him". So we fasted and petitioned our God about this, and he answered our prayer (Ezra 8:21-23).

> Then Ezra withdrew from before the house of God and went to the room of Jehohanan son of Eliashib. While he was there, he ate no food and drank no water, because he continued to mourn over the unfaithfulness of the exiles. A proclamation was then issued throughout Judah and Jerusalem for all the exiles to assemble in Jerusalem. Anyone who failed to appear within three days would forfeit all his property, in accordance with the decision of the officials and elders, and would himself be expelled from the assembly of the exiles (Ezra 10:6-8).

> When Mordecai learned of all that had been done, he tore his clothes, put on sackcloth and ashes, and went out into the city, wailing loudly and bitterly. But he went only as far as the king's gate, because no one clothed in sackcloth was allowed to enter it. In every province to which the edict and order of the king came, there was great mourning among the Jews, with fasting, weeping and wailing. Many lay in sackcloth and ashes (Est. 4:1-3).

We all face problems in our lives, but our attitude is too often focused upon the problem which only exacerbates the problem instead of focusing on the solution. The purpose of the Ezra Fast is to "untie the cords of the yoke" in your life (Isa. 58:6) and its goal is to ask the Holy Spirit to give us wisdom in confronting the problems. As His servants, we have His power available for us, through His Spirit, "this is the word of the Lord to Zerubbabel: 'Not by might nor by power, but by my Spirit', says the Lord Almighty" (Zech. 4:6). We all face every day struggles, trials and tribulations, but as we walk daily with the Lord we will find peace and protection through Jesus Christ. Those who trust in their own strength will be put to shame, but those who place their trust in the Lord and follow his commands and precepts will be will know His protection under the shadow of His wings (Ezra 8:22).[54]

Therefore, we can see that the purpose of the Ezra Fast was to "untie the cords of the yoke". In Ezra, we can see that the priests, Levites and many men had been "tied" to foreign women who had lead them astray from God and had contaminate the holy seed or remnant. Through the Ezra Fast we dedicate ourselves wholeheartedly to God so that His purpose can be realized within our lives.

The following questions are a guide to help you "untie the cords of the yoke" in your life and find freedom from the contaminating effects of sin and free to dedicate our lives to the Lord. They will also assist you in applying the Ezra Fast to your personal life. It is vital that you pray and ask the Holy Spirit for guidance and direction, wisdom, and the best course of action as you complete the Ezra Fast.

---

[54] Brooks, *Summarized* Bible, 94.

1. What lessons can we learn from the Ezra Fast?

2. Which lesson has had the greatest impact on your life? Explain.

3. How is the Ezra Fast relevant today?

4. What is your purpose in the Ezra Fast? Be specific. I am fasting to:

5. What spiritual power and breakthrough do you desire to unlock through the Ezra Fast?

6. If you experienced this spiritual breakthrough, how would your life be different? How would your relationships (family, friends, church) be different or affected by this spiritual breakthrough? Be specific.

7. How can your faith be increased and/or strengthened through the Ezra Fast? How will you be benefited by having your faith increased and/or strengthened?

8. What other benefits, whether physical, emotional, relational, psychological, and spiritual do you desire to achieve during the Ezra Fast?

9. What might you discover about yourself during the Ezra Fast?

10. How could the Ezra Fast change your life?

11. What steps would you take to bring out these changes in your life? Who should be involved and to what extent?

12. Describe the burden that Ezra needed to confront, which resulted in the Ezra fast?

13. Describe the underlying cause of the burden for which you are caring and desire to find a solution.

14. Write down some principles from the Word of God that can be applied to this situation?

15. Evaluate the facts and determine the best course of action to take. Make sure to allow time for the Holy Spirit to speak to you.

16. What length of time (days) and hours each day will you commit to during the Ezra Fast? When do you plan to begin and end your fast?

Prayer

Fasting is one of the spiritual disciplines that the Lord has established for you to achieve the spiritual power and breakthrough not only within your life but also in the lives of those whom are close to your heart. I acknowledge that I have become too comfortable in my current state of living and I sense you Holy Spirit calling me to confront the issues that I have been avoiding and find the freedom to live solely for Jesus Christ. Help me through the Ezra Fast to break free from the bondages that have been controlling my life for too long. Therefore, prayerfully consider and write a prayer that you will address to the Lord that reflects a new commitment and dedication to Him.

The Ezra Fast Journal

As you progress through this fast, write down any insights the Lord speaks to you, spiritual growth, and personal thoughts to further reflect upon in your walk with the Lord.

The Samuel Fast

Please read the following Scripture reference and then respond to the questions that follow.

> It was a long time, twenty years in all, that the ark remained at Kiriath Jearim, and all the people of Israel mourned and sought after the Lord. And Samuel said to the whole house of Israel, "If you are returning to the Lord with all your hearts, then rid yourselves of the foreign gods and the Ashtoreths and commit yourselves to the Lord and serve him only, and he will deliver you out of the hand of the Philistines". So the Israelites put away their Baals and Ashtoreths, and served the Lord only. Then Samuel said, "Assemble all Israel at Mizpah and I will intercede with the Lord for you". When they had assembled at Mizpah, they drew water and poured it out before the Lord. On that day they fasted and there they confessed, "We have sinned against the Lord". And Samuel was leader of Israel at Mizpah. When the Philistines heard that Israel had assembled at Mizpah, the rulers of the Philistines came up to attack them. And when the Israelites heard of it, they were afraid because of the Philistines. They said to Samuel, "Do not stop crying out to the Lord our God for us, that he may rescue us from the hand of the Philistines". Then Samuel took a suckling lamb and offered it up as a whole burnt offering to the Lord. He cried out to the Lord on Israel's behalf, and the Lord answered him. While Samuel was sacrificing the burnt offering, the Philistines drew near to engage Israel in battle. But that day the Lord thundered with loud thunder against the Philistines and threw them into such a panic that they were routed before the Israelites. The men of Israel rushed out of Mizpah and pursued the Philistines, slaughtering them along the way to a point below Beth Car. Then Samuel took a stone and set it up between Mizpah and Shen. He named it Ebenezer, saying, "Thus far has the Lord helped us". So the Philistines were subdued and did not invade Israelite territory again. Throughout Samuel's lifetime, the hand of the Lord was against the Philistines. The towns from Ekron to Gath that the Philistines had captured from Israel were restored to her, and Israel delivered the neighboring territory from the power of the Philistines. And there was peace between Israel and the Amorites. Samuel continued as judge over Israel all the days of his life. From year to year he went on a circuit from Bethel to Gilgal to Mizpah, judging Israel in all those places. But he always went back to Ramah, where his home was, and there he also judged Israel. And he built an altar there to the Lord (1 Sam. 7:2-17).

The purpose of the Samuel Fast is designed to bring liberty to the oppressed (Isa. 58:6). When we become conscious that the Lord seems to be distant because of our sin and that we cannot continue to live as we have lived, then we must take that step of repentance and receive assurance that renewed prosperity and deliverance is there for us. The Samuel Fast includes both corporate and individual revival.[55]

Matthew Henry wrote,

> When God intends great mercy for his people the first thing he does is to set them a praying; thus he seeks to destroy their enemies by stirring them up to seek to him that he would do it for them; because, though he has proposed it and promised it, and it is for his own glory to do it, yet he will *for this be enquired of by the house of Israel.*[56]

> This is what the Sovereign Lord says: Once again I will yield to the plea of the house of Israel and do this for them: I will make their people as numerous as sheep, as numerous as the flocks for

---

[55] Brooks, *Summarized* Bible, 58.

[56] Zechariah 12:9-14, In Matthew Henry, *Matthew Henry's Commentary on the Whole Bible: Complete and Unabridged in One Volume* (Peabody, MA: Hendrickson Publishers, 1994).

offerings at Jerusalem during her appointed feasts. So will the ruined cities be filled with flocks of people. Then they will know that I am the Lord (Eze. 36:37-38).

Throughout the great revivals of history, fasting and prayer have always been the key components. The Samuel Fast explores the relationship between fasting and revival.

The following questions are a guide to help you identify areas within your life that have placed you in bondage to sin, such as: sinful habits, demonic influences, and memories to name a few and find freedom to live a healthy and prosperous life. We also seek the Lord for the spiritual direction so that we can be set free from enslavement to sin, defeat all strongholds and dethrone all established idols. They will also assist you in applying the Samuel Fast to your personal life. It is vital that you pray and ask the Holy Spirit to give you the guidance and direction, wisdom, and the best course of action as you complete the Samuel Fast.

1. What lessons can we learn from the Samuel Fast?

____

____

2. Which lesson has had the greatest impact on your life? Explain.

____

____

3. How is the Samuel Fast relevant today?

____

____

4. What is your purpose in the Samuel Fast? Be specific. I am fasting to:

____

____

5. What spiritual power and breakthrough do you desire to unlock through the Samuel Fast?

____

____

6. If you experienced this spiritual breakthrough, how would your life be different? How would your relationships (family, friends, church) be different or affected by this spiritual breakthrough? Be specific.

____

____

7. How can your faith be increased and/or strengthened through the Samuel Fast? How will you be benefited by having your faith increased and/or strengthened?

____

____

8. What other benefits, whether physical, emotional, relational, psychological, and spiritual do you desire to achieve during the Samuel Fast?

____

____

9. What might you discover about yourself during the Samuel Fast?

____

____

10. How could the Samuel Fast change your life?

____

____

11. What steps would you take to bring out these changes in your life? Who should be involved and to what extent?

____

____

____

12. How does the expression "times of refreshing may come from the presence of the Lord" describe revival? In what ways do you need a time of refreshing?

____

____

13. What role did the Samuel Fast have in the national revival in Israel?

____

____

14. In order to experience revival, it is imperative that we identify the root of our bondage to sin which can hinder revival.

____

____

15. What signs do you see in your own life, your church, community, and nation that suggest the need for revival?

____

____

16. If you were to fast for revival, what changes would you anticipate in your life, church, community, and nation?

____

____

17. List the necessary steps that would need to be taken to bring about a revival in your own life, your church, community, and nation.

____

____

18. Are there noticeable changes that God has begun to make changes in your life, family, church, community, and nation?

____

19. What length of time (days) and hours each day will you commit to during the Samuel Fast? When do you plan to begin and end your fast?

Prayer

Fasting is one of the spiritual disciplines that the Lord has established for you to achieve the spiritual power and breakthrough not only within your life but also in the lives of those whom are close to your heart. I acknowledge that I have become too comfortable in my current state of living and I sense you Holy Spirit calling me to confront the issues that I have been avoiding and find the freedom to live solely for Jesus Christ. Help me through the Samuel Fast to break free from the bondages that have been controlling my life for too long. Therefore, prayerfully consider and write a prayer that you will address to the Lord that reflects a new commitment and dedication to Him.

The Samuel Fast Journal

As you progress through this fast, write down any insights the Lord speaks to you, spiritual growth, and personal thoughts to further reflect upon in your walk with the Lord.

The Elijah Fast

Please read the following Scripture reference and then respond to the questions that follow.

> Now Ahab told Jezebel everything Elijah had done and how he had killed all the prophets with the sword. So Jezebel sent a messenger to Elijah to say, "May the gods deal with me, be it ever so severely, if by this time tomorrow I do not make your life like that of one of them". Elijah was afraid and ran for his life. When he came to Beersheba in Judah, he left his servant there, while he himself went a day's journey into the wilderness. He came to a broom bush, sat down under it and prayed that he might die. "I have had enough, Lord", he said. "Take my life; I am no better than my ancestors". Then he lay down under the bush and fell asleep. All at once an angel touched him and said, "Get up and eat". He looked around, and there by his head was some bread baked over hot coals, and a jar of water. He ate and drank and then lay down again. The angel of the Lord came back a second time and touched him and said, "Get up and eat, for the journey is too much for you". So he got up and ate and drank. Strengthened by that food, he traveled forty days and forty nights until he reached Horeb, the mountain of God. There he went into a cave and spent the night (1 Kgs. 19:1-9).

The purpose of the Elijah Fast is to "break every yoke" (Isa. 58:6) in your life. The prophet Isaiah says, "In that day their burden will be lifted from your shoulders, their yoke from your neck; the yoke will be broken because you have grown so fat" (Isa. 10:27). The adjective used for "fat" שָׁמֵן *šāmēn* does not refer to obesity but well-being and prosperity to the point that a person has turned away from Yahweh who had given them prosperity. They had become so well-fed and healthy that they no longer needed God to sustain them.[57] Elmer L. Towns defines a habit as a "behavior pattern acquired by frequent repetition reflected in regular or increased performance".[58]

The prophet Elijah has sometimes been viewed as "super saint", a person who had a close relationship with God, and lived a life that surpassed others in their walk with the Lord. However, the New Testament describes Elijah as "a man just like us" (Jas. 5:17). It is interesting how we often tend to hide our inner pain, struggles, and pretend that everything is perfect. But, we must realize that God is omniscient and knows our heart, which cannot be hidden from Him. Like Elijah, many of us find our source of life and joy in doing ministry, yet cannot comprehend how we become discouraged, depressed, and emotionally distressed.

The following questions are a guide to help you "break every yoke "especially in relation to negative emotions and find freedom over mental and emotional issues and anything that dominates our thoughts, cognitive perception, and false belief systems. The Elijah Fast is specifically directed towards negative emotions like, "I am worthless", "nobody loves me", "I will never amount to anything", or "I'm a failure". They will also assist you in applying the Elijah Fast to your personal life. It is vital that you pray and ask the Holy Spirit to give you the guidance and direction, wisdom, and the best course of action as you complete the Elijah Fast.

---

[57] שָׁמֵן *šāmēn*, "2410", In Harris, Archer Jr., and Waltke, eds, *Theological Wordbook of the Old Testament*, 938.

[58] Elmer L. Towns, *Fasting for Spiritual Breakthrough* (Ventura, CA: Regal Books, 1996), 192.

1. What lessons can we learn from the Elijah Fast?

____

____

2. Which lesson has had the greatest impact on your life? Explain.

____

____

3. How is the Elijah Fast relevant today?

____

____

4. What is your purpose in the Elijah Fast? Be specific. I am fasting to:

____

____

5. What spiritual power and breakthrough do you desire to unlock through the Elijah Fast?

____

____

6. If you experienced this spiritual breakthrough, how would your life be different? How would your relationships (family, friends, church) be different or affected by this spiritual breakthrough? Be specific.

____

____

7. How can your faith be increased and/or strengthened through the Elijah Fast? How will you be benefited by having your faith increased and/or strengthened?

____

8. What other benefits, whether physical, emotional, relational, psychological, and spiritual do you desire to achieve during the Elijah Fast?

9. What might you discover about yourself during the Elijah Fast?

10. How could the Elijah Fast change your life?

11. What steps would you take to bring out these changes in your life? Who should be involved and to what extent?

12. What is your greatest personal concern causing you mental and/or emotional anguish? Briefly describe.

13. Even though Elijah had an emotional problem, God used him in a powerful way on Mount Carmel. Describe how his emotional problem was manifested. Are there times in your own life when you feel like Elijah? Explain.

14. Elmer L. Towns states four signs that contribute to emotional distress: (1) negative self-image; (2) low self-image; (3) threatening self-image; (4) self-rejection.[59] Do you identify with one or more of these signs? State and explain. How do these sign(s) contribute to your emotional state of being?

____

____

15. Describe how the Elijah Fast might help you cope with this emotional distress?

____

____

16. Like Elijah, do you find yourself becoming discouraged, depressed, and emotionally distressed following a major spiritual victory and/or achievement and wonder why the joy of the Lord is absent? Describe.

____

____

17. Do you sometimes depend upon past victories and achievements to sustain you through subsequent ministry opportunities? Briefly explain. How could you become better equipped for present ministry?

____

____

The Word of God gives us the steps to break "every yoke", create new behaviours, and achieve personal and emotional freedom in your life.

> Through these he has given us his very great and precious promises, so that through them you may participate in the divine nature and escape the corruption in the world caused by evil desires. For this very reason, make every effort to add to your faith goodness; and to goodness, knowledge; and to knowledge, self-control; and to self-control, perseverance; and to perseverance, godliness; and to godliness, brotherly kindness; and to brotherly kindness, love. For if you possess these qualities in increasing measure, they will keep you from being ineffective and unproductive in your knowledge of our Lord Jesus Christ (2 Pet. 1:4-8).

The apostle Peter presents seven distinguishing traits of walking the Christian life. Peter begins by affirming that as Christians, our new birth in Jesus Christ becomes the foundation on which we begin to build our freedom in Christ. We must remember that this is a daily walk with the Lord and as Peter states

[59] Towns, *Fasting for Spiritual Breakthrough*, 84.

to "escape the corruption in the world caused by evil desires" literally to be "out of reach of pursuit", "being acquitted", "to escape the accusations", or "escape by flight".[60] We are to escape the "evil desires" or strong cravings that lead to corruption, decay, or ruin. Peter exhorts believers to "make every effort to add" meaning "to supply or increase in spiritual dimensions".[61]

He makes it very clear that believers mature only as they cultivate these spiritual virtues in harmony with the other virtues in connection with the life and relationship of Jesus Christ (cf. Gal. 5:22-23).[62] The virtues that believers are instructed to add to their faith include: (1) goodness; (2) knowledge; (3) self-control; (4) perseverance; (5) godliness; (6) brotherly kindness; and (7) love. It is as we follow these virtues in harmony and through the power of the Holy Spirit that we can break the destructive cycle of "every yoke" and emotional distress and achieve and live a life of freedom in Jesus Christ.

18. What destructive habits, thoughts, and behaviours will be the focus of your Elijah Fast?

____

____

19. What will be your course of action that will bring the necessary transformation to your attitude, behaviour, and/or habit?

____

____

20. What positive thought, attitude, and behaviour would you like to replace your former destructive habit or emotional distress?

____

____

21. What length of time (days) and hours each day will you commit to during the Elijah Fast? When do you plan to begin and end your fast?

____

60 ἀποφεύγω *apopheugō* "662", In Gilbrant, ed., *The Complete Biblical Library Greek-English Dictionary, Alpha-Gamma* (Springfield, MO: Complete Biblical Library, 1991), WORD*search* CROSS e-book. Gilbrant, ed., *The Complete Biblical Library, Hebrews-Jude* (Springfield, IL: World Library Press, Inc., 1989), WORD*search* CROSS e-book, 323. ἐπιθυμίᾳ *epithumia*, 1924, In Gilbrant, ed., *The Complete Biblical Library Greek-English Dictionary, Delta-Epsilon* (Springfield, MO: Complete Biblical Library, 1991), WORD*search* CROSS e-book.

61 ἐπιχορηγήσατε *epichorēgēsate* "2007", In Gilbrant, ed., *The Complete Biblical Library Greek-English Dictionary, Delta-Epsilon* (Springfield, MO: Complete Biblical Library, 1991), WORDsearch CROSS e-book.

62 Warren W. Wiersbe, *The Bible Exposition Commentary*, Vol. 2 (Wheaton, IL: Victor Books, 1996), 438. Towns, *Fasting for Spiritual Breakthrough*, 92f.

Prayer

Fasting is one of the spiritual disciplines that the Lord has established for you to achieve the spiritual power and breakthrough not only within your life but also in the lives of those whom are close to your heart. I acknowledge that I have become too comfortable in my current state of living and I sense you Holy Spirit calling me to confront the issues that I have been avoiding and find the freedom to live solely for Jesus Christ. Help me through the Elijah Fast to break free from the bondages that have been controlling my life for too long. Therefore, prayerfully consider and write a prayer that you will address to the Lord that reflects a new commitment and dedication to Him.

The Elijah Fast Journal

As you progress through this fast, write down any insights the Lord speaks to you, spiritual growth, and personal thoughts to further reflect upon in your walk with the Lord.

The Widow's Fast

Please read the following Scripture references and then respond to the questions that follow.

Some time later the brook dried up because there had been no rain in the land. Then the word of the Lord came to him: "Go at once to Zarephath of Sidon and stay there. I have commanded a widow in that place to supply you with food". So he went to Zarephath. When he came to the town gate, a widow was there gathering sticks. He called to her and asked, "Would you bring me a little water in a jar so I may have a drink?" As she was going to get it, he called, "And bring me, please, a piece of bread". "As surely as the Lord your God lives", she replied, "I don't have any bread—only a handful of flour in a jar and a little oil in a jug. I am gathering a few sticks to take home and make a meal for myself and my son, that we may eat it—and die". Elijah said to her, "Don't be afraid. Go home and do as you have said. But first make a small cake of bread for me from what you have and bring it to me, and then make something for yourself and your son. For this is what the Lord, the God of Israel, says: 'The jar of flour will not be used up and the jug of oil will not run dry until the day the Lord gives rain on the land'". She went away and did as Elijah had told her. So there was food every day for Elijah and for the woman and her family. For the jar of flour was not used up and the jug of oil did not run dry, in keeping with the word of the Lord spoken by Elijah. Some time later the son of the woman who owned the house became ill. He grew worse and worse, and finally stopped breathing. She said to Elijah, "What do you have against me, man of God? Did you come to remind me of my sin and kill my son?" "Give me your son", Elijah replied. He took him from her arms, carried him to the upper room where he was staying, and laid him on his bed. Then he cried out to the Lord, "O Lord my God, have you brought tragedy also upon this widow I am staying with, by causing her son to die?" Then he stretched himself out on the boy three times and cried to the Lord, "O Lord my God, let this boy's life return to him!" The Lord heard Elijah's cry, and the boy's life returned to him, and he lived. Elijah picked up the child and carried him down from the room into the house. He gave him to his mother and said, "Look, your son is alive!" Then the woman said to Elijah, "Now I know that you are a man of God and that the word of the Lord from your mouth is the truth" (1 Kgs. 17:7-24).

There was also a prophetess, Anna, the daughter of Phanuel, of the tribe of Asher. She was very old; she had lived with her husband seven years after her marriage, and then was a widow until she was eighty-four. She never left the temple but worshiped night and day, fasting and praying (Lk. 2:36-37).

The Widow's Fast is designed as a means of meeting the humanitarian needs of others. It is about sacrificing our physical necessities to provide for the poor and needy. The widow did not have much but she gave up her food to help the prophet. A selfless fast of this type requires faith and trust in God. As already noted, there are many benefits of fasting. One of these benefits includes that through fasting we have extra resources to be allocated to towards helping those who are poor, needy, less fortunate, in need of a helping hand, or just have a hard time coping with life. This is also one of the purposes of God in fasting. The following context is a great example of obedience and God's intervention to meet the needs of those involved.

The following questions are a guide to help you take the focus off of yourself and to focus on the physical, emotional, and spiritual needs of others and find joy and freedom in helping the poor and needy in the basic necessities of life. They will also assist you in applying the Widow's Fast to your personal life. It is vital that you pray and ask the Holy Spirit to give you the guidance and direction, wisdom, and the best course of action as you complete the Widow's Fast.

1. What lessons can we learn from the Widow's Fast?

____

____

2. Which lesson has had the greatest impact on your life? Explain.

____

____

3. How is the Widow's Fast relevant today?

____

____

4. What is your purpose in the Widow's Fast? Be specific. I am fasting to:

____

____

5. What spiritual power and breakthrough do you desire to unlock through the Widow's Fast?

____

____

6. If you experienced this spiritual breakthrough, how would your life be different? How would your relationships (family, friends, church) be different or affected by this spiritual breakthrough? Be specific.

____

____

____

7. How can your faith be increased and/or strengthened through the Widow's Fast? How will you be benefited by having your faith increased and/or strengthened?

8. What other benefits, whether physical, emotional, relational, psychological, and spiritual do you desire to achieve during the Widow's Fast?

9. What might you discover about yourself during the Widow's Fast?

10. How could the Widow's Fast change your life?

11. What steps would you take to bring out these changes in your life? Who should be involved and to what extent?

12. Through the Widow's Fast we become more aware of the physical, emotional, and spiritual needs of others. Who do you know that needs assistance in providing for their family?

13. Name five specific needs in your church and five specific needs in your community that would motivate you to fast and pray for them.

Your Church	**Your Community**
1. ____________________	1. ____________________
2. ____________________	2. ____________________
3. ____________________	3. ____________________
4. ____________________	4. ____________________
5. ____________________	5. ____________________

14. Which of these ten needs seem to be the greatest concern in your church and community?

____

____

15. While you follow the Widow's Fast, how can the money you save be used to help some of needs stated above?

____

____

16. Take some time to modify your budget, what changes could you make to allocate some of your resources to help those who are less fortunate?

____

____

17. What length of time (days) and hours each day will you commit to during the Widow's Fast? When do you plan to begin and end your fast?

____

____

____

Prayer

Fasting is one of the spiritual disciplines that the Lord has established for you to achieve the spiritual power and breakthrough not only within your life but also in the lives of those whom are close to your heart. I acknowledge that I have become too comfortable in my current state of living and I sense you Holy Spirit calling me to confront the issues that I have been avoiding and find the freedom to live solely for Jesus Christ. Help me through the Widow's Fast to break free from the bondages that have been controlling my life for too long. Therefore, prayerfully consider and write a prayer that you will address to the Lord that reflects a new commitment and dedication to Him.

____

____

____

____

____

The Widow's Fast Journal

As you progress through this fast, write down any insights the Lord speaks to you, spiritual growth, and personal thoughts to further reflect upon in your walk with the Lord.

____

____

____

____

____

____

____

____

Chapter 6: The Fasts of Isaiah 58 Continued

This chapter is a continuation of Chapter 5 on the fasts of Isaiah 58 and the context in which the fasting occurs. Each fast concludes by reflecting and responding to questions relevant to each fast.

The Apostle Paul Fast

Please read the following Scripture reference and then respond to the questions that follow.

> Meanwhile, Saul was still breathing out murderous threats against the Lord's disciples. He went to the high priest and asked him for letters to the synagogues in Damascus, so that if he found any there who belonged to the Way, whether men or women, he might take them as prisoners to Jerusalem. As he neared Damascus on his journey, suddenly a light from heaven flashed around him. He fell to the ground and heard a voice say to him, "Saul, Saul, why do you persecute me?" "Who are you, Lord?" Saul asked. "I am Jesus, whom you are persecuting", he replied. "Now get up and go into the city, and you will be told what you must do". The men traveling with Saul stood there speechless; they heard the sound but did not see anyone. Saul got up from the ground, but when he opened his eyes he could see nothing. So they led him by the hand into Damascus. For three days he was blind, and did not eat or drink anything. In Damascus there was a disciple named Ananias. The Lord called to him in a vision, "Ananias!" "Yes, Lord", he answered. The Lord told him, "Go to the house of Judas on Straight Street and ask for a man from Tarsus named Saul, for he is praying. In a vision he has seen a man named Ananias come and place his hands on him to restore his sight". "Lord", Ananias answered, "I have heard many reports about this man and all the harm he has done to your saints in Jerusalem. And he has come here with authority from the chief priests to arrest all who call on your name". But the Lord said to Ananias, "Go! This man is my chosen instrument to carry my name before the Gentiles and their kings and before the people of Israel. I will show him how much he must suffer for my name". Then Ananias went to the house and entered it. Placing his hands on Saul, he said, "Brother Saul, the Lord—Jesus, who appeared to you on the road as you were coming here—has sent me so that you may see again and be filled with the Holy Spirit". Immediately, something like scales fell from Saul's eyes, and he could see again. He got up and was baptized, and after taking some food, he regained his strength. Saul spent several days with the disciples in Damascus. At once he began to preach in the synagogues that Jesus is the Son of God. All those who heard him were astonished and asked, "Isn't he the man who raised havoc in Jerusalem among those who call on this name? And hasn't he come here to take them as prisoners to the chief priests?" Yet Saul grew more and more powerful and baffled the Jews living in Damascus by proving that Jesus is the Christ (Acts 9:1-22).

The purpose of the Apostle Paul Fast is to gain insight in the process of making important decisions, find solutions to problems, seek God's wisdom concerning serious life issues or direction in life (Isa. 58:8). Fasting prepares us for transformation, insight, and decision-making (Acts 9:9-19). If we fast for decision-making and insight, God will reveal His will to us.

The following questions are a guide to help you discern the best course of action, receive wisdom, and find the freedom to make sound decisions. They will also assist you in applying the Apostle Paul Fast to your personal life. It is vital that you pray and ask the Holy Spirit to give you the guidance and direction, wisdom, and the best course of action as you complete the Apostle Paul Fast.

If any of you lacks wisdom, he should ask God, who gives generously to all without finding fault, and it will be given to him. But when he asks, he must believe and not doubt, because he who doubts is like a wave of the sea, blown and tossed by the wind. That man should not think he will receive anything from the Lord; he is a double-minded man, unstable in all he does (Jas. 1:5-8).

1. What lessons can we learn from the Apostle Paul Fast?

____

____

2. Which lesson has had the greatest impact on your life? Explain.

____

____

3. How is the Apostle Paul Fast relevant today?

____

____

4. What is your purpose in the Apostle Paul Fast? Be specific. I am fasting to:

____

____

5. What spiritual power and breakthrough do you desire to unlock through the Apostle Paul Fast?

____

____

6. If you experienced this spiritual breakthrough, how would your life be different? How would your relationships (family, friends, church) be different or affected by this spiritual breakthrough? Be specific.

____

____

7. How can your faith be increased and/or strengthened through the Apostle Paul Fast? How will you be benefited by having your faith increased and/or strengthened?

____

____

8. What other benefits, whether physical, emotional, relational, psychological, and spiritual do you desire to achieve during the Apostle Paul Fast?

____

____

9. What might you discover about yourself during the Apostle Paul Fast?

____

____

10. How could the Apostle Paul Fast change your life?

____

____

11. What steps would you take to bring out these changes in your life? Who should be involved and to what extent?

____

____

12. Have you prayed for and received God's direction in making a decision in the past? State some of the important decisions that you will need to make in near future.

____

____

13. Which of these decisions could be the focus for the Saint Paul Fast (Acts 13:1-4)?

____

14. How will you devote your time while fasting?

15. How has God revealed guidance and direction to when making decisions in past situations? Make sure to allow the Lord to speak to you in other ways.

16. What things in your life today that could possibly hinder the Lord from speaking to you?

17. Whom do you usually consult for advice in making decisions?

18. How could you be prepared to and respond to those who do not understand your decision? Make sure that before you move ahead in implementing your decision to know the conviction of the Lord and have the support of those involved in your decision (e.g., spouse, family).

19. Ask the Holy Spirit to reveal any and all specific problems that need clarification as to the direction. Write down them down, acknowledge them, and then ask the Lord to remove them.

20. What biblical principles are applicable to your current decision?

____

____

21. Ask the Holy Spirit to reveal to you any possible improvement to your decision? How?

____

____

22. Do you feel convicted that this is the best decision? Briefly explain this conviction.

____

____

23. Write down the steps in order that are involved in executing this decision?

____

____

24. What length of time (days) and hours each day will you commit to during the Apostle Paul Fast? When do you plan to begin and end your fast?

____

____

The Word of God gives us the guidance we need in making those tough decisions. However, He has also given us resources, such as:

- He directs us by counsel with friends (cf. Pr. 11:14).
- He sovereignly guides (cf. Rom. 8:28).
- He directs us inwardly (cf. Acts 16:6; Rom. 8:14).
- He directs us by opportunities (cf. 1 Cor. 16:9).
- He directs us when we have a yielded spirit (cf. Rom. 12:1-2).
- He directs us through our spiritual gifts (cf. 1 Cor. 7:7).
- He directs us through our common sense (cf. Pr. 16:9).
- He guides us through prayer.
- He directs us through fasting.[63]

[63] Towns, *Fasting for Spiritual Breakthrough*, 113.

Prayer

Fasting is one of the spiritual disciplines that the Lord has established for you to achieve the spiritual power and breakthrough not only within your life but also in the lives of those whom are close to your heart. I acknowledge that I have become too comfortable in my current state of living and I sense you Holy Spirit calling me to confront the issues that I have been avoiding and find the freedom to live solely for Jesus Christ. Help me through the Apostle Paul Fast to break free from the bondages that have been controlling my life for too long. Therefore, prayerfully consider and write a prayer that you will address to the Lord that reflects a new commitment and dedication to Him.

The Apostle Paul's Fast Journal

As you progress through this fast, write down any insights the Lord speaks to you, spiritual growth, and personal thoughts to further reflect upon in your walk with the Lord.

The Daniel Fast

Please read the following Scripture references and then respond to the questions that follow.

But Daniel resolved not to defile himself with the royal food and wine, and he asked the chief official for permission not to defile himself this way. Now God had caused the official to show favor and compassion to Daniel, but the official told Daniel, "I am afraid of my lord the king, who has assigned your food and drink. Why should he see you looking worse than the other young men your age? The king would then have my head because of you". Daniel then said to the guard whom the chief official had appointed over Daniel, Hananiah, Mishael and Azariah, "Please test your servants for ten days: Give us nothing but vegetables to eat and water to drink. Then compare our appearance with that of the young men who eat the royal food, and treat your servants in accordance with what you see". So he agreed to this and tested them for ten days. At the end of the ten days they looked healthier and better nourished than any of the young men who ate the royal food. So the guard took away their choice food and the wine they were to drink and gave them vegetables instead. To these four young men God gave knowledge and understanding of all kinds of literature and learning. And Daniel could understand visions and dreams of all kinds (Dan. 1:8-17).

In the first year of Darius son of Xerxes (a Mede by descent), who was made ruler over the Babylonian kingdom—in the first year of his reign, I, Daniel, understood from the Scriptures, according to the word of the Lord given to Jeremiah the prophet, that the desolation of Jerusalem would last seventy years. So I turned to the Lord God and pleaded with him in prayer and petition, in fasting, and in sackcloth and ashes. I prayed to the Lord my God and confessed: "O Lord, the great and awesome God, who keeps his covenant of love with all who love him and obey his commands, we have sinned and done wrong. We have been wicked and have rebelled; we have turned away from your commands and laws. We have not listened to your servants the prophets, who spoke in your name to our kings, our princes and our fathers, and to all the people of the land. "Lord, you are righteous, but this day we are covered with shame—the men of Judah and people of Jerusalem and all Israel, both near and far, in all the countries where you have scattered us because of our unfaithfulness to you. O Lord, we and our kings, our princes and our fathers are covered with shame because we have sinned against you. The Lord our God is merciful and forgiving, even though we have rebelled against him; we have not obeyed the Lord our God or kept the laws he gave us through his servants the prophets. All Israel has transgressed your law and turned away, refusing to obey you. "Therefore the curses and sworn judgments written in the Law of Moses, the servant of God, have been poured out on us, because we have sinned against you. You have fulfilled the words spoken against us and against our rulers by bringing upon us great disaster. Under the whole heaven nothing has ever been done like what has been done to Jerusalem. Just as it is written in the Law of Moses, all this disaster has come upon us, yet we have not sought the favor of the Lord our God by turning from our sins and giving attention to your truth. The Lord did not hesitate to bring the disaster upon us, for the Lord our God is righteous in everything he does; yet we have not obeyed him. "Now, O Lord our God, who brought your people out of Egypt with a mighty hand and who made for yourself a name that endures to this day, we have sinned, we have done wrong. O Lord, in keeping with all your righteous acts, turn away your anger and your wrath from Jerusalem, your city, your holy hill. Our sins and the iniquities of our fathers have made Jerusalem and your people an object of scorn to all those around us. "Now, our God, hear the prayers and petitions of your servant. For your sake, O Lord, look with favor on your desolate sanctuary. Give ear, O God, and hear; open your eyes and see the desolation of the city that bears your Name. We do not make requests of you because we are righteous, but because of your great mercy. O Lord, listen! O Lord, forgive! O

Lord, hear and act! For your sake, O my God, do not delay, because your city and your people bear your Name" (Dan. 9:1-19).

In the third year of Cyrus king of Persia, a revelation was given to Daniel (who was called Belteshazzar). Its message was true and it concerned a great war. The understanding of the message came to him in a vision. At that time I, Daniel, mourned for three weeks. I ate no choice food; no meat or wine touched my lips; and I used no lotions at all until the three weeks were over. On the twenty-fourth day of the first month, as I was standing on the bank of the great river, the Tigris, I looked up and there before me was a man dressed in linen, with a belt of the finest gold around his waist. His body was like chrysolite, his face like lightning, his eyes like flaming torches, his arms and legs like the gleam of burnished bronze, and his voice like the sound of a multitude. I, Daniel, was the only one who saw the vision; the men with me did not see it, but such terror overwhelmed them that they fled and hid themselves. So I was left alone, gazing at this great vision; I had no strength left, my face turned deathly pale and I was helpless. Then I heard him speaking, and as I listened to him, I fell into a deep sleep, my face to the ground. A hand touched me and set me trembling on my hands and knees. He said, "Daniel, you who are highly esteemed, consider carefully the words I am about to speak to you, and stand up, for I have now been sent to you". And when he said this to me, I stood up trembling. Then he continued, "Do not be afraid, Daniel. Since the first day that you set your mind to gain understanding and to humble yourself before your God, your words were heard, and I have come in response to them. But the prince of the Persian kingdom resisted me twenty-one days. Then Michael, one of the chief princes, came to help me, because I was detained there with the king of Persia. Now I have come to explain to you what will happen to your people in the future, for the vision concerns a time yet to come" (Dan. 10:1-14).

The purpose of the Daniel Fast is to improve health and for your "healing to quickly appear" and to seek God's favour (Isa. 58:8). The principle here is that through fasting we can receive physical, emotional, psychological healing for our bodies and divine knowledge and understanding.

The following questions are a guide to help you receive your healing and appropriate the favour of God upon your life. It is through the Daniel Fast that we find freedom in mind, body, and spirit and divine insight into living a healthier lifestyle. They will also assist you in applying the Daniel Fast to your personal life. It is vital that you pray and ask the Holy Spirit to give you the guidance and direction, wisdom, and the best course of action as you complete the Daniel Fast. Make sure that you fast as a spiritual vow to the Lord for His answer. Your vow is an external test that reflects an internal desire. The Daniel Fast should be done to understand the role that sin has in keeping you from receiving your healing.

1. What lessons can we learn from the Daniel Fast?

____

____

2. Which lesson has had the greatest impact on your life? Explain.

____

3. How is the Daniel Fast relevant today? What dietary lifestyle would the Daniel Fast be called today? How can the Daniel Fast contribute to the healing process?

4. What is your purpose in the Daniel Fast? Be specific. I am fasting to:

5. What spiritual power and breakthrough do you desire to unlock through the Daniel Fast?

6. If you experienced this spiritual breakthrough, how would your life be different? How would your relationships (family, friends, church) be different or affected by this spiritual breakthrough? Be specific.

7. How can your faith be increased and/or strengthened through the Daniel Fast? How will you be benefited by having your faith increased and/or strengthened?

8. What other benefits, whether physical, emotional, relational, psychological, and spiritual do you desire to achieve during the Daniel Fast?

9. What might you discover about yourself during the Daniel Fast?

10. How could the Daniel Fast change your life?

11. What steps would you take to bring out these changes in your life? Who should be involved and to what extent?

12. When the Israelites were in bondage to the Egyptians how did the Lord use a specific diet to prevent them from getting diseases common to the Egyptians?

13. What foods would need to be eliminated or added to your diet? (cf. Daniel 1, 10).

14. What is the purpose behind the specific foods that are eaten in the Daniel Fast?

15. In what ways can fasting help the body rejuvenate itself?

16. Can fasting help in the treatment of some medical conditions, food addictions and/or improve a person's emotional and mental state?

____

____

17. Take an inventory of your present diet. Do you see any specific problems? If so, are there any potential risks?

____

____

18. In what ways could an improved diet and lifestyle help you to better serve the Lord and others?

____

____

19. How will you respond if there is no improvement in your health after completing the Daniel Fast?

____

____

20. Is there a specific dietary issue that you hope will be resolved through the Daniel Fast?

____

____

21. What new spiritual insights have you received as a result of your Daniel Fast?

____

____

22. What steps will you take to insure that your health will remain strong and free of disease and sickness?

____

23. What length of time (days) and hours each day will you commit to during the Daniel Fast? When do you plan to begin and end your fast?

Prayer

Fasting is one of the spiritual disciplines that the Lord has established for you to achieve the spiritual power and breakthrough not only within your life but also in the lives of those whom are close to your heart. I acknowledge that I have become too comfortable in my current state of living and I sense you Holy Spirit calling me to confront the issues that I have been avoiding and find the freedom to live solely for Jesus Christ. Help me through the Daniel Fast to break free from the bondages that have been controlling my life for too long. Therefore, prayerfully consider and write a prayer that you will address to the Lord that reflects a new commitment and dedication to Him.

The Daniel Fast Journal

As you progress through this fast, write down any insights the Lord speaks to you, spiritual growth, and personal thoughts to further reflect upon in your walk with the Lord.

The King Darius Fast

Please read the following Scripture reference and then respond to the questions that follow.

So the king gave the order, and they brought Daniel and threw him into the lions' den. The king said to Daniel, "May your God, whom you serve continually, rescue you!" A stone was brought and placed over the mouth of the den, and the king sealed it with his own signet ring and with the rings of his nobles, so that Daniel's situation might not be changed. Then the king returned to his palace and spent the night without eating and without any entertainment being brought to him. And he could not sleep. At the first light of dawn, the king got up and hurried to the lions' den. When he came near the den, he called to Daniel in an anguished voice, "Daniel, servant of the living God, has your God, whom you serve continually, been able to rescue you from the lions?" Daniel answered, "May the king live forever! My God sent his angel, and he shut the mouths of the lions. They have not hurt me, because I was found innocent in his sight. Nor have I ever done any wrong before you, Your Majesty". The king was overjoyed and gave orders to lift Daniel out of the den. And when Daniel was lifted from the den, no wound was found on him, because he had trusted in his God (Dan. 6:16-23).

The King Darius Fast portrays a distraught King who was emotionally distressed as he was deceived by his administrators and satraps to issue a decree that according to Persian Law could not be changed. In fulfilling the decree, King Darius has Daniel thrown into the lion's den and is so agitated that he could not sleep the entire night "and spent the night without eating and without any entertainment being brought to him" (cf. Xerxes' sleepless night, Est. 6:1). It was a customary among the ancients—Greeks and Romans—to have music and dancing girls at their meals. However, King Darius refrained from eating, possibly due to grieving the probable death of his friend there was no entertainment דַּחֲוָה *dachăwāh.* How could King Darius enjoy the pleasures of a king while his close friend Daniel was fighting for his life in the lion's den? We can see in this context the Psalmist David speaking of being in the midst of lions as he flees from King Saul into a cave, "I am in the midst of lions; I lie among ravenous beasts—men whose teeth are spears and arrows, whose tongues are sharp swords" (Ps. 57:4).[64]

This story concludes with the pagan King Darius acknowledging the universal sovereignty of the God of Israel as he states, "May your God, whom you serve continually, rescue you!" "At the first light of dawn", King Darius rushes to the lion's den and "in an anguished voice" calls out to Daniel expecting the worst, "Daniel, servant of the living God, has your God, whom you serve continually, been able to rescue you from the lions?" The King discovers that Daniel is alive, well, and untouched by the lions.

Daniel uses the Hebrew phrase חֱיִי לְעָלְמִיןמַלְכָּא *malkā' lĕ'olĕmîn ḥĕyî*, which literally means "O king unto eternity live" and then the Hebrew phrase טְאֵב שַׂגִּיאמַלְכָּא *malkā' śaggy' te'fiv*, which denotes the dramatic elevation of emotions as King Darius hears Daniel's voice since the Lord had "shut the mouths of the lions. They have not hurt me, because I was found innocent in his sight. Nor have I ever

---

[64] דַּחֲוָה *dachăwāh* "A1816", In Gilbrant, ed., *The Complete Biblical Library Hebrew-English Dictionary, Gimel-Zayin* (Springfield, IL: World Library Press, Inc., 1998), WORDsearch CROSS e-book. "Daniel 6:18", In Albert Barnes, *Albert Barnes' Notes on the Bible*, Rick Meyers e-Sword Version 10.1.0, 2012.

done any wrong before you, Your Majesty". The author of Daniel uses the Hebrew noun זָכוּ *zākhû* for innocence meaning "one who has moral innocence" and likewise speaks of "purity in God's sight". Daniel was saved from imminent death because of his character, integrity, flawless life, and his reverential fear of the Lord.[65]

King Darius responds by giving the guards orders to lift Daniel from the lion's den and "no wound was found on him". This experience demonstrated to the king and everyone that faith in God who is sovereign overall and will deliver His people who place their trust in Him. King Darius then follow Old Testament Law regarding anyone who maliciously bears false witness "then do to him as he intended to do to his brother" (Deut. 19:19). King Darius decrees that men throughout his kingdom must honour Daniel. This Old Testament Law was also enforced in the case of Haman who was hung on the gallows that he had built for Mordecai (cf. Est. 7).[66]

The following questions are a guide to help you to choose between good and evil in everything that you do on a daily basis. King Darius could have avoided this whole situation if he had truly seen the character, integrity, and godly life of Daniel and not allowed himself to be deceived by his 120 satraps and three administrators. These governmental officials had become so jealous and envious of the favour of God upon Daniel's life that the evil within them surfaced and they maliciously sought to bring harm to him. The story of Daniel in the lion's den illustrates the good and evil that exists within our lives, the sovereignty of God, the perils of living a godly life, and that all things work together for good.

> The good man brings good things out of the good stored up in him, and the evil man brings evil things out of the evil stored up in him. But I tell you that men will have to give account on the day of judgment for every careless word they have spoken. For by your words you will be acquitted, and by your words you will be condemned" (Mt. 12:35-37).
>
> Dear friends, I urge you, as aliens and strangers in the world, to abstain from sinful desires, which war against your soul. Live such good lives among the pagans that, though they accuse you of doing wrong, they may see your good deeds and glorify God on the day he visits us (1 Pet. 2:11-12).
>
> And we know that in all things God works for the good of those who love him, who have been called according to his purpose (Rom. 8:28).

---

[65] This Hebrew adjective is used "of anger (Dan. 2:12), fear (5:9; 7:28), remorse (6:14) and joy (v. 23). In each instance, an exceptional level of the emotion is demonstrated by the subject". שַׂגִּיא *saggî'* "A7895", In Gilbrant, ed., *The Complete Biblical Library Hebrew-English Dictionary, Sin-Taw.* זָכוּ *zākû* "2708", In Harris, Archer Jr., and Waltke, eds, *Theological Wordbook of the Old Testament*, 1015. זָכוּ *zākhû* "A2219", In Gilbrant, ed., *The Complete Biblical Library Hebrew-English Dictionary, Gimel-Zayin.* טְאֵב *te'ſiv* "A2976", In Gilbrant, ed., *The Complete Biblical Library Hebrew-English Dictionary, Heth-Yodh* (Springfield, IL: World Library Press, Inc., 1998), WORD*search* CROSS e-book.

[66] Walvoord and Zuck, eds., *The Bible Knowledge Commentary*, Vol. 1, 1349. Mays, ed., *Harper's Bible Commentary*, 701. Richards, *The Bible Reader's Companion*, electronic ed., 518.

You will find the freedom and joy as you choose behaviours that follow the precepts of the Word of God. They will also assist you in applying the King Darius Fast to your personal life. It is vital that you pray and ask the Holy Spirit to give you the guidance and direction, wisdom, and the best course of action as you complete the King Darius Fast.

1. What lessons can we learn from the King Darius Fast?

____

____

2. Which lesson has had the greatest impact on your life? Explain.

____

____

3. How is the King Darius Fast relevant today?

____

____

4. What is your purpose in the King Darius Fast? Be specific. I am fasting to:

____

____

5. What spiritual power and breakthrough do you desire to unlock through the King Darius Fast?

____

____

6. If you experienced this spiritual breakthrough, how would your life be different? How would your relationships (family, friends, church) be different or affected by this spiritual breakthrough? Be specific.

____

____

7. How can your faith be increased and/or strengthened through the King Darius Fast? How will you be benefited by having your faith increased and/or strengthened?

____

____

8. What other benefits, whether physical, emotional, relational, psychological, and spiritual do you desire to achieve during the King Darius Fast?

____

____

9. What might you discover about yourself during the King Darius Fast?

____

____

10. How could the King Darius Fast change your life?

____

____

11. What steps would you take to bring out these changes in your life? Who should be involved and to what extent?

____

____

12. What steps can you take to guard yourself from becoming emotionally distressed like King Darius?

____

____

13. What length of time (days) and hours each day will you commit to during the King Darius Fast? When do you plan to begin and end your fast?

____

Prayer

Fasting is one of the spiritual disciplines that the Lord has established for you to achieve the spiritual power and breakthrough not only within your life but also in the lives of those whom are close to your heart. I acknowledge that I have become too comfortable in my current state of living and I sense you Holy Spirit calling me to confront the issues that I have been avoiding and find the freedom to live solely for Jesus Christ. Help me through the King Darius Fast to break free from the bondages that have been controlling my life for too long. Therefore, prayerfully consider and write a prayer that you will address to the Lord that reflects a new commitment and dedication to Him.

The King Darius Fast Journal

As you progress through this fast, write down any insights the Lord speaks to you, spiritual growth, and personal thoughts to further reflect upon in your walk with the Lord.

The John the Baptist Fast

Please read the following Scripture references and then respond to the questions that follow.

> John's clothes were made of camel's hair, and he had a leather belt around his waist. His food was locusts and wild honey. People went out to him from Jerusalem and all Judea and the whole region of the Jordan. Confessing their sins, they were baptized by him in the Jordan River (Mt. 3:4-6).
>
> He will be a joy and delight to you, and many will rejoice because of his birth, for he will be great in the sight of the Lord. He is never to take wine or other fermented drink, and he will be filled with the Holy Spirit even before he is born. He will bring back many of the people of Israel to the Lord their God. And he will go on before the Lord, in the spirit and power of Elijah, to turn the hearts of the parents to their children and the disobedient to the wisdom of the righteous—to make ready a people prepared for the Lord" (Lk. 1:14-17).

The purpose of the John the Baptist Fast is to enhance your testimony and influence for Jesus Christ and empower you to become a true witness and influence others to receive salvation through Jesus Christ. (Isa. 58:8). Fasting sets us apart from the world and to have an influential testimony (Lk. 1:15; Mt. 3:4). If we fast for the influence of our testimony, God will use us. As Christians we have been called to follow Jesus and publicly acknowledge our separation from sin, an unending tenacity to bring forth fruit unto God, and consecration to His service.

The following questions are a guide to help empower your witness for Jesus Christ and give you a greater boldness to preach the Word of God. They will also assist you in applying the John the Baptist Fast to your personal life. It is vital that you pray and ask the Holy Spirit to give you the guidance and direction, wisdom, and the best course of action as you complete the John the Baptist Fast.

1. What lessons can we learn from the John the Baptist Fast?

___

___

2. Which lesson has had the greatest impact on your life? Explain.

___

___

3. How is the John the Baptist Fast relevant today?

___

___

4. What is your purpose in the John the Baptist Fast? Be specific. I am fasting to:

____

____

5. What spiritual power and breakthrough do you desire to unlock through the John the Baptist Fast?

____

____

6. If you experienced this spiritual breakthrough, how would your life be different? How would your relationships (family, friends, church) be different or affected by this spiritual breakthrough? Be specific.

____

____

7. How can your faith be increased and/or strengthened through the John the Baptist Fast? How will you be benefited by having your faith increased and/or strengthened?

____

____

8. What other benefits, whether physical, emotional, relational, psychological, and spiritual do you desire to achieve during the John the Baptist Fast?

____

____

9. What might you discover about yourself during the John the Baptist Fast?

____

____

10. How could the John the Baptist Fast change your life?

____

11. What steps would you take to bring out these changes in your life? Who should be involved and to what extent?

12. How can the John the Baptist Fast silence those who criticize our testimony and influence for the Lord?

13. The heart of fasting is about crucifying anything that hinders us from developing a more intimate relationship with the Lord. How does this spirit of sacrifice affect the nature of your fast?

14. How did fasting impact the ministry of John the Baptist?

15. How did fasting reflect John the Baptist's intimacy and commitment to God?

16. In what ways would fasting impact your reputation and ministry?

17. Take a moment to evaluate your present influence on others. What areas do you need to allow the Holy Spirit to bring necessary transformation?

____

____

18. What is the specific area in your life that you desire to change in the John the Baptist Fast? Be specific.

____

____

19. What length of time (days) and hours each day will you commit to during the John the Baptist Fast? When do you plan to begin and end your fast?

____

____

Prayer

Fasting is one of the spiritual disciplines that the Lord has established for you to achieve the spiritual power and breakthrough not only within your life but also in the lives of those whom are close to your heart. I acknowledge that I have become too comfortable in my current state of living and I sense you Holy Spirit calling me to confront the issues that I have been avoiding and find the freedom to live solely for Jesus Christ. Help me through the John the Baptist Fast to break free from the bondages that have been controlling my life for too long. Therefore, prayerfully consider and write a prayer that you will address to the Lord that reflects a new commitment and dedication to Him.

____

____

____

____

____

The John the Baptist Fast Journal

As you progress through this fast, write down any insights the Lord speaks to you, spiritual growth, and personal thoughts to further reflect upon in your walk with the Lord.

The Esther Fast

Please read the following Scripture references and then respond to the questions that follow.

> When Mordecai learned of all that had been done, he tore his clothes, put on sackcloth and ashes, and went out into the city, wailing loudly and bitterly. But he went only as far as the king's gate, because no one clothed in sackcloth was allowed to enter it. In every province to which the edict and order of the king came, there was great mourning among the Jews, with fasting, weeping and wailing. Many lay in sackcloth and ashes (Est. 4:1-3).
>
> When Esther's words were reported to Mordecai, he sent back this answer: "Do not think that because you are in the king's house you alone of all the Jews will escape. For if you remain silent at this time, relief and deliverance for the Jews will arise from another place, but you and your father's family will perish. And who knows but that you have come to your royal position for such a time as this?" Then Esther sent this reply to Mordecai: "Go, gather together all the Jews who are in Susa, and fast for me. Do not eat or drink for three days, night or day. I and my attendants will fast as you do. When this is done, I will go to the king, even though it is against the law. And if I perish, I perish". So Mordecai went away and carried out all of Esther's instructions (Est. 4:12-17).
>
> So Queen Esther, daughter of Abihail, along with Mordecai the Jew, wrote with full authority to confirm this second letter concerning Purim. And Mordecai sent letters to all the Jews in the 127 provinces of the kingdom of Xerxes—words of goodwill and assurance—to establish these days of Purim at their designated times, as Mordecai the Jew and Queen Esther had decreed for them, and as they had established for themselves and their descendants in regard to their times of fasting and lamentation. Esther's decree confirmed these regulations about Purim, and it was written down in the records (Est. 9:29-32).

The final fast spoken of in Isaiah 58 is the Esther Fast, "the glory of the Lord will be your rear guard" (Isa. 58:8). The purpose of the Esther Fast is to protect us from an attack of the devil and for continual protection against satanic forces. The Lord guarantees that fasting according to what Isaiah has previously stated will result in the restoration of health, protection, and access to himself in prayer; an abundance of divine blessing (cf. Isa. 59:9; 60:1).[67]

Fasting opens the door to God's favour and protects us from evil or evil people (Est. 4:16). If we fast for protection and deliverance from the evil, we are become "untouchable" until God calls us home. The purpose of the Esther Fast is to protect us from the Evil One (Isa. 58:8). The Book of Esther emphasizes that when God seems to have hidden Himself from His people, He can be found by those who earnestly seek Him.

Jewish women were expected to be quiet, serve in the home, and marginalized with respect to religious and political issues. However, this was not the case with Esther, a Jewish woman, who followed the Lord's direction in breaking cultural norms to risk her life to deliver her people from apparent annihilation. Whatever your place in life, wherever you are in your walk with the Lord, He can use you if you are willing, available, and ready since He desires to use you for His glory when others are afraid to

[67] Gaebelein, ed., *The Expositor's Bible Commentary, Volume 6*, 322.

even consider.[68] The Book of Esther demonstrates what will be the "lot" of everyone who hates the Jews, His people. The Lord Himself will arise, defend His people, and judge their enemies,

> I will take vengeance on my adversaries and repay those who hate me. I will make my arrows drunk with blood, while my sword devours flesh: the blood of the slain and the captives, the heads of the enemy leaders". Rejoice, O nations, with his people, for he will avenge the blood of his servants; he will take vengeance on his enemies and make atonement for his land and people (Deut. 32:41-43).

It is in this respect that the Book of Esther is seen prophetically of Yahweh's ultimate triumph over the enemies of His chosen people, as the prophet Isaiah states,

> no weapon forged against you will prevail, and you will refute every tongue that accuses you. This is the heritage of the servants of the Lord, and this is their vindication from me, declares the Lord (Isa. 54:17).

As in the life and calling of Esther, we should reflect upon our present circumstances and ask the Lord regarding the purpose, the lesson He wants us to learn, and make a difference in your community and/or church. The Lord has brought you to your present circumstance, like He did with Esther, to take you out of your comfort zone "for such a time as this".[69]

The following questions are a guide to help us understand that the Lord is not only our protector from the attacks of the enemy, but He is also sustains us, restores our health, pours out His divine blessings upon His children, and the source of ultimate freedom. They will also assist you in applying the Esther Fast to your personal life. It is vital that you pray and ask the Holy Spirit to give you the guidance and direction, wisdom, and the best course of action as you complete the Esther Fast.

1. What lessons can we learn from the Esther Fast?

____

____

2. Which lesson has had the greatest impact on your life? Explain.

____

____

____

[68] "Chapter 50", In Elmer L. Towns, *A Journey Through The Old Testament: The Story of how God Developed His People in the Old Testament* (Fort Worth, TX: Harcourt Brace Custom Publishers, 1989).

[69] Brooks, *Summarized* Bible, 99-100.

3. How is the Esther Fast relevant today?

4. What is your purpose in the Esther Fast? Be specific. I am fasting to:

5. What spiritual power and breakthrough do you desire to unlock through the Esther Fast?

6. If you experienced this spiritual breakthrough, how would your life be different? How would your relationships (family, friends, church) be different or affected by this spiritual breakthrough? Be specific.

7. How can your faith be increased and/or strengthened through the Esther Fast? How will you be benefited by having your faith increased and/or strengthened?

8. What other benefits, whether physical, emotional, relational, psychological, and spiritual do you desire to achieve during the Esther Fast?

9. What might you discover about yourself during the Esther Fast?

10. How could the Esther Fast change your life?

11. What steps would you take to bring out these changes in your life? Who should be involved and to what extent?

12. The Book of Esther is a story of a woman taking a stand for what is right and "if I perish, I perish" (Est. 4:16). Likewise, taking a stand for Christ can be costly. State some of the dangers that Christians face today.

13. Are you presently encountering personal danger? Briefly explain. How can fasting help you to be victorious over this personal and present danger? Be specific in your prayer requests.

14. It is interesting that many Christians do not believe in evil forces or demonic spirits. Why do you think many Christians struggle with the reality that there are evil forces at work in our world?

15. What is the difference between the Esther Fast and the final petition of the Lord's Prayer, "deliver us from the evil one" (Mt. 6:13)?

16. Even though the name of God is does not appear in the Book of Esther, the providence of God is evident throughout Esther. Explain how God protected Esther and the Jews from immanent annihilation.

17. For whom will you be fasting if not for yourself? This could be for someone in a difficult situation or someone in a unique ministry situation.

18. What length of time (days) and hours each day will you commit to during the Esther Fast? When do you plan to begin and end your fast?

Prayer

Fasting is one of the spiritual disciplines that the Lord has established for you to achieve the spiritual power and breakthrough not only within your life but also in the lives of those whom are close to your heart. I acknowledge that I have become too comfortable in my current state of living and I sense you Holy Spirit calling me to confront the issues that I have been avoiding and find the freedom to live solely for Jesus Christ. Help me through the Esther Fast to break free from the bondages that have been controlling my life for too long. Therefore, prayerfully consider and write a prayer that you will address to the Lord that reflects a new commitment and dedication to Him.

The Esther Fast Journal

As you progress through this fast, write down any insights the Lord speaks to you, spiritual growth, and personal thoughts to further reflect upon in your walk with the Lord.

Summary Questions to the Fasts of Isaiah 58

1. What are the primary themes throughout the Fasts of Isaiah 58? Name them in order of prominence.

2. What does this show you regarding the types of sins that have affected God's people throughout history?

3. To what degree are these sins or wickedness still prevalent within your personal life, family, community, city, and/or nation?

4. What are the primary lessons that we can learn from the Fasts of Isaiah 58?

5. Which fast was the *most* meaningful to you? Why?

6. Which fast was the *least* meaningful to you? Why?

7. How does your understanding of true fasting as described in the Fasts of Isaiah 58, change the way in which you perceive and respond to your community and culture?

8. What steps do you need to take to live a life of abundance and freedom from the "sin that so easily entangles"?

   Therefore, since we are surrounded by such a great cloud of witnesses, let us throw off everything that hinders and the sin that so easily entangles, and let us run with perseverance the race marked out for us. Let us fix our eyes on Jesus, the author and perfecter of our faith, who for the joy set before him endured the cross, scorning its shame, and sat down at the right hand of the throne of God. Consider him who endured such opposition from sinful men, so that you will not grow weary and lose heart (Heb. 12:1-3).

The Fasts of Isaiah 58 Journal

Take some time to reflect on these fasts. What are some of the common themes that were the most relevant to you? How can finding victory in these areas transform your life?

Chapter 7: The Fasts of the Prophetical Books

The purpose of this chapter is to present the fasts that are included in the prophetical books and the context in which the fasting occurs. Each fast concludes by reflecting and responding to questions relevant to each fast.

Fasting in the prophetical books is seen as the prophets speak out against purely external fasting that seeks to obtain an automatic entrance and hearing with the Lord (Isa. 58:1-12; cf. Jer. 14:11-12; Zech. 7). From the prophet's perspective, fasting was the humbling the soul, which lead to moral action and was rejected where there was strife, disobedience, and selfish motives. The Lord does not submit merely because someone is afflicting their body in one form or another. A true fast, as revealed in Isaiah 58, is seen as people sought to live righteously, grow deeper in their relationship with the Lord, and helped to take care of the poor and the needy.

Like the Old Testament prophets, Jesus opposed the flamboyant fasting of the Pharisees, and viewed fasting as a means of achieving humility and reflecting the Word of God (Mt. 6:16-18). Fasting in the prophetical books concludes with the final salvation of the Lord when the months of fasting will be turned into feasts of joy and gladness (Zech. 8:19).[70]

The Jeremiah Fast

Please read the following Scripture reference and then respond to the questions that follow.

> In the fourth year of Jehoiakim son of Josiah king of Judah, this word came to Jeremiah from the Lord: "Take a scroll and write on it all the words I have spoken to you concerning Israel, Judah and all the other nations from the time I began speaking to you in the reign of Josiah till now. Perhaps when the people of Judah hear about every disaster I plan to inflict on them, each of them will turn from his wicked way; then I will forgive their wickedness and their sin". So Jeremiah called Baruch son of Neriah, and while Jeremiah dictated all the words the Lord had spoken to him, Baruch wrote them on the scroll. Then Jeremiah told Baruch, "I am restricted; I cannot go to the Lord's temple. So you go to the house of the Lord on a day of fasting and read to the people from the scroll the words of the Lord that you wrote as I dictated. Read them to all the people of Judah who come in from their towns. Perhaps they will bring their petition before the Lord, and each will turn from his wicked ways, for the anger and wrath pronounced against this people by the Lord are great". Baruch son of Neriah did everything Jeremiah the prophet told him to do; at the Lord's temple he read the words of the Lord from the scroll. In the ninth month of the fifth year of Jehoiakim son of Josiah king of Judah, a time of fasting before the Lord was proclaimed for all the people in Jerusalem and those who had come from the towns of Judah (Jer. 36:1-9).

---

[70] "Fasting", In D. R. W. Wood and I. Howard Marshall, eds., *New Bible Dictionary*, 3rd ed (Downers Grove, IL: InterVarsity Press, 1996), 364. Gerhard Kittel, Gerhard Friedrich and Geoffrey William Bromiley, eds., *Theological Dictionary of the New Testament: Abridged in One Volume* (Grand Rapids, MI: William B. Eerdmans Publishing Company, 1985), 632-33. Gerhard Kittel, Geoffrey W. Bromiley and Gerhard Friedrich, eds., *Theological Dictionary of the New Testament*, electronic ed., Vol. 4 (Grand Rapids, MI: William B. Eerdmans Publishing Company, 1964), 927-30. "Fasting", In Chad Brand, Charles Draper, Archie England et al., eds., *Holman Illustrated Bible Dictionary* (Nashville, TN: Holman Bible Publishers, 2003), 560.

There seems to be no definite reason for the Jeremiah Fast except that the Babylonians are capturing and destroying the towns of Philistia, especially Ashkelon. However, could it be that the purpose for corporate fasting was that Jeremiah chose the day of the largest gathering to have the Word of the Lord read concerning "every disaster I plan to inflict on them, each of them will turn from his wicked way; then I will forgive their wickedness and their sin". The use of the noun for "wicked" רָשָׁע *rāshā'* is quite significant since it is the opposite of being righteous, and someone who is wicked gushes evil from with, craving evil with their whole being.[71]

The following questions are a guide to help you to see what wicked ways are within you, repent and receive the Lord's forgiveness and find the freedom to live the abundant life the Lord has prepared for you. They will also assist you in applying the Jeremiah Fast to your personal life. It is vital that you pray and ask the Holy Spirit to give you the guidance and direction, wisdom, and the best course of action as you complete the Jeremiah Fast.

1. What lessons can we learn from the Jeremiah Fast?

___

___

2. Which lesson has had the greatest impact on your life? Explain.

___

___

3. How is the Jeremiah Fast relevant today?

___

___

4. What is your purpose in the Jeremiah Fast? Be specific. I am fasting to:

___

___

[71] רָשָׁע *rāshā'* "7857", In Gilbrant, ed., *The Complete Biblical Library Hebrew-English Dictionary, Pe-Resh* (Springfield, IL: World Library Press, Inc., 1998), WORD*search* CROSS e-book. רָשָׁע *rāshā'* "2222", In Harris, Archer Jr., and Waltke, eds, *Theological Wordbook of the Old Testament*, 863.

5. What spiritual power and breakthrough do you desire to unlock through the Jeremiah Fast?

____

____

6. If you experienced this spiritual breakthrough, how would your life be different? How would your relationships (family, friends, church) be different or affected by this spiritual breakthrough? Be specific.

____

____

7. How can your faith be increased and/or strengthened through the Jeremiah Fast? How will you be benefited by having your faith increased and/or strengthened?

____

____

8. What other benefits, whether physical, emotional, relational, psychological, and spiritual do you desire to achieve during the Jeremiah Fast?

____

____

9. What might you discover about yourself during the Jeremiah Fast?

____

____

10. How could the Jeremiah Fast change your life?

____

____

____

11. What steps would you take to bring out these changes in your life? Who should be involved and to what extent?

12. Take a moment to ask the Holy Spirit to reveal any "wickedness" in your life? Do you sometimes feel guilt, shame, or simply wrong-doing—against yourself or another person? This could refer to an action and/or behaviour committed against God (Ex. 2:13; Num. 35:31)

13. Ask the Lord to help to expose and to breakthrough this wickedness in your life. In what ways has this wickedness affected you and others?

14. Ask the Lord to help you decide what type of fast is the most relevant to break this cycle of wickedness in your life?

15. Ask the Holy Spirit to reveal any form of corporate wickedness in your church that needs to be repented of. If you believe that there is, it is advised that this remain part of your personal prayer. Ask the Holy Spirit to reveal it to others so that it does not cause further issues.

16. Likewise, ask the Holy Spirit to reveal any form of wickedness in your community that needs to be repented of. If you believe that there is, speak with your pastor and in accordance with him or her follow their leading in breaking wickedness within your community.

17. What length of time (days) and hours each day will you commit to during the Jeremiah Fast? When do you plan to begin and end your fast?

Prayer

Fasting is one of the spiritual disciplines that the Lord has established for you to achieve the spiritual power and breakthrough not only within your life but also in the lives of those whom are close to your heart. I acknowledge that I have become too comfortable in my current state of living and I sense you Holy Spirit calling me to confront the issues that I have been avoiding and find the freedom to live solely for Jesus Christ. Help me through the Jeremiah Fast to break free from the bondages that have been controlling my life for too long. Therefore, prayerfully consider and write a prayer that you will address to the Lord that reflects a new commitment and dedication to Him.

The Jeremiah Fast Journal

As you progress through this fast, write down any insights the Lord speaks to you, spiritual growth, and personal thoughts to further reflect upon in your walk with the Lord.

The Joel Fast

Please read the following Scripture references and then respond to the questions that follow.

> Put on sackcloth, O priests, and mourn; wail, you who minister before the altar. Come, spend the night in sackcloth, you who minister before my God; for the grain offerings and drink offerings are withheld from the house of your God. Declare a holy fast; call a sacred assembly. Summon the elders and all who live in the land to the house of the Lord your God, and cry out to the Lord (Joel 1:13-14).

> "Even now", declares the Lord, "return to me with all your heart, with fasting and weeping and mourning". Rend your heart and not your garments. Return to the Lord your God, for he is gracious and compassionate, slow to anger and abounding in love, and he relents from sending calamity. Who knows? He may turn and have pity and leave behind a blessing—grain offerings and drink offerings for the Lord your God. Blow the trumpet in Zion, declare a holy fast, call a sacred assembly. Gather the people, consecrate the assembly; bring together the elders, gather the children, those nursing at the breast. Let the bridegroom leave his room and the bride her chamber. Let the priests, who minister before the Lord, weep between the temple porch and the altar. Let them say, "Spare your people, O Lord. Do not make your inheritance an object of scorn, a byword among the nations. Why should they say among the peoples, 'Where is their God?'" (Joel 2:12-17).

Today when we see and hear of natural disasters such as, earthquakes, floods, tsunamis, hurricanes, tornados, volcanic eruption and the like, we believe them to be "acts of God". This means that no human had control over this event happening. However, in biblical times, especially the Old Testament, many of these natural disasters were an "act of God", which can be defined as the sovereignty of God over nature which teaches a spiritual lesson. The sovereignty of God in sending the infestation of locusts is demonstrated most powerfully in the Book of Joel like no other book. These locusts had stripped the land of everything leading the prophet Joel to call the entire nation of Israel to fasting and prayer (1:13-14).

On a deeper level, this locust infestation illustrated the coming "Day of the Lord", which is seen in Scripture as divine judgment. The Book of Joel presents God's urgent call to His people "return to me with all your heart, with fasting and weeping and mourning" (Joel 2:12) and concludes with one of the most recognized Old Testament promises that God will pour out His spirit upon all flesh, judge all pagan nations, and bless His people. The images seen in Joel and his urgent call for reform should remind us that our relationship with the Lord takes precedence over issues and concerns in life. The prophet stresses that when we become too preoccupied with the cares of worldly things, that this should be a clue that our focus has drifted away from God and we must "return to me with all your heart, with fasting and weeping and mourning". In the end, sin brings God's judgment; yet with God's justice there is also great mercy.[72]

The following questions are a guide to help you remember that our relationship with the Lord is our highest priority and when the concerns of life take precedence in our lives we need to repent and "rend your heart" in wholehearted commitment to the Lord. Then you will find freedom from the judgment of God and receive His great mercy. They will also assist you in applying the Joel Fast to your personal life.

[72] Richards, *The Bible Reader's Companion*, electronic ed., 531. Brooks, *Summarized* Bible, 197.

It is vital that you pray and ask the Holy Spirit to give you the guidance and direction, wisdom, and the best course of action as you complete the Joel Fast.

1. What lessons can we learn from the Joel Fast?

____

____

2. Which lesson has had the greatest impact on your life? Explain.

____

____

3. How is the Joel Fast relevant today?

____

____

4. What is your purpose in the Joel Fast? Be specific. I am fasting to:

____

____

5. What spiritual power and breakthrough do you desire to unlock through the Joel Fast?

____

____

6. If you experienced this spiritual breakthrough, how would your life be different? How would your relationships (family, friends, church) be different or affected by this spiritual breakthrough? Be specific.

____

____

____

7. How can your faith be increased and/or strengthened through the Joel Fast? How will you be benefited by having your faith increased and/or strengthened?

____

____

8. What other benefits, whether physical, emotional, relational, psychological, and spiritual do you desire to achieve during the Joel Fast?

____

____

9. What might you discover about yourself during the Joel Fast?

____

____

10. How could the Joel Fast change your life?

____

____

11. What steps would you take to bring out these changes in your life? Who should be involved and to what extent?

____

____

12. Like the people of the early eighth century, do you feel as though you have fallen into spiritual infidelity and moral corruption and/or have been lacerated mentally or emotionally? Explain in which ways that you feel that this has happened. How can fasting bring you back into a right relationship with God?

____

____

13. Joel's message addressed the spiritual bankruptcy of the people. Do you find yourself in a similar situation where you feel like you have become spiritually bankrupt? How can fasting bring you back into a right relationship with God?

____

____

14. Are you presently experiencing trials and suffering and have you become complacent and forgotten the Lord Chief attributes? State which attributes that you have forgotten. How do these attributes affect your relationship with God?

____

____

15. Have you neglected to live a life of walking in daily repentance and dependence upon God? Joel appealed for the people to live with a broken and contrite heart which is the only soil in which the regenerated soul can grow. Why is this the only soil on which the soul can grow? What is the condition of your soil? Explain.

____

____

16. What length of time (days) and hours each day will you commit to during the Joel Fast? When do you plan to begin and end your fast?

____

____

Prayer

Fasting is one of the spiritual disciplines that the Lord has established for you to achieve the spiritual power and breakthrough not only within your life but also in the lives of those whom are close to your heart. I acknowledge that I have become too comfortable in my current state of living and I sense you Holy Spirit calling me to confront the issues that I have been avoiding and find the freedom to live solely for Jesus Christ. Help me through the Joel Fast to break free from the bondages that have been controlling my life for too long. Therefore, prayerfully consider and write a prayer that you will address to the Lord that reflects a new commitment and dedication to Him.

The Joel Fast Journal

As you progress through this fast, write down any insights the Lord speaks to you, spiritual growth, and personal thoughts to further reflect upon in your walk with the Lord.

The Nineveh Fast

Please read the following Scripture reference and then respond to the questions that follow.

> Then the word of the Lord came to Jonah a second time: "Go to the great city of Nineveh and proclaim to it the message I give you". Jonah obeyed the word of the Lord and went to Nineveh. Now Nineveh was a very important city—a visit required three days. On the first day, Jonah started into the city. He proclaimed: "Forty more days and Nineveh will be overturned". The Ninevites believed God. They declared a fast, and all of them, from the greatest to the least, put on sackcloth. When the news reached the king of Nineveh, he rose from his throne, took off his royal robes, covered himself with sackcloth and sat down in the dust. Then he issued a proclamation in Nineveh: "By the decree of the king and his nobles: Do not let any man or beast, herd or flock, taste anything; do not let them eat or drink. But let man and beast be covered with sackcloth. Let everyone call urgently on God. Let them give up their evil ways and their violence. Who knows? God may yet relent and with compassion turn from his fierce anger so that we will not perish". When God saw what they did and how they turned from their evil ways, he had compassion and did not bring upon them the destruction he had threatened (Jon. 3:1-10).

It is interesting that the prophet Jonah was afraid that the people of Nineveh would repent and the Lord would relent, which troubled him.

> But Jonah was greatly displeased and became angry. He prayed to the Lord, "O Lord, is this not what I said when I was still at home? That is why I was so quick to flee to Tarshish. I knew that you are a gracious and compassionate God, slow to anger and abounding in love, a God who relents from sending calamity (Jon. 4:1-2).

Even though the Book of Jonah depicts simplicity in its story line, it contains a wealth of spiritual lessons like few other Old Testament books.

1. The timing of Jonah's call occurred during the reign of Jeroboam II.
2. It was also during this same reign that the prophetic ministry of Amos took place. As Jonah confronts Israel's elite and rebukes them for their social injustices, so Amos pronounces judgment and called for Israel to repent of their wicked practices.
3. Jonah reveals that God uses believers to carry out His plan to spread the news of God's hatred of sin and to tell of His grace to those who repent and turn to Him in faith.
4. Although God's messengers may reject His will, God does not abandon His plans. Through God's control of events, His servants will experience His discipline in order to bring them to obedience.
5. Since no one can hide from God, each person must faithfully do God's will and share the message that God has given to him or her.
6. Limiting God's compassion to His covenant people is a great misunderstanding of God's love and will lead to a great misunderstanding of His will for the believer.[73]

The Book of Jonah portrays God in a threefold manner:

1. He is profoundly attentive to the well-being of people from all nations, just not His people Israel;

[73] Samuel J. Schultz and Gary V. Smith, *Exploring the Old Testament* (Wheaton, IL: Crossway Books, 2001), 153.

2. He is merciful and gracious with the behaviour of his prophet Jonah;
3. He is the God of a second chance, even though Jonah wilfully disobeyed God's commands.

The significance of the Book of Jonah is seen in the merciful and gracious acts of God. Moreover, Jonah's mission to Nineveh is portrayed as mission and spiritual lesson for His own people. Jonah, God warns His people and gives them time to repent before judgment comes. Jonah reveals God's character as being immutable. However, when the people "turned from their evil ways", He "had compassion and did not bring upon them the destruction he had threatened" (Jon. 3:10). "Repentance in man is a change of will. Repentance in God is God willing a change".[74]

The following questions are a guide to help you remember that we serve a God who is longsuffering, abounding in grace and mercy. However, God only gives people a period of time to repent, "Forty more days and Nineveh will be overturned" (Jon. 3:4). Then you will find freedom from the judgment of God and receive His great mercy and compassion. They will also assist you in applying the Nineveh Fast to your personal life. It is vital that you pray and ask the Holy Spirit to give you the guidance and direction, wisdom, and the best course of action as you complete the Nineveh Fast.

1. What lessons can we learn from the Nineveh Fast?

____

____

2. Which lesson has had the greatest impact on your life? Explain.

____

____

3. How is the Nineveh Fast relevant today?

____

____

4. What is your purpose in the Nineveh Fast? Be specific. I am fasting to:

____

____

---

[74] Brooks, *Summarized* Bible, 202. Richards, *The Bible Reader's Companion*, electronic ed., 546.

5. What spiritual power and breakthrough do you desire to unlock through the Nineveh Fast?

____

____

6. If you experienced this spiritual breakthrough, how would your life be different? How would your relationships (family, friends, church) be different or affected by this spiritual breakthrough? Be specific.

____

____

7. How can your faith be increased and/or strengthened through the Nineveh Fast? How will you be benefited by having your faith increased and/or strengthened?

____

____

8. What other benefits, whether physical, emotional, relational, psychological, and spiritual do you desire to achieve during the Nineveh Fast?

____

____

9. What might you discover about yourself during the Nineveh Fast?

____

____

10. How could the Nineveh Fast change your life?

____

____

____

11. What steps would you take to bring out these changes in your life? Who should be involved and to what extent?

____

____

12. Take a moment to examine yourself to see if there is any "wickedness" in your life? Do you sometimes feel guilty of wrong-doing—especially against another person? This could refer to an action and/or behaviour done against God (Ex. 2:13; Num. 35:31).

____

____

13. Ask the Lord to reveal, expose, and to breakthrough this wickedness in your life. How has this wickedness affected you and others?

____

____

14. Like Nineveh, is there wickedness in the city in which you live that requires a corporate or city-wide fast? Would it be possible to bring the churches together for a time of fasting? Explain.

____

____

15. What wickedness would be the focus of this fast? If this fast was successful, how would that change your city or community?

____

____

16. What length of time (days) and hours each day will you commit to during the Nineveh Fast? When do you plan to begin and end your fast?

____

____

Prayer

Fasting is one of the spiritual disciplines that the Lord has established for you to achieve the spiritual power and breakthrough not only within your life but also in the lives of those whom are close to your heart. I acknowledge that I have become too comfortable in my current state of living and I sense you Holy Spirit calling me to confront the issues that I have been avoiding and find the freedom to live solely for Jesus Christ. Help me through the Nineveh Fast to break free from the bondages that have been controlling my life for too long. Therefore, prayerfully consider and write a prayer that you will address to the Lord that reflects a new commitment and dedication to Him.

____

____

____

____

____

The Nineveh Fast Journal

As you progress through this fast, write down any insights the Lord speaks to you, spiritual growth, and personal thoughts to further reflect upon in your walk with the Lord.

____

____

____

____

____

____

____

____

The Fasts of Jewish Captivity

Please read the following Scripture references and then respond to the questions that follow.

> In the fourth year of King Darius, the word of the Lord came to Zechariah on the fourth day of the ninth month, the month of Kislev. The people of Bethel had sent Sharezer and Regem-Melek, together with their men, to entreat the Lord by asking the priests of the house of the Lord Almighty and the prophets, "Should I mourn and fast in the fifth month, as I have done for so many years?" Then the word of the Lord Almighty came to me: "Ask all the people of the land and the priests, 'When you fasted and mourned in the fifth and seventh months for the past seventy years, was it really for me that you fasted? And when you were eating and drinking, were you not just feasting for yourselves? Are these not the words the Lord proclaimed through the earlier prophets when Jerusalem and its surrounding towns were at rest and prosperous, and the Negev and the western foothills were settled?'". "This is what the Lord Almighty says: 'Administer true justice; show mercy and compassion to one another. Do not oppress the widow or the fatherless, the alien or the poor. In your hearts do not think evil of each other'" (Zech. 7:1-10).

> This is what the Lord Almighty says: "The fasts of the fourth, fifth, seventh and tenth months will become joyful and glad occasions and happy festivals for Judah. Therefore love truth and peace" (Zech. 8:19).

The fasts of Zechariah chapter 7 help us to understand that when we present our petitions to the Lord we need to anticipate a response from Him. We must realize that just because we fast does not obligate the Lord to give us what we have asked for because of fasting. In fasting, we must remember that it includes self-examination and repentance of our wickedness and/or sins. In everything we do, we must ask ourselves, I am doing this from God's perspective, identifying with His purposes, desires, and concerns for my life or am I doing this from selfish reasons. To Zechariah, it was about true religion that will "administer true justice; show mercy and compassion to one another. Do not oppress the widow or the fatherless, the alien or the poor. In your hearts do not think evil of each other" (Zech. 7:9-10). The shift in the emphasis of true religion from ritual to ethics is characteristic of the later prophets (cf. Isa. 1:11-14; 61:1, 8; Am. 5:10-15, 21-24; Mic. 6:6-8).[75]

The following questions are a guide to help you realize that fasting does obligate a response from the Lord. However, He is not moved by an external demonstration of piety. In fasting we must always ask, who are we fasting for: the Lord to bring about inner transformation or for ourselves for selfish reasons. You will find freedom when in everything we do, we do it as unto the Lord, which is the only thing that matters. They will also assist you in applying the Fasts of Jewish Captivity to your personal life. It is vital

---

[75] Richards, *The Bible Reader's Companion*, electronic ed., 579. Franklin H. Paschall and Herschel H. Hobbs, *The Teacher's Bible Commentary: A Concise, Thorough Interpretation of the Entire Bible Designed Especially for Sunday School Teachers* (Nashville, TN: Broadman and Holman Publishers, 1972), 578. "The Minor Prophets", In David S. Dockery, ed., *Holman Concise Bible Commentary: Simple, Straightforward Commentary on Every Book of the Bible* (Nashville, TN: Broadman & Holman Publishers, 1998), 387. Brooks, *Summarized* Bible, 211. <http:// www.enterthebible.org/resourcelink.aspx ?rid=343>. Accessed on December 10, 2013.

that you pray and ask the Holy Spirit to give you the guidance and direction, wisdom, and the best course of action as you complete the Fasts of Jewish Captivity.

1. What lessons can we learn from the Fasts of Jewish Captivity?

___

___

2. Which lesson has had the greatest impact on your life? Explain.

___

___

3. How are the Fasts of Jewish Captivity relevant today?

___

___

4. What is your purpose in the Fasts of Jewish Captivity? Be specific. I am fasting to:

___

___

5. What spiritual power and breakthrough do you desire to unlock through the Fasts of Jewish Captivity?

___

___

6. If you experienced this spiritual breakthrough, how would your life be different? How would your relationships (family, friends, church) be different or affected by this spiritual breakthrough? Be specific.

___

___

7. How can your faith be increased and/or strengthened through the Fasts of Jewish Captivity? How will you be benefited by having your faith increased and/or strengthened?

____

____

8. What other benefits, whether physical, emotional, relational, psychological, and spiritual do you desire to achieve during the Fasts of Jewish Captivity?

____

____

9. What might you discover about yourself during the Fasts of Jewish Captivity?

____

____

10. How could the Fasts of Jewish Captivity change your life?

____

____

11. What steps would you take to bring out these changes in your life? Who should be involved and to what extent?

____

____

12. As we have seen in this study on Zechariah, the purpose of chapters 7 and 8 was to exhort the people to live righteously in response to their past judgment and future glory. How can the Zechariah Fast encourage you to live a righteous life in today's world?

____

____

____

13. How can a personal and/or corporate fast help you and the church in which you attend in spiritual renewal?

____

____

14. Zechariah responds to an inquiry concerning fasting (7:1-3) in four messages (7:4, 8; 8:1, 18). How can these messages be applied to your relationship with God? How would these messages change the way in which you live your life?

____

____

15. According to 8:19, the question included all the fasts commemorating major events related to the fall and destruction of Jerusalem and the temple, namely, the "fasts of the fourth, fifth, seventh and tenth months". What kind of major events in your life or in your church can be commemorated on a regular basis? How would this commemoration change your life and/or your church?

____

____

16. As with so much religious activity, God is left out. Zechariah's word from the Lord was that Jewish fasting had been nothing but a hypocritical ritual motivated by self-interest rather than the genuine sorrow for sin and the desire to renew their faithfulness to God. How is God left out of the picture in your life? How can fasting help to restore and rebuilt your spiritual life?

____

____

17. What length of time (days) and hours each day will you commit to during the Fasts of Jewish Captivity? When do you plan to begin and end your fast?

____

____

____

Prayer

Fasting is one of the spiritual disciplines that the Lord has established for you to achieve the spiritual power and breakthrough not only within your life but also in the lives of those whom are close to your heart. I acknowledge that I have become too comfortable in my current state of living and I sense you Holy Spirit calling me to confront the issues that I have been avoiding and find the freedom to live solely for Jesus Christ. Help me through the Fasts of Jewish Captivity to break free from the bondages that have been controlling my life for too long. Therefore, prayerfully consider and write a prayer that you will address to the Lord that reflects a new commitment and dedication to Him.

____

____

____

____

____

The Fasts of Jewish Captivity Journal

As you progress through this fast, write down any insights the Lord speaks to you, spiritual growth, and personal thoughts to further reflect upon in your walk with the Lord.

____

____

____

____

____

____

____

____

Summary Questions to the Fasts of the Prophetical Books

1. What are the primary themes throughout the Fasts of the Prophetical Books? Name them in order of prominence.

____

____

2. What does this show you regarding the types of sins that have affected God's people throughout history?

____

____

3. To what degree are these sins or wickedness still prevalent within your personal life, family, community, city, and/or nation?

____

____

4. What are the primary lessons that we can learn from the Fasts of the Prophetical Books?

____

____

5. Which fast was the *most* meaningful to you? Why?

____

____

6. Which fast was the *least* meaningful to you? Why?

____

____

____

7. How does your understanding of true fasting, as described in the Fasts of the Prophetical Books, change the way in which you perceive and respond to our community and culture?

8. What steps do you need to take to live a life of abundance and freedom from the "sin that so easily entangles"?

   Therefore, since we are surrounded by such a great cloud of witnesses, let us throw off everything that hinders and the sin that so easily entangles, and let us run with perseverance the race marked out for us. Let us fix our eyes on Jesus, the author and perfecter of our faith, who for the joy set before him endured the cross, scorning its shame, and sat down at the right hand of the throne of God. Consider him who endured such opposition from sinful men, so that you will not grow weary and lose heart (Heb. 12:1-3).

The Fasts of the Prophetical Books Journal

Take some time to reflect on these fasts. What are some of the common themes that were the most relevant to you? How can finding victory in these areas transform your life?

Chapter 8: The Fasts of the New Testament

The purpose of this chapter is to present the fasts that are included in the New Testament and the context in which the fasting occurs. This chapter begins by reflecting and responding to questions on fasting from the New Testament. Each fast concludes by reflecting and responding to questions relevant to each fast.

In the New Testament, Jesus established fasting along with giving and prayer as the foundational spiritual disciplines to be practiced throughout all of history. Since fasting was established by Jesus it must become an integral part of our lives and the ministry He has called us to if we are going to live the victorious, abundant life that He has promised those who are His children. The following fasts of biblical characters present various purposes for fasting and the context in which the fasting occurs.

Personal Reflections from the New Testament

In the New Testament, the foundation for fasting was commanded by Jesus in the Sermon on the Mount as He states "when"

> When you fast, do not look somber as the hypocrites do, for they disfigure their faces to show men they are fasting. I tell you the truth, they have received their reward in full. But when you fast, put oil on your head and wash your face, so that it will not be obvious to men that you are fasting, but only to your Father, who is unseen; and your Father, who sees what is done in secret, will reward you (Mt. 6:16-18).

Fasting parallels the practice of prayer; the two are often conjoined. At various points in history, societal conditions have brought the church to fast and pray to bring about necessary nationwide spiritual and political transformation. Each fast presents the context and purpose in which the fasting occurs and then concludes by completing the relevant "Personal Reflections" section.[76]

1. Briefly describe the practice of fasting in the New Testament?

____

____

2. How does your understanding of fasting in the New Testament practice influence you to practice the spiritual discipline of fasting today?

____

____

---

[76] "Fast", In Barry and Wentz, eds., *Lexham Bible Dictionary*. "Fast, Fasting", In Freedman, ed., *The Anchor Yale Bible Dictionary*, Vol. 2, 773. Tylor, *Primitive Culture*, Vol. 2, 410.

3. What did Jesus teach His disciples concerning fasting?

____

____

4. What did the Apostle Paul teach his disciples concerning fasting?

____

____

5. For what reasons did the New Testament Church practice fasting?

____

____

6. How did the Early Church practice the discipline of fasting?

____

____

7. What parts of their practice are you likely to incorporate into your personal discipline of fasting?

____

____

8. What conditions in the church today might motivate you to fast for revival?

____

____

9. What conditions in society today might motivate you to fast?

____

____

10. What political conditions in society today might motivate you to fast?

Prayer

Heavenly Father, I recognize that I have not been faithful in practicing the spiritual discipline of fasting as I should and I need Your help to create a pattern of fasting on a regular basis. Help me to be a person like your servant David who was "a man after my own heart" (Acts 13:22) and a person who hungers and thirsts for You (Mt. 5:6). Therefore, prayerfully consider and write a prayer that you will address to the Lord that reflects a new commitment and dedication to Him.

Personal Reflections from the New Testament Journal

Write down any insights the Lord speaks to you regarding spiritual growth and personal thoughts to further reflect upon in your walk with the Lord.

The Bridegroom or the Jesus Fast

Please read the following Scripture references and then respond to the questions that follow.

> Then John's disciples came and asked him, "How is it that we and the Pharisees fast, but your disciples do not fast?" Jesus answered, "How can the guests of the bridegroom mourn while he is with them? The time will come when the bridegroom will be taken from them; then they will fast. "No one sews a patch of unshrunk cloth on an old garment, for the patch will pull away from the garment, making the tear worse. Neither do men pour new wine into old wineskins. If they do, the skins will burst, the wine will run out and the wineskins will be ruined. No, they pour new wine into new wineskins, and both are preserved" (Mt. 9:14-17)

> Now John's disciples and the Pharisees were fasting. Some people came and asked Jesus, "How is it that John's disciples and the disciples of the Pharisees are fasting, but yours are not?" Jesus answered, "How can the guests of the bridegroom fast while he is with them? They cannot, so long as they have him with them. But the time will come when the bridegroom will be taken from them, and on that day they will fast. "No one sews a patch of unshrunk cloth on an old garment. If he does, the new piece will pull away from the old, making the tear worse. And no one pours new wine into old wineskins. If he does, the wine will burst the skins, and both the wine and the wineskins will be ruined. No, he pours new wine into new wineskins" (Mk. 2:18-22).

> They said to him, "John's disciples often fast and pray, and so do the disciples of the Pharisees, but yours go on eating and drinking". Jesus answered, "Can you make the guests of the bridegroom fast while he is with them? But the time will come when the bridegroom will be taken from them; in those days they will fast". He told them this parable: "No one tears a patch from a new garment and sews it on an old one. If he does, he will have torn the new garment, and the patch from the new will not match the old. And no one pours new wine into old wineskins. If he does, the new wine will burst the skins, the wine will run out and the wineskins will be ruined. No, new wine must be poured into new wineskins. And no one after drinking old wine wants the new, for he says, 'The old is better'" (Lk 5:33-39).

The principle presented in the Bridegroom or the Jesus Fast is that fasting increases our spiritual capacity. Jesus fasted for 40 days before He started His public ministry. Jesus set the example for His disciples and believers today to practice on a continual basis?

The following questions are a guide to help empower you in your spiritual capacity for ministry. Whether you are beginning a new ministry or have been in ministry for a period of years the Bridegroom or the Jesus Fast can empower you for ministry. You will find the freedom and joy you desire for ministry when you commit yourself to the Lord in the task at hand.

> Trust in the LORD with all your heart and lean not on your own understanding; in all your ways acknowledge him, and he will make your paths straight (Pr. 3:5-6).

They will also assist you in applying the Bridegroom or the Jesus Fast to your personal life. It is vital that you pray and ask the Holy Spirit to give you the guidance and direction, wisdom, and the best course of action as you complete the Bridegroom or the Jesus Fast.

1. What lessons can we learn from the Bridegroom or the Jesus Fast?

2. Which lesson has had the greatest impact on your life? Explain.

3. How is the Bridegroom or the Jesus Fast relevant today?

4. What is your purpose in the Bridegroom or the Jesus Fast? Be specific. I am fasting to:

5. What spiritual power and breakthrough do you desire to unlock through the Bridegroom or the Jesus Fast?

6. If you experienced this spiritual breakthrough, how would your life be different? How would your relationships (family, friends, church) be different or affected by this spiritual breakthrough? Be specific.

7. How can your faith be increased and/or strengthened through the Bridegroom or the Jesus Fast? How will you be benefited by having your faith increased and/or strengthened?

8. What other benefits, whether physical, emotional, relational, psychological, and spiritual do you desire to achieve during the Bridegroom or the Jesus Fast?

9. What might you discover about yourself during the Bridegroom or the Jesus Fast?

10. How could the Bridegroom or the Jesus Fast change your life?

11. What steps would you take to bring out these changes in your life? Who should be involved and to what extent?

12. Does it seem like you often feel a lack of strength, energy, or enthusiasm in accomplishing what the Lord has called you to do? Do you need to be empowered from the Lord? Reflect on a few situations where you operated in your own strength. How could have the outcome have been different if you had asked the Lord for His strength?

13. Have you begun or will begin a new task without seeking God's strength and guidance? How can fasting bring God's strength and guidance? What difference will it make in the task at hand?

14. Take a moment to compare moving forward in a new task without God's strength and guidance and what it may have been the result through fasting?

____

____

15. How might the church in which you attend benefit from the Bridegroom or the Jesus Fast?

____

____

16. What length of time (days) and hours each day will you commit to during the Bridegroom or the Jesus Fast? When do you plan to begin and end your fast?

____

____

Prayer

Fasting is one of the spiritual disciplines that the Lord has established for you to achieve the spiritual power and breakthrough not only within your life but also in the lives of those whom are close to your heart. I acknowledge that I have become too comfortable in my current state of living and I sense you Holy Spirit calling me to confront the issues that I have been avoiding and find the freedom to live solely for Jesus Christ. Help me through the Bridegroom or the Jesus Fast to break free from the bondages that have been controlling my life for too long. Therefore, prayerfully consider and write a prayer that you will address to the Lord that reflects a new commitment and dedication to Him.

____

____

____

____

____

____

The Bridegroom or the Jesus Fast Journal

As you progress through this fast, write down any insights the Lord speaks to you, spiritual growth, and personal thoughts to further reflect upon in your walk with the Lord.

The Cornelius Fast

Please read the following Scripture reference and then respond to the questions that follow.

Cornelius answered: "Four days ago I was in my house praying at this hour, at three in the afternoon. Suddenly a man in shining clothes stood before me and said, 'Cornelius, God has heard your prayer and remembered your gifts to the poor" (Acts 10:30-31).

The prophet Joel prophesied that before the day of the Lord that, "And afterward, I will pour out my Spirit on all people. Your sons and daughters will prophesy, your old men will dream dreams, your young men will see visions" (Joel 2:28). Solomon in the Book of Proverbs states, "Where there is no revelation (vision), the people cast off restraint" (Pr. 29:18). The Hebrew verb used for "people cast off restraint" is the verb יִפָּרַע *yippāraʿ* from the verb פָּרַע *pāraʿ* meaning "they will get out of control". For example, while Moses was on Mount Sinai and received the Ten Commandments, Aaron allowed the Israelites to "cast off restraint" resulting in practicing pagan rituals; "Moses saw that the people were running wild and that Aaron had let them get out of control and so become a laughingstock to their enemies" (Ex. 32:25). This verb is used six times in the Book of Proverbs (Pr. 1:25; 4:15; 8:33; 13:18; 15:32; 29:18) and "willful rejection of wise instruction which results in suffering such consequences as poverty and shame". The King James Version uses "perish" instead of "cast off restraint" and those who reject wise instruction will follow the path of the wicked (Pr. 4:15).[77] As Cornelius was praying and fasting he had a vision which establishes an exciting turning point in the history of the church—Gentiles now hear and respond to the gospel and become part of the church.

The following questions are a guide to help you receive a fresh vision that could be the beginning of a new move of the Lord in your life, family, ministry, or your involvement in your community. You will find the freedom and joy you desire when you continually look to the Lord for a fresh vision for ministry, "Where there is no revelation, the people cast off restraint; but blessed is he who keeps the law" (Pr. 29:18). They will also assist you in applying the Cornelius Fast to your personal life. It is vital that you pray and ask the Holy Spirit to give you the guidance and direction, wisdom, and the best course of action as you complete the Cornelius Fast.

1. What lessons can we learn from the Cornelius Fast?

____

____

2. Which lesson has had the greatest impact on your life? Explain.

____

[77] פָּרַע *pāraʿ* "6797", In Gilbrant, ed., *The Complete Biblical Library Hebrew-English Dictionary, Pe-Resh.*

3. How is the Cornelius Fast relevant today?

4. What is your purpose in the Cornelius Fast? Be specific. I am fasting to:

5. What spiritual power and breakthrough do you desire to unlock through the Cornelius Fast?

6. If you experienced this spiritual breakthrough, how would your life be different? How would your relationships (family, friends, church) be different or affected by this spiritual breakthrough? Be specific.

7. How can your faith be increased and/or strengthened through the Cornelius Fast? How will you be benefited by having your faith increased and/or strengthened?

8. What other benefits, whether physical, emotional, relational, psychological, and spiritual do you desire to achieve during the Cornelius Fast?

9. What might you discover about yourself during the Cornelius Fast?

____

____

10. How could the Cornelius Fast change your life?

____

____

11. What steps would you take to bring out these changes in your life? Who should be involved and to what extent?

____

____

12. When is the last time that while you were fasting and/or praying that you had a vision? Briefly describe the vision.

____

____

13. Who was involved in that vision (i.e., you, family, church)? What happened to that vision?

____

____

14. What is the vision for the church in which you attend? Is it a fresh vision? When was the last time that a fresh vision was given in your church?

____

____

15. Ask the Lord to give you a fresh vision. This could refer to you, your family, or your church. Briefly state your vision.

____

16. What length of time (days) and hours each day will you commit to during the Cornelius Fast? When do you plan to begin and end your fast?

Prayer

Fasting is one of the spiritual disciplines that the Lord has established for you to achieve the spiritual power and breakthrough not only within your life but also in the lives of those whom are close to your heart. I acknowledge that I have become too comfortable in my current state of living and I sense you Holy Spirit calling me to confront the issues that I have been avoiding and find the freedom to live solely for Jesus Christ. Help me through the Cornelius Fast to break free from the bondages that have been controlling my life for too long. Therefore, prayerfully consider and write a prayer that you will address to the Lord that reflects a new commitment and dedication to Him.

The Cornelius Fast Journal

As you progress through this fast, write down any insights the Lord speaks to you, spiritual growth, and personal thoughts to further reflect upon in your walk with the Lord.

The Elder's Fast

Please read the following Scripture references and then respond to the questions that follow.

In the church at Antioch there were prophets and teachers: Barnabas, Simeon called Niger, Lucius of Cyrene, Manaen (who had been brought up with Herod the tetrarch) and Saul. While they were worshiping the Lord and fasting, the Holy Spirit said, "Set apart for me Barnabas and Saul for the work to which I have called them". So after they had fasted and prayed, they placed their hands on them and sent them off (Acts 13:1-3).

They preached the good news in that city and won a large number of disciples. Then they returned to Lystra, Iconium and Antioch, strengthening the disciples and encouraging them to remain true to the faith. "We must go through many hardships to enter the kingdom of God", they said. Paul and Barnabas appointed elders for them in each church and, with prayer and fasting, committed them to the Lord, in whom they had put their trust. After going through Pisidia, they came into Pamphylia, 25 and when they had preached the word in Perga, they went down to Attalia (Acts 14:21-25).

Our God is committed to guide believers by His Spirit who earnestly seek to do His will. Guidance in the Old Testament could be found in the moral and ritual laws provided in the Pentateuch. When guidance was needed in national or personal circumstances, God used the Urim and Thummim (Ex. 28-29) or prophets (Deut. 18) to determine who would lead an attack in battle. In the New Testament, guidance and direction is provided by the Holy Spirit who indwells believers (Acts 20:22; Rom. 8:14). Whenever we are faced with making difficult decisions, we need to be sensitive to the leading of the Holy Spirit who will give us the peace we need as long as we are moving in God's chosen way.[78]

The following questions are a guide to help you to be sensitive to the guidance and direction of the Holy Spirit in making important decisions, especially when commissioning people into ministry. You will find the freedom and joy you desire when you look to the Holy Spirit to guide and direct us and follow His ways in what we do. They will also assist you in applying the Elder's Fast to your personal life. It is vital that you pray and ask the Holy Spirit to give you the guidance and direction, wisdom, and the best course of action as you complete the Elder's Fast.

1. What lessons can we learn from the Elder's Fast?

____

____

2. Which lesson has had the greatest impact on your life? Explain.

____

[78] Richards, *The Bible Reader's Companion*, electronic ed., 720.

3. How is the Elder's Fast relevant today?

4. What is your purpose in the Elder's Fast? Be specific. I am fasting to:

5. What spiritual power and breakthrough do you desire to unlock through the Elder's Fast?

6. If you experienced this spiritual breakthrough, how would your life be different? How would your relationships (family, friends, church) be different or affected by this spiritual breakthrough? Be specific.

7. How can your faith be increased and/or strengthened through the Elder's Fast? How will you be benefited by having your faith increased and/or strengthened?

8. What other benefits, whether physical, emotional, relational, psychological, and spiritual do you desire to achieve during the Elder's Fast?

9. What might you discover about yourself during the Elder's Fast?

10. How could the Elder's Fast change your life?

11. What steps would you take to bring out these changes in your life? Who should be involved and to what extent?

12. Define in your own words the two styles of leadership described in the Elder's Fast.

13. Which style of leadership do you or the leadership of the church in which you attend adhere to? What affect does this style of leadership have upon you and others?

14. What does the Word of God have to say about this style of leadership? How did Jesus model this style of leadership?

15. What steps can we take to ensure that we follow the guidance and direction of the Holy Spirit?

16. What length of time (days) and hours each day will you commit to during the Elder's Fast? When do you plan to begin and end your fast?

Prayer

Fasting is one of the spiritual disciplines that the Lord has established for you to achieve the spiritual power and breakthrough not only within your life but also in the lives of those whom are close to your heart. I acknowledge that I have become too comfortable in my current state of living and I sense you Holy Spirit calling me to confront the issues that I have been avoiding and find the freedom to live solely for Jesus Christ. Help me through the Elder's Fast to break free from the bondages that have been controlling my life for too long. Therefore, prayerfully consider and write a prayer that you will address to the Lord that reflects a new commitment and dedication to Him.

The Elder's Fast Journal

As you progress through this fast, write down any insights the Lord speaks to you, spiritual growth, and personal thoughts to further reflect upon in your walk with the Lord.

Summary Questions to the Fasts of the New Testament

1. What are the primary themes throughout the Fasts of the New Testament? Name them in order of prominence.

2. What does this show you regarding the types of sins that have affected God's people throughout history?

3. To what degree are these sins or wickedness still prevalent within your personal life, family, community, city, and/or nation?

4. What are the primary lessons that we can learn from the Fasts of the New Testament?

5. Which fast was the *most* meaningful to you? Why?

6. Which fast was the *least* meaningful to you? Why?

7. How does your understanding of true fasting, as described in the Fasts of the New Testament, change the way in which you perceive and respond to our community and culture?

____

____

8. What steps do you need to take to live a life of abundance and freedom from the "sin that so easily entangles"?

   Therefore, since we are surrounded by such a great cloud of witnesses, let us throw off everything that hinders and the sin that so easily entangles, and let us run with perseverance the race marked out for us. Let us fix our eyes on Jesus, the author and perfecter of our faith, who for the joy set before him endured the cross, scorning its shame, and sat down at the right hand of the throne of God. Consider him who endured such opposition from sinful men, so that you will not grow weary and lose heart (Heb. 12:1-3).

____

____

The Fasts of the New Testament Journal

Take some time to reflect on these fasts. What are some of the common themes that were the most relevant to you? How can finding victory in these areas transform your life?

____

____

____

____

____

____

____

____

Chapter 9: Thematic Fasts

The purpose of this chapter is to present the numerous examples of thematic fasting that can be found in Scripture. These thematic fasts include receiving healing, preventing individual and national crisis, preventing divine judgment, experiencing the power of God, fasting to humble oneself, sorrow and mourning, and divine direction. Each fast concludes by reflecting and responding to questions relevant to each fast.

Fasting to Receive Healing

Please read the following Scripture references and then respond to the questions that follow.

> But to Hannah he gave a double portion because he loved her, and the Lord had closed her womb. And because the Lord had closed her womb, her rival kept provoking her in order to irritate her. This went on year after year. Whenever Hannah went up to the house of the Lord, her rival provoked her till she wept and would not eat. Elkanah her husband would say to her, "Hannah, why are you weeping? Why don't you eat? Why are you downhearted? Don't I mean more to you than ten sons?" Once when they had finished eating and drinking in Shiloh, Hannah stood up. Now Eli the priest was sitting on a chair by the doorpost of the Lord's temple. In bitterness of soul Hannah wept much and prayed to the Lord. And she made a vow, saying, "O Lord Almighty, if you will only look upon your servant's misery and remember me, and not forget your servant but give her a son, then I will give him to the Lord for all the days of his life, and no razor will ever be used on his head". . . . She said, "May your servant find favor in your eyes". Then she went her way and ate something, and her face was no longer downcast. Early the next morning they arose and worshiped before the Lord and then went back to their home at Ramah. Elkanah lay with Hannah his wife, and the Lord remembered her. So in the course of time Hannah conceived and gave birth to a son. She named him Samuel, saying, "Because I asked the Lord for him" (1 Sam. 1:5-11, 18-20).

> After Nathan had gone home, the LORD struck the child that Uriah's wife had borne to David, and he became ill. David pleaded with God for the child. He fasted and went into his house and spent the nights lying on the ground. The elders of his household stood beside him to get him up from the ground, but he refused, and he would not eat any food with them. . . . His servants asked him, "Why are you acting this way? While the child was alive, you fasted and wept, but now that the child is dead, you get up and eat!" He answered, "While the child was still alive, I fasted and wept. I thought, 'Who knows? The LORD may be gracious to me and let the child live'. But now that he is dead, why should I fast? Can I bring him back again? I will go to him, but he will not return to me" (2 Sam. 12:15-17, 21-23).

> Then your light will break forth like the dawn, and your healing will quickly appear; then your righteousness will go before you, and the glory of the LORD will be your rear guard (Isa. 58:8).

> For three days he was blind, and did not eat or drink anything. . . . Then Ananias went to the house and entered it. Placing his hands on Saul, he said, "Brother Saul, the Lord—Jesus, who appeared to you on the road as you were coming here—has sent me so that you may see again and be filled with the Holy Spirit". Immediately, something like scales fell from Saul's eyes, and he could see again. He got up and was baptized, and after taking some food, he regained his strength (Acts 9:9, 17-19).

1. What lessons can we learn from Fasting to Receive Healing?

2. Which lesson has had the greatest impact on your life? Explain.

3. How is Fasting to Receive Healing relevant today?

4. What is your purpose in Fasting to Receive Healing? Be specific. I am fasting to:

5. What spiritual power and breakthrough do you desire to unlock through Fasting to Receive Healing?

6. If you experienced this spiritual breakthrough, how would your life be different? How would your relationships (family, friends, church) be different or affected by this spiritual breakthrough? Be specific.

7. How can your faith be increased and/or strengthened through Fasting to Receive Healing? How will you be benefited by having your faith increased and/or strengthened?

8. What other benefits, whether physical, emotional, relational, psychological, and spiritual do you desire to achieve during Fasting to Receive Healing?

9. What might you discover about yourself during Fasting to Receive Healing?

10. How could Fasting to Receive Healing change your life?

11. What steps would you take to bring out these changes in your life? Who should be involved and to what extent?

12. What length of time (days) and hours each day will you commit to during Fasting to Receive Healing? When do you plan to begin and end your fast?

Prayer

Fasting is one of the spiritual disciplines that the Lord has established for you to achieve the spiritual power and breakthrough not only within your life but also in the lives of those whom are close to your heart. I acknowledge that I have become too comfortable in my current state of living and I sense you Holy Spirit calling me to confront the issues that I have been avoiding and find the freedom to live solely for Jesus Christ. Help me through the fasting to receive healing to break free from the bondages that have been controlling my life for too long. Therefore, prayerfully consider and write a prayer that you will address to the Lord that reflects a new commitment and dedication to Him.

Fasting to Receive Healing Journal

As you progress through this fast, write down any insights the Lord speaks to you, spiritual growth, and personal thoughts to further reflect upon in your walk with the Lord.

Fasting to Receive a Solution to Individual / National Crisis

Please read the following Scripture references and then respond to the questions that follow.

When they had assembled at Mizpah, they drew water and poured it out before the LORD. On that day they fasted and there they confessed, "We have sinned against the LORD". And Samuel was leader of Israel at Mizpah (1 Sam. 7:6).

The Ninevites believed God. They declared a fast, and all of them, from the greatest to the least, put on sackcloth. When the news reached the king of Nineveh, he rose from his throne, took off his royal robes, covered himself with sackcloth and sat down in the dust. Then he issued a proclamation in Nineveh: "By the decree of the king and his nobles: Do not let any man or beast, herd or flock, taste anything; do not let them eat or drink. But let man and beast be covered with sackcloth. Let everyone call urgently on God. Let them give up their evil ways and their violence. Who knows? God may yet relent and with compassion turn from his fierce anger so that we will not perish". When God saw what they did and how they turned from their evil ways, he had compassion and did not bring upon them the destruction he had threatened. But Jonah was greatly displeased and became angry (Jon. 3:5-4:1).

The word of the LORD that came to Joel son of Pethuel. Hear this, you elders; listen, all who live in the land. Has anything like this ever happened in your days or in the days of your forefathers? Tell it to your children, and let your children tell it to their children, and their children to the next generation. What the locust swarm has left the great locusts have eaten; what the great locusts have left the young locusts have eaten; what the young locusts have left other locusts have eaten. Wake up, you drunkards, and weep! Wail, all you drinkers of wine; wail because of the new wine, for it has been snatched from your lips. A nation has invaded my land, powerful and without number; it has the teeth of a lion, the fangs of a lioness. It has laid waste my vines and ruined my fig trees. It has stripped off their bark and thrown it away, leaving their branches white. Mourn like a virgin in sackcloth grieving for the husband of her youth. Grain offerings and drink offerings are cut off from the house of the LORD. The priests are in mourning, those who minister before the LORD. The fields are ruined, the ground is dried up; the grain is destroyed, the new wine is dried up, the oil fails. Despair, you farmers, wail, you vine growers; grieve for the wheat and the barley, because the harvest of the field is destroyed. The vine is dried up and the fig tree is withered; the pomegranate, the palm and the apple tree—all the trees of the field—are dried up. Surely the joy of mankind is withered away. Put on sackcloth, O priests, and mourn; wail, you who minister before the altar. Come, spend the night in sackcloth, you who minister before my God; for the grain offerings and drink offerings are withheld from the house of your God. Declare a holy fast; call a sacred assembly. Summon the elders and all who live in the land to the house of the LORD your God, and cry out to the LORD. Alas for that day! For the day of the LORD is near; it will come like destruction from the Almighty. Has not the food been cut off before our very eyes—joy and gladness from the house of our God? The seeds are shriveled beneath the clods. The storehouses are in ruins, the granaries have been broken down, for the grain has dried up. How the cattle moan! The herds mill about because they have no pasture; even the flocks of sheep are suffering. To you, O LORD, I call, for fire has devoured the open pastures and flames have burned up all the trees of the field. Even the wild animals pant for you; the streams of water have dried up and fire has devoured the open pastures (Joel 1:1-20).

Blow the trumpet in Zion; sound the alarm on my holy hill. Let all who live in the land tremble, for the day of the LORD is coming. It is close at hand—a day of darkness and gloom, a day of clouds and blackness. Like dawn spreading across the mountains a large and mighty army comes, such as never was of old nor ever will be in ages to come. Before them fire devours, behind them a flame blazes. Before them the land is like the garden of Eden, behind them, a desert waste—nothing escapes them. They have the appearance of horses; they gallop along like cavalry. With a noise like that of chariots they leap over the mountaintops, like a crackling fire consuming stubble, like a mighty army drawn up for battle. At the sight of them, nations are in anguish; every face turns pale. They charge like warriors; they scale walls like soldiers. They all march in line, not swerving from their course. They do not jostle each other; each marches straight ahead. They plunge through defenses without breaking ranks. They rush upon the city; they run along the wall. They climb into the houses; like thieves they enter through the windows. Before them the earth shakes, the sky trembles, the sun and moon are darkened, and the stars no longer shine. The LORD thunders at the head of his army; his forces are beyond number, and mighty are those who obey his command. The day of the LORD is great; it is dreadful. Who can endure it? "Even now", declares the LORD, "return to me with all your heart, with fasting and weeping and mourning". Rend your heart and not your garments. Return to the LORD your God, for he is gracious and compassionate, slow to anger and abounding in love, and he relents from sending calamity. Who knows? He may turn and have pity and leave behind a blessing—grain offerings and drink offerings for the LORD your God. Blow the trumpet in Zion, declare a holy fast, call a sacred assembly. Gather the people, consecrate the assembly; bring together the elders, gather the children, those nursing at the breast. Let the bridegroom leave his room and the bride her chamber. Let the priests, who minister before the LORD, weep between the temple porch and the altar. Let them say, "Spare your people, O LORD. Do not make your inheritance an object of scorn, a byword among the nations. Why should they say among the peoples, 'Where is their God?'" Then the LORD will be jealous for his land and take pity on his people. The LORD will reply to them: "I am sending you grain, new wine and oil, enough to satisfy you fully; never again will I make you an object of scorn to the nations. "I will drive the northern army far from you, pushing it into a parched and barren land, with its front columns going into the eastern sea and those in the rear into the western sea. And its stench will go up; its smell will rise". Surely he has done great things. Be not afraid, O land; be glad and rejoice. Surely the LORD has done great things. Be not afraid, O wild animals, for the open pastures are becoming green. The trees are bearing their fruit; the fig tree and the vine yield their riches. Be glad, O people of Zion, rejoice in the LORD your God, for he has given you the autumn rains in righteousness. He sends you abundant showers, both autumn and spring rains, as before. The threshing floors will be filled with grain; the vats will overflow with new wine and oil. "I will repay you for the years the locusts have eaten—the great locust and the young locust, the other locusts and the locust swarm—my great army that I sent among you. You will have plenty to eat, until you are full, and you will praise the name of the LORD your God, who has worked wonders for you; never again will my people be shamed. Then you will know that I am in Israel, that I am the LORD your God, and that there is no other; never again will my people be shamed. "And afterward, I will pour out my Spirit on all people. Your sons and daughters will prophesy, your old men will dream dreams, your young men will see visions. Even on my servants, both men and women, I will pour out my Spirit in those days. I will show wonders in the heavens and on the earth, blood and fire and billows of smoke. The sun will be turned to darkness and the moon to blood before the coming of the great and dreadful day of the LORD. And everyone who calls on the name of the LORD will be saved; for on Mount Zion and in Jerusalem there will be deliverance, as the LORD has said, among the survivors whom the LORD calls (Joel 2:1-32).

1. What lessons can we learn from Fasting to Receive a Solution to Individual / National Crisis?

2. Which lesson has had the greatest impact on your life? Explain.

3. How is Fasting to Receive a Solution to Individual / National Crisis relevant today?

4. What is your purpose in Fasting to Receive a Solution to Individual / National Crisis? Be specific. I am fasting to:

5. What spiritual power and breakthrough do you desire to unlock through Fasting to Receive a Solution to Individual / National Crisis?

6. If you experienced this spiritual breakthrough, how would your life be different? How would your relationships (family, friends, church) be different or affected by this spiritual breakthrough? Be specific.

7. How can your faith be increased and/or strengthened through Fasting to Receive a Solution to Individual / National Crisis? How will you be benefited by having your faith increased and/or strengthened?

8. What other benefits, whether physical, emotional, relational, psychological, and spiritual do you desire to achieve during Fasting to Receive a Solution to Individual / National Crisis?

9. What might you discover about yourself during Fasting to Receive a Solution to Individual / National Crisis?

10. How could Fasting to Receive a Solution to Individual / National Crisis change your life?

11. What steps would you take to bring out these changes in your life? Who should be involved and to what extent?

12. What is the individual crisis that you or our family are presently seeking a solution?

13. What is one of the most pressing national crisis that is having an affect upon you, your family, your church, or your community? How should you respond to this national crisis?

14. Write out the steps that you would take to help to eleviate the national crisis. Who should be involved and to what extent?

____

____

15. How could periodic fasting help to prevent individual / national crisis from beginning?

____

____

16. What length of time (days) and hours each day will you commit to during Fasting to Receive a Solution to Individual / National Crisis? When do you plan to begin and end your fast?

____

____

Prayer

Fasting is one of the spiritual disciplines that the Lord has established for you to achieve the spiritual power and breakthrough not only within your life but also in the lives of those whom are close to your heart. I acknowledge that I have become too comfortable in my current state of living and I sense you Holy Spirit calling me to confront the issues that I have been avoiding and find the freedom to live solely for Jesus Christ. Help me through the fasting to prevent individual / national crisis to break free from the bondages that have been controlling my life for too long. Therefore, prayerfully consider and write a prayer that you will address to the Lord that reflects a new commitment and dedication to Him.

____

____

____

____

____

____

Fasting to Receive a Solution to Individual / National Crisis Journal

As you progress through this fast, write down any insights the Lord speaks to you, spiritual growth, and personal thoughts to further reflect upon in your walk with the Lord.

Fasting to Prevent Divine Judgment

Please read the following Scripture references and then respond to the questions that follow.

Then once again I fell prostrate before the LORD for forty days and forty nights; I ate no bread and drank no water, because of all the sin you had committed, doing what was evil in the LORD's sight and so provoking him to anger. . . . I lay prostrate before the LORD those forty days and forty nights because the LORD had said he would destroy you (Deut. 9:18, 25).

Then you will call, and the LORD will answer; you will cry for help, and he will say: Here am I. "If you do away with the yoke of oppression, with the pointing finger and malicious talk, and if you spend yourselves in behalf of the hungry and satisfy the needs of the oppressed, then your light will rise in the darkness, and your night will become like the noonday (Isa. 58:9-10).

1. What lessons can we learn from Fasting to Prevent Divine Judgment?

____

____

2. Which lesson has had the greatest impact on your life? Explain.

____

____

3. How is Fasting to Prevent Divine Judgment relevant today?

____

____

4. What is your purpose in Fasting to Prevent Divine Judgment? Be specific. I am fasting to:

____

____

5. What spiritual power and breakthrough do you desire to unlock through Fasting to Prevent Divine Judgment?

____

____

6. If you experienced this spiritual breakthrough, how would your life be different? How would your relationships (family, friends, church) be different or affected by this spiritual breakthrough? Be specific.

____

____

7. How can your faith be increased and/or strengthened through Fasting to Prevent Divine Judgment? How will you be benefited by having your faith increased and/or strengthened?

____

____

8. What other benefits, whether physical, emotional, relational, psychological, and spiritual do you desire to achieve during Fasting to Prevent Divine Judgment?

____

____

9. What might you discover about yourself during Fasting to Prevent Divine Judgment?

____

____

10. How could Fasting to Prevent Divine Judgment change your life?

____

____

11. What steps would you take to bring out these changes in your life? Who should be involved and to what extent?

____

____

____

12. How serious is the situation that you would need to commit to fasting to prevent divine judgment? This does not necessarily refer to you, but to a group of people like the contexts stated above.

____

____

13. Do you feel that the seriousness of this situation could have been to some extent avoided if you would have dealt with this issue earlier? What would you have done?

____

____

14. Write out the steps that you would take to stop this situation from becoming so serious. Who should be involved and to what extent?

____

____

15. How could periodic fasting help to prevent divine judgment from beginning?

____

____

16. What length of time (days) and hours each day will you commit to during Fasting to Prevent Divine Judgment? When do you plan to begin and end your fast?

____

____

Prayer

Fasting is one of the spiritual disciplines that the Lord has established for you to achieve the spiritual power and breakthrough not only within your life but also in the lives of those whom are close to your heart. I acknowledge that I have become too comfortable in my current state of living and I sense you Holy Spirit calling me to confront the issues that I have been avoiding and find the freedom to live solely for Jesus Christ. Help me through the fasting to prevent divine judgment to break free from the bondages that have been controlling my life for too long. Therefore, prayerfully consider and write a prayer that you will address to the Lord that reflects a new commitment and dedication to Him.

Fasting to Prevent Divine Judgment Journal

As you progress through this fast, write down any insights the Lord speaks to you, spiritual growth, and personal thoughts to further reflect upon in your walk with the Lord.

Fasting to Experience God's Power

We all desire to experience the power of God in new and fresh ways on a continual basis. However, we often feel as though something is hindering us from growing deeper in our relationship with the Lord and struggle to break free from these obstacles. Fasting takes our focus off of ourselves and opens us to experience God's power. You can find anecdotal testimonies of people who have experienced God's power in miraculous ways as a result of fasting.

1. What lessons can we learn from Fasting to Experience God's Power?

____

____

2. Which lesson has had the greatest impact on your life? Explain.

____

____

3. How is Fasting to Experience God's Power relevant today?

____

____

4. What is your purpose in Fasting to Experience God's Power? Be specific. I am fasting to:

____

____

5. What spiritual power and breakthrough do you desire to unlock through Fasting to Experience God's Power?

____

____

____

____

6. If you experienced this spiritual breakthrough, how would your life be different? How would your relationships (family, friends, church) be different or affected by this spiritual breakthrough? Be specific.

____

____

7. How can your faith be increased and/or strengthened through Fasting to Experience God's Power? How will you be benefited by having your faith increased and/or strengthened?

____

____

8. What other benefits, whether physical, emotional, relational, psychological, and spiritual do you desire to achieve during Fasting to Experience God's Power?

____

____

9. What might you discover about yourself during Fasting to Experience God's Power?

____

____

10. How could Fasting to Experience God's Power change your life?

____

____

11. What steps would you take to bring out these changes in your life? Who should be involved and to what extent?

____

____

____

12. How could periodic fasting help you to experience God's power on a continual basis?

13. What length of time (days) and hours each day will you commit to during Fasting to Experience God's Power? When do you plan to begin and end your fast?

Prayer

Fasting is one of the spiritual disciplines that the Lord has established for you to achieve the spiritual power and breakthrough not only within your life but also in the lives of those whom are close to your heart. I acknowledge that I have become too comfortable in my current state of living and I sense you Holy Spirit calling me to confront the issues that I have been avoiding and find the freedom to live solely for Jesus Christ. Help me through the fasting to experience God's power to break free from the bondages that have been controlling my life for too long. Therefore, prayerfully consider and write a prayer that you will address to the Lord that reflects a new commitment and dedication to Him.

Fasting to Experience God's Power Journal

As you progress through this fast, write down any insights the Lord speaks to you, spiritual growth, and personal thoughts to further reflect upon in your walk with the Lord.

Fasting to Humble Oneself

Please read the following Scripture references and then respond to the questions that follow.

> Yet when they were ill, I put on sackcloth and humbled myself with fasting. When my prayers returned to me unanswered, I went about mourning as though for my friend or brother. I bowed my head in grief as though weeping for my mother (Ps. 35:13-14).

> When I weep and fast, I must endure scorn; when I put on sackcloth, people make sport of me (Ps. 69:10-11).

David was known for fasting, wearing sackcloth, and humbling himself when his enemies became sick. Yet when he received no response from the Lord he mourned and wept for them. Moreover, when he faced difficult times, his enemies mocked and ridiculed him (Ps. 35:15-16). He experienced injustice and sought the Lord for assistance who had not responded and pleaded "O Lord, how long will you look on?" When the Lord answered his plea, he stated "I will give you thanks in the great assembly; among throngs of people I will praise you" (Ps. 35:18).

1. What lessons can we learn from Fasting to Humble Oneself?

____

____

2. Which lesson has had the greatest impact on your life? Explain.

____

____

3. How is Fasting to Humble Oneself relevant today?

____

____

4. What is your purpose in Fasting to Humble Oneself ? Be specific. I am fasting to:

____

____

____

5. What spiritual power and breakthrough do you desire to unlock through Fasting to Humble Oneself?

____

____

6. If you experienced this spiritual breakthrough, how would your life be different? How would your relationships (family, friends, church) be different or affected by this spiritual breakthrough? Be specific.

____

____

7. How can your faith be increased and/or strengthened through Fasting to Humble Oneself? How will you be benefited by having your faith increased and/or strengthened?

____

____

8. What other benefits, whether physical, emotional, relational, psychological, and spiritual do you desire to achieve during Fasting to Humble Oneself?

____

____

9. What might you discover about yourself during Fasting to Humble Oneself?

____

____

10. How could Fasting to Humble Oneself change your life?

____

____

____

11. What steps would you take to bring out these changes in your life? Who should be involved and to what extent?

____

____

12. Like David, for whom are you humbling yourself. Why? What results do you hope to achieve?

____

____

13. What did Jesus teach that we should do towards our enemies? (Mt. 5:43-48)

____

____

14. What length of time (days) and hours each day will you commit to during Fasting to Humble Oneself? When do you plan to begin and end your fast?

____

____

Prayer

Fasting is one of the spiritual disciplines that the Lord has established for you to achieve the spiritual power and breakthrough not only within your life but also in the lives of those whom are close to your heart. I acknowledge that I have become too comfortable in my current state of living and I sense you Holy Spirit calling me to confront the issues that I have been avoiding and find the freedom to live solely for Jesus Christ. Help me through fasting to humble myself to break free from the bondages that have been controlling my life for too long. Therefore, prayerfully consider and write a prayer that you will address to the Lord that reflects a new commitment and dedication to Him.

____

____

____

Fasting to Humble Oneself Journal

As you progress through this fast, write down any insights the Lord speaks to you, spiritual growth, and personal thoughts to further reflect upon in your walk with the Lord.

Fasting in Sorrow and Mourning

Please read the following Scripture reference and then respond to the questions that follow.

So she wrote letters in Ahab's name, placed his seal on them, and sent them to the elders and nobles who lived in Naboth's city with him. In those letters she wrote: "Proclaim a day of fasting and seat Naboth in a prominent place among the people. But seat two scoundrels opposite him and have them testify that he has cursed both God and the king. Then take him out and stone him to death". So the elders and nobles who lived in Naboth's city did as Jezebel directed in the letters she had written to them. They proclaimed a fast and seated Naboth in a prominent place among the people. Then two scoundrels came and sat opposite him and brought charges against Naboth before the people, saying, "Naboth has cursed both God and the king". So they took him outside the city and stoned him to death. Then they sent word to Jezebel: "Naboth has been stoned and is dead" (1 Kgs. 21:8-14).

When Ahab received the prophetic judgment (1 Kgs. 21:27-29) spoken through Elijah, he humbled himself before the Lord by tearing his clothes (Est. 4:1; Job 1:20), wearing sackcloth (Gen. 37:34; 1 Kgs. 20:31-32; Est. 4:1; Neh. 9:1; Dan. 9:3), and fasting (Neh. 9:1; Dan. 9:3), which demonstrated a deep sense of sorrow and mourning for his behaviour. However, God was not completely merciful to Ahab, and his son Joram suffered the consequences of his actions (2 Kgs. 9:24-26; 10:17). His wife, Queen Jezebel, refused to repent of her wicked actions and suffered the fullest extent of what the Lord had promised without mercy (2 Kgs. 9:30-37).

1. What lessons can we learn from Fasting in Sorrow and Mourning?

____

____

2. Which lesson has had the greatest impact on your life? Explain.

____

____

3. How is Fasting in Sorrow and Mourning relevant today?

____

____

4. What is your purpose in Fasting in Sorrow and Mourning? Be specific. I am fasting to:

____

5. What spiritual power and breakthrough do you desire to unlock through Fasting in Sorrow and Mourning?

6. If you experienced this spiritual breakthrough, how would your life be different? How would your relationships (family, friends, church) be different or affected by this spiritual breakthrough? Be specific.

7. How can your faith be increased and/or strengthened through Fasting in Sorrow and Mourning? How will you be benefited by having your faith increased and/or strengthened?

8. What other benefits, whether physical, emotional, relational, psychological, and spiritual do you desire to achieve during Fasting in Sorrow and Mourning?

9. What might you discover about yourself during Fasting in Sorrow and Mourning?

10. How could Fasting in Sorrow and Mourning change your life?

11. What steps would you take to bring out these changes in your life? Who should be involved and to what extent?

______

______

12. In this context, do you relate more to Ahab or Jezebel? Have you stood by while someone committed a wicked act against another person or were you the person committing the act? Explain.

______

______

13. What was your response to the situation? What would you do or not do if this happened again?

______

______

14. What length of time (days) and hours each day will you commit to during Fasting in Sorrow and Mourning? When do you plan to begin and end your fast?

______

______

Prayer

Fasting is one of the spiritual disciplines that the Lord has established for you to achieve the spiritual power and breakthrough not only within your life but also in the lives of those whom are close to your heart. I acknowledge that I have become too comfortable in my current state of living and I sense you Holy Spirit calling me to confront the issues that I have been avoiding and find the freedom to live solely for Jesus Christ. Help me through fasting in sorrow and mourning to break free from the bondages that have been controlling my life for too long. Therefore, prayerfully consider and write a prayer that you will address to the Lord that reflects a new commitment and dedication to Him.

______

______

______

Fasting in Sorrow and Mourning Journal

As you progress through this fast, write down any insights the Lord speaks to you, spiritual growth, and personal thoughts to further reflect upon in your walk with the Lord.

Fasting for Divine Direction

Please read the following Scripture references and then respond to the questions that follow.

Then the Israelites, all the people, went up to Bethel, and there they sat weeping before the LORD. They fasted that day until evening and presented burnt offerings and fellowship offerings to the LORD. And the Israelites inquired of the LORD. (In those days the ark of the covenant of God was there, with Phinehas son of Eleazar, the son of Aaron, ministering before it.) They asked, "Shall we go up again to battle with Benjamin our brother, or not?" The LORD responded, "Go, for tomorrow I will give them into your hands" (Jdg. 20:26-28).

Alarmed, Jehoshaphat resolved to inquire of the LORD, and he proclaimed a fast for all Judah. [4] The people of Judah came together to seek help from the LORD; indeed, they came from every town in Judah to seek him (2 Chr. 20:3-4).

There, by the Ahava Canal, I proclaimed a fast, so that we might humble ourselves before our God and ask him for a safe journey for us and our children, with all our possessions. I was ashamed to ask the king for soldiers and horsemen to protect us from enemies on the road, because we had told the king, "The gracious hand of our God is on everyone who looks to him, but his great anger is against all who forsake him". So we fasted and petitioned our God about this, and he answered our prayer (Ezra 8:21-23).

In the church at Antioch there were prophets and teachers: Barnabas, Simeon called Niger, Lucius of Cyrene, Manaen (who had been brought up with Herod the tetrarch) and Saul. While they were worshiping the Lord and fasting, the Holy Spirit said, "Set apart for me Barnabas and Saul for the work to which I have called them". So after they had fasted and prayed, they placed their hands on them and sent them off (Acts 13:1-3).

They preached the good news in that city and won a large number of disciples. Then they returned to Lystra, Iconium and Antioch, strengthening the disciples and encouraging them to remain true to the faith. "We must go through many hardships to enter the kingdom of God", they said. Paul and Barnabas appointed elders for them in each church and, with prayer and fasting, committed them to the Lord, in whom they had put their trust. After going through Pisidia, they came into Pamphylia, and when they had preached the word in Perga, they went down to Attalia (Acts 14:21-25).

1. What lessons can we learn from Fasting for Divine Direction?

____

____

2. Which lesson has had the greatest impact on your life? Explain.

____

____

3. How is Fasting for Divine Direction relevant today?

---

4. What is your purpose in Fasting for Divine Direction? Be specific. I am fasting to:

---

5. What spiritual power and breakthrough do you desire to unlock through Fasting for Divine Direction?

---

6. If you experienced this spiritual breakthrough, how would your life be different? How would your relationships (family, friends, church) be different or affected by this spiritual breakthrough? Be specific.

---

7. How can your faith be increased and/or strengthened through Fasting for Divine Direction? How will you be benefited by having your faith increased and/or strengthened?

---

8. What other benefits, whether physical, emotional, relational, psychological, and spiritual do you desire to achieve during Fasting for Divine Direction?

---

9. What might you discover about yourself during Fasting for Divine Direction?

---

10. How could Fasting for Divine Direction change your life?

11. What steps would you take to bring out these changes in your life? Who should be involved and to what extent?

12. In what ways is this fast similar to or different from the Moses Fast and the Jehoshaphat Fast?

13. Are there personal and/or familial issues that you are in search for divine direction?

14. Are there issues within your church or community that need divine direction? If so, who would be involved? What steps would you take?

15. What length of time (days) and hours each day will you commit to during Fasting for Divine Direction? When do you plan to begin and end your fast?

Prayer

Fasting is one of the spiritual disciplines that the Lord has established for you to achieve the spiritual power and breakthrough not only within your life but also in the lives of those whom are close to your heart. I acknowledge that I have become too comfortable in my current state of living and I sense you Holy Spirit calling me to confront the issues that I have been avoiding and find the freedom to live solely for Jesus Christ. Help me through fasting for divine direction to break free from the bondages that have been controlling my life for too long. Therefore, prayerfully consider and write a prayer that you will address to the Lord that reflects a new commitment and dedication to Him.

____

____

____

____

____

Fasting for Divine Direction Journal

As you progress through this fast, write down any insights the Lord speaks to you, spiritual growth, and personal thoughts to further reflect upon in your walk with the Lord.

____

____

____

____

____

____

____

____

Chapter 10: Thematic Fasting Continued

This chapter is a continuation of Chapter 9 on thematic fasting. These fast include remorse over committed sin, spiritual deliverance, revival, renewal, righteousness, material provision, God rejecting fasting, and fasting to find freedom from emotional distress. Each fast concludes by reflecting and responding to questions relevant to each fast.

Fasting for Remorse over Committed Sin

Please read the following Scripture reference and then respond to the questions that follow.

> Then the word of the LORD came to Elijah the Tishbite: "Go down to meet Ahab king of Israel, who rules in Samaria. He is now in Naboth's vineyard, where he has gone to take possession of it. Say to him, 'This is what the LORD says: Have you not murdered a man and seized his property?' Then say to him, 'This is what the LORD says: In the place where dogs licked up Naboth's blood, dogs will lick up your blood—yes, yours!'" Ahab said to Elijah, "So you have found me, my enemy!" "I have found you", he answered, "because you have sold yourself to do evil in the eyes of the LORD. 'I am going to bring disaster on you. I will consume your descendants and cut off from Ahab every last male in Israel—slave or free. I will make your house like that of Jeroboam son of Nebat and that of Baasha son of Ahijah, because you have provoked me to anger and have caused Israel to sin'. "And also concerning Jezebel the LORD says: 'Dogs will devour Jezebel by the wall of Jezreel'. "Dogs will eat those belonging to Ahab who die in the city, and the birds of the air will feed on those who die in the country". (There was never a man like Ahab, who sold himself to do evil in the eyes of the LORD, urged on by Jezebel his wife. He behaved in the vilest manner by going after idols, like the Amorites the LORD drove out before Israel.) When Ahab heard these words, he tore his clothes, put on sackcloth and fasted. He lay in sackcloth and went around meekly. Then the word of the LORD came to Elijah the Tishbite: "Have you noticed how Ahab has humbled himself before me? Because he has humbled himself, I will not bring this disaster in his day, but I will bring it on his house in the days of his son" (1 Kgs. 21:17-29).

Please refer to the earlier discussion on fasting in sorrow and mourning and also to the Queen Jezebel which further describes this context. In this context, Queen Jezebel coveted Naboth's vineyard and devised a plan to acquire property that was not God's will for them. Moreover, when we covet anything that belongs to someone else, we may be sure that a curse will follow. After all, covetousness is the root of all sin. It was the first sin that was committed in the Garden of Eden (Gen. 3:6), the first sin upon entering the Promised Land (Jos. 7:21), and the first sin in the early Church (Acts 5:1-3).

1. What lessons can we learn from Fasting for Remorse over Committed Sin?

____

____

2. Which lesson has had the greatest impact on your life? Explain.

____

3. How is Fasting for Remorse over Committed Sin relevant today?

4. What is your purpose in Fasting for Remorse over Committed Sin? Be specific. I am fasting to:

5. What spiritual power and breakthrough do you desire to unlock through Fasting for Remorse over Committed Sin?

6. If you experienced this spiritual breakthrough, how would your life be different? How would your relationships (family, friends, church) be different or affected by this spiritual breakthrough? Be specific.

7. How can your faith be increased and/or strengthened through Fasting for Remorse over Committed Sin? How will you be benefited by having your faith increased and/or strengthened?

8. What other benefits, whether physical, emotional, relational, psychological, and spiritual do you desire to achieve during Fasting for Remorse over Committed Sin?

9. What might you discover about yourself during Fasting for Remorse over Committed Sin?

____

____

10. How could Fasting for Remorse over Committed Sin change your life?

____

____

11. What steps would you take to bring out these changes in your life? Who should be involved and to what extent?

____

____

12. What are some of the things that you covet or have coveted? How did coveting this thing affect yourself and others?

____

____

13. Did someone, like Jezebel, influence you to covet something that belonged to another person or was it only your decision? Describe the circumstances surrounding this covetousness.

____

____

14. How could it have been avoided? Describe the triggers that led you to commit such an act.

____

____

15. Like Ahab did you repent of your covetousness? Did you make restitution for what you had done? If not, why not?

____

16. How should you respond if / when similar circumstances arise?

17. What length of time (days) and hours each day will you commit to during Fasting for Remorse over Committed Sin? When do you plan to begin and end your fast?

Prayer

Fasting is one of the spiritual disciplines that the Lord has established for you to achieve the spiritual power and breakthrough not only within your life but also in the lives of those whom are close to your heart. I acknowledge that I have become too comfortable in my current state of living and I sense you Holy Spirit calling me to confront the issues that I have been avoiding and find the freedom to live solely for Jesus Christ. Help me through fasting for remorse over committed sin to break free from the bondages that have been controlling my life for too long. Therefore, prayerfully consider and write a prayer that you will address to the Lord that reflects a new commitment and dedication to Him.

Fasting for Remorse over Committed Sin Journal

As you progress through this fast, write down any insights the Lord speaks to you, spiritual growth, and personal thoughts to further reflect upon in your walk with the Lord.

Fasting for Spiritual Deliverance

Please read the following Scripture references and then respond to the questions that follow.

Alarmed, Jehoshaphat resolved to inquire of the LORD, and he proclaimed a fast for all Judah. The people of Judah came together to seek help from the LORD; indeed, they came from every town in Judah to seek him (2 Chr. 20:3-4).

Is not this the kind of fasting I have chosen: to loose the chains of injustice and untie the cords of the yoke, to set the oppressed free and break every yoke? (Isa. 58:6).

But this kind does not go out except by prayer and fasting (Mt. 17:21).

He replied, "This kind can come out only by prayer and fasting" (Mk. 9:29).

1. What lessons can we learn from Fasting for Spiritual Deliverance?

____

____

2. Which lesson has had the greatest impact on your life? Explain.

____

____

3. How is Fasting for Spiritual Deliverance relevant today?

____

____

4. What is your purpose in Fasting for Spiritual Deliverance? Be specific. I am fasting to:

____

____

5. What spiritual power and breakthrough do you desire to unlock through Fasting for Spiritual Deliverance?

____

____

6. If you experienced this spiritual breakthrough, how would your life be different? How would your relationships (family, friends, church) be different or affected by this spiritual breakthrough? Be specific.

____

____

7. How can your faith be increased and/or strengthened through Fasting for Spiritual Deliverance? How will you be benefited by having your faith increased and/or strengthened?

____

____

8. What other benefits, whether physical, emotional, relational, psychological, and spiritual do you desire to achieve during Fasting for Spiritual Deliverance?

____

____

9. What might you discover about yourself during Fasting for Spiritual Deliverance?

____

____

10. How could Fasting for Spiritual Deliverance change your life?

____

____

11. What steps would you take to bring out these changes in your life? Who should be involved and to what extent?

____

____

____

12. What kind of spiritual deliverance so you seek through this fast? How long have you felt as though you were living in bondage?

____

____

13. Did someone, like Jezebel, influence you to covet something that belonged to another person or was it only your decision? Describe the circumstances surrounding this covetousness.

____

____

14. How could it have been avoided? Describe the triggers that led you to commit such an act.

____

____

15. Like Ahab did you repent of your covetousness? Did you make restitution for what you had done? If not, why not?

____

____

16. How should you respond if / when similar circumstances arise?

____

____

17. What length of time (days) and hours each day will you commit to during Fasting for Spiritual Deliverance? When do you plan to begin and end your fast?

____

____

____

Prayer

Fasting is one of the spiritual disciplines that the Lord has established for you to achieve the spiritual power and breakthrough not only within your life but also in the lives of those whom are close to your heart. I acknowledge that I have become too comfortable in my current state of living and I sense you Holy Spirit calling me to confront the issues that I have been avoiding and find the freedom to live solely for Jesus Christ. Help me through fasting for spiritual deliverance to break free from the bondages that have been controlling my life for too long. Therefore, prayerfully consider and write a prayer that you will address to the Lord that reflects a new commitment and dedication to Him.

____

____

____

____

____

Fasting for Spiritual Deliverance Journal

As you progress through this fast, write down any insights the Lord speaks to you, spiritual growth, and personal thoughts to further reflect upon in your walk with the Lord.

____

____

____

____

____

____

____

____

Fasting for Revival, Renewal, and Righteousness

Please read the following Scripture references and then respond to the questions that follow.

There was also a prophetess, Anna, the daughter of Phanuel, of the tribe of Asher. She was very old; she had lived with her husband seven years after her marriage, and then was a widow until she was eighty-four. She never left the temple but worshiped night and day, fasting and praying (Lk. 2:36-37).

The word of the LORD that came to Joel son of Pethuel. Hear this, you elders; listen, all who live in the land. Has anything like this ever happened in your days or in the days of your forefathers? Tell it to your children, and let your children tell it to their children, and their children to the next generation. What the locust swarm has left the great locusts have eaten; what the great locusts have left the young locusts have eaten; what the young locusts have left other locusts have eaten. Wake up, you drunkards, and weep! Wail, all you drinkers of wine; wail because of the new wine, for it has been snatched from your lips. A nation has invaded my land, powerful and without number; it has the teeth of a lion, the fangs of a lioness. It has laid waste my vines and ruined my fig trees. It has stripped off their bark and thrown it away, leaving their branches white. Mourn like a virgin in sackcloth grieving for the husband of her youth. Grain offerings and drink offerings are cut off from the house of the LORD. The priests are in mourning, those who minister before the LORD. The fields are ruined, the ground is dried up; the grain is destroyed, the new wine is dried up, the oil fails. Despair, you farmers, wail, you vine growers; grieve for the wheat and the barley, because the harvest of the field is destroyed. The vine is dried up and the fig tree is withered; the pomegranate, the palm and the apple tree—all the trees of the field—are dried up. Surely the joy of mankind is withered away. Put on sackcloth, O priests, and mourn; wail, you who minister before the altar. Come, spend the night in sackcloth, you who minister before my God; for the grain offerings and drink offerings are withheld from the house of your God. Declare a holy fast; call a sacred assembly. Summon the elders and all who live in the land to the house of the LORD your God, and cry out to the LORD. Alas for that day! For the day of the LORD is near; it will come like destruction from the Almighty. Has not the food been cut off before our very eyes—joy and gladness from the house of our God? The seeds are shriveled beneath the clods. The storehouses are in ruins, the granaries have been broken down, for the grain has dried up. How the cattle moan! The herds mill about because they have no pasture; even the flocks of sheep are suffering. To you, O LORD, I call, for fire has devoured the open pastures and flames have burned up all the trees of the field. Even the wild animals pant for you; the streams of water have dried up and fire has devoured the open pastures (Joel 1:1-20).

Blow the trumpet in Zion; sound the alarm on my holy hill. Let all who live in the land tremble, for the day of the LORD is coming. It is close at hand—a day of darkness and gloom, a day of clouds and blackness. Like dawn spreading across the mountains a large and mighty army comes, such as never was of old nor ever will be in ages to come. Before them fire devours, behind them a flame blazes. Before them the land is like the garden of Eden, behind them, a desert waste—nothing escapes them. They have the appearance of horses; they gallop along like cavalry. With a noise like that of chariots they leap over the mountaintops, like a crackling fire consuming stubble, like a mighty army drawn up for battle. At the sight of them, nations are in anguish; every face turns pale. They charge like warriors; they scale walls like soldiers. They all march in line, not swerving from their course. They do not jostle each other; each marches straight ahead. They plunge through defenses without breaking ranks. They rush upon the city; they run along the wall. They climb into the houses; like thieves they enter through the windows. Before them the earth shakes, the sky trembles, the sun and moon are darkened, and the stars no longer shine.

The LORD thunders at the head of his army; his forces are beyond number, and mighty are those who obey his command. The day of the LORD is great; it is dreadful. Who can endure it? "Even now", declares the LORD, "return to me with all your heart, with fasting and weeping and mourning". Rend your heart and not your garments. Return to the LORD your God, for he is gracious and compassionate, slow to anger and abounding in love, and he relents from sending calamity. Who knows? He may turn and have pity and leave behind a blessing—grain offerings and drink offerings for the LORD your God. Blow the trumpet in Zion, declare a holy fast, call a sacred assembly. Gather the people, consecrate the assembly; bring together the elders, gather the children, those nursing at the breast. Let the bridegroom leave his room and the bride her chamber. Let the priests, who minister before the LORD, weep between the temple porch and the altar. Let them say, "Spare your people, O LORD. Do not make your inheritance an object of scorn, a byword among the nations. Why should they say among the peoples, 'Where is their God?'" Then the LORD will be jealous for his land and take pity on his people. The LORD will reply to them: "I am sending you grain, new wine and oil, enough to satisfy you fully; never again will I make you an object of scorn to the nations. "I will drive the northern army far from you, pushing it into a parched and barren land, with its front columns going into the eastern sea and those in the rear into the western sea. And its stench will go up; its smell will rise". Surely he has done great things. Be not afraid, O land; be glad and rejoice. Surely the LORD has done great things. Be not afraid, O wild animals, for the open pastures are becoming green. The trees are bearing their fruit; the fig tree and the vine yield their riches. Be glad, O people of Zion, rejoice in the LORD your God, for he has given you the autumn rains in righteousness. He sends you abundant showers, both autumn and spring rains, as before. The threshing floors will be filled with grain; the vats will overflow with new wine and oil. "I will repay you for the years the locusts have eaten—the great locust and the young locust, the other locusts and the locust swarm—my great army that I sent among you. You will have plenty to eat, until you are full, and you will praise the name of the LORD your God, who has worked wonders for you; never again will my people be shamed. Then you will know that I am in Israel, that I am the LORD your God, and that there is no other; never again will my people be shamed. "And afterward, I will pour out my Spirit on all people. Your sons and daughters will prophesy, your old men will dream dreams, your young men will see visions. Even on my servants, both men and women, I will pour out my Spirit in those days. I will show wonders in the heavens and on the earth, blood and fire and billows of smoke. The sun will be turned to darkness and the moon to blood before the coming of the great and dreadful day of the LORD. And everyone who calls on the name of the LORD will be saved; for on Mount Zion and in Jerusalem there will be deliverance, as the LORD has said, among the survivors whom the LORD calls (Joel 2:1-32).

1. What lessons can we learn from Fasting for Revival, Renewal, and Righteousness?

____

____

2. Which lesson has had the greatest impact on your life? Explain.

____

____

3. How is Fasting for Revival, Renewal, and Righteousness relevant today?

____

____

4. What is your purpose in Fasting for Revival, Renewal, and Righteousness? Be specific. I am fasting to:

____

____

5. What spiritual power and breakthrough do you desire to unlock through Fasting for Revival, Renewal, and Righteousness?

____

____

6. If you experienced this spiritual breakthrough, how would your life be different? How would your relationships (family, friends, church) be different or affected by this spiritual breakthrough? Be specific.

____

____

7. How can your faith be increased and/or strengthened through Fasting for Revival, Renewal, and Righteousness? How will you be benefited by having your faith increased and/or strengthened?

____

____

8. What other benefits, whether physical, emotional, relational, psychological, and spiritual do you desire to achieve during Fasting for Revival, Renewal, and Righteousness?

____

____

9. What might you discover about yourself during Fasting for Revival, Renewal, and Righteousness?

____

____

10. How could Fasting for Revival, Renewal, and Righteousness change your life?

____

____

11. What steps would you take to bring out these changes in your life? Who should be involved and to what extent?

____

____

12. How does the expression "times of refreshing may come from the presence of the Lord" describe revival?

____

____

13. What role did this fast have in the national revival in Israel?

____

____

14. In order to experience revival, it is imperative that we identify the root of our bondage to sin which can hinder revival.

____

____

15. What signs do you see in your own life, your church, community, and nation that suggest the need for revival?

____

____

16. If you were to fast for revival, what changes would you anticipate in your life, church, community, and nation?

____

____

17. List the necessary steps that would need to be taken to bring about a revival in your own life, your church, community, and nation.

____

____

18. Are there noticeable changes that God has begun to make changes in your life, family, church, community, and nation?

____

____

19. What length of time (days) and hours each day will you commit to during Fasting for Revival, Renewal, and Righteousness? When do you plan to begin and end your fast?

____

____

Prayer

Fasting is one of the spiritual disciplines that the Lord has established for you to achieve the spiritual power and breakthrough not only within your life but also in the lives of those whom are close to your heart. I acknowledge that I have become too comfortable in my current state of living and I sense you Holy Spirit calling me to confront the issues that I have been avoiding and find the freedom to live solely for Jesus Christ. Help me through fasting for revival, renewal, and righteousness to break free from the bondages that have been controlling my life for too long. Therefore, prayerfully consider and write a prayer that you will address to the Lord that reflects a new commitment and dedication to Him.

____

____

____

Fasting for Revival, Renewal, and Righteousness Journal

As you progress through this fast, write down any insights the Lord speaks to you, spiritual growth, and personal thoughts to further reflect upon in your walk with the Lord.

Fasting for Material Provision

Please read the following Scripture reference and then respond to the questions that follow.

Are they servants of Christ? (I am out of my mind to talk like this.) I am more. I have worked much harder, been in prison more frequently, been flogged more severely, and been exposed to death again and again. Five times I received from the Jews the forty lashes minus one. Three times I was beaten with rods, once I was stoned, three times I was shipwrecked, I spent a night and a day in the open sea, I have been constantly on the move. I have been in danger from rivers, in danger from bandits, in danger from my own countrymen, in danger from Gentiles; in danger in the city, in danger in the country, in danger at sea; and in danger from false brothers. I have labored and toiled and have often gone without sleep; I have known hunger and thirst and have often gone without food; I have been cold and naked. Besides everything else, I face daily the pressure of my concern for all the churches (2 Cor. 11:23-28).

1. What lessons can we learn from Fasting for Material Provision?

____

____

2. Which lesson has had the greatest impact on your life? Explain.

____

____

3. How is Fasting for Material Provision relevant today?

____

____

4. What is your purpose in Fasting for Material Provision? Be specific. I am fasting to:

____

____

5. What spiritual power and breakthrough do you desire to unlock through Fasting for Material Provision?

____

____

6. If you experienced this spiritual breakthrough, how would your life be different? How would your relationships (family, friends, church) be different or affected by this spiritual breakthrough? Be specific.

____

____

7. How can your faith be increased and/or strengthened through Fasting for Material Provision? How will you be benefited by having your faith increased and/or strengthened?

____

____

8. What other benefits, whether physical, emotional, relational, psychological, and spiritual do you desire to achieve during Fasting for Material Provision?

____

____

9. What might you discover about yourself during Fasting for Material Provision?

____

____

10. How could Fasting for Material Provision change your life?

____

____

11. What steps would you take to bring out these changes in your life? Who should be involved and to what extent?

____

____

____

12. What hardships are presently facing that you need a financial breakthrough?

____

____

13. What length of time (days) and hours each day will you commit to during Fasting for Material Provision? When do you plan to begin and end your fast?

____

____

Prayer

Fasting is one of the spiritual disciplines that the Lord has established for you to achieve the spiritual power and breakthrough not only within your life but also in the lives of those whom are close to your heart. I acknowledge that I have become too comfortable in my current state of living and I sense you Holy Spirit calling me to confront the issues that I have been avoiding and find the freedom to live solely for Jesus Christ. Help me through fasting for material provision to break free from the bondages that have been controlling my life for too long. Therefore, prayerfully consider and write a prayer that you will address to the Lord that reflects a new commitment and dedication to Him.

____

____

____

____

____

Fasting for Material Provision Journal

As you progress through this fast, write down any insights the Lord speaks to you, spiritual growth, and personal thoughts to further reflect upon in your walk with the Lord.

____

____

Fasting Rejected By God

Please read the following Scripture references and then respond to the questions that follow.

Your fasting ends in quarreling and strife, and in striking each other with wicked fists. You cannot fast as you do today and expect your voice to be heard on high. Is this the kind of fast I have chosen, only a day for a man to humble himself? Is it only for bowing one's head like a reed and for lying on sackcloth and ashes? Is that what you call a fast, a day acceptable to the LORD? (Isa. 58:4-5).

Although they fast, I will not listen to their cry; though they offer burnt offerings and grain offerings, I will not accept them. Instead, I will destroy them with the sword, famine and plague (Jer. 14:12).

Ask all the people of the land and the priests, "When you fasted and mourned in the fifth and seventh months for the past seventy years, was it really for me that you fasted?" (Zech. 7:5).

1. What lessons can we learn from Fasting Rejected By God?

____

____

2. Which lesson has had the greatest impact on your life? Explain.

____

____

3. How is Fasting Rejected By God relevant today?

____

____

4. What is your purpose in Fasting Rejected By God? Be specific. I am fasting to:

____

____

5. What spiritual power and breakthrough do you desire to unlock through Fasting Rejected By God?

____

____

6. If you experienced this spiritual breakthrough, how would your life be different? How would your relationships (family, friends, church) be different or affected by this spiritual breakthrough? Be specific.

____

____

7. How can your faith be increased and/or strengthened through Fasting Rejected By God? How will you be benefited by having your faith increased and/or strengthened?

____

____

8. What other benefits, whether physical, emotional, relational, psychological, and spiritual do you desire to achieve during Fasting Rejected By God?

____

____

9. What might you discover about yourself during Fasting Rejected By God?

____

____

10. How could Fasting Rejected By God change your life?

____

____

11. What steps would you take to bring out these changes in your life? Who should be involved and to what extent?

____

____

____

12. Have you ever fasted and felt as though your fasting was done in vain or that God was silent and did not respond to you? What needs to be changed so that the Lord would listen to you and your purpose for fasting?

13. What length of time (days) and hours each day will you commit to during Fasting Rejected By God? When do you plan to begin and end your fast?

Prayer

Fasting is one of the spiritual disciplines that the Lord has established for you to achieve the spiritual power and breakthrough not only within your life but also in the lives of those whom are close to your heart. I acknowledge that I have become too comfortable in my current state of living and I sense you Holy Spirit calling me to confront the issues that I have been avoiding and find the freedom to live solely for Jesus Christ. Help me through the Lord rejecting your fast to break free from the bondages that have been controlling my life for too long. Therefore, prayerfully consider and write a prayer that you will address to the Lord that reflects a new commitment and dedication to Him.

Fasting Rejected By God Journal

As you progress through this fast, write down any insights the Lord speaks to you, spiritual growth, and personal thoughts to further reflect upon in your walk with the Lord.

Fasting Due to Emotional Distress

Please read the following Scripture references and then respond to the questions that follow.

Then Jacob tore his clothes, put on sackcloth and mourned for his son many days. All his sons and daughters came to comfort him, but he refused to be comforted. "No", he said, "in mourning will I go down to the grave to my son". So his father wept for him (Gen. 37:34-35).

But to Hannah he gave a double portion because he loved her, and the LORD had closed her womb. And because the LORD had closed her womb, her rival kept provoking her in order to irritate her. This went on year after year. Whenever Hannah went up to the house of the LORD, her rival provoked her till she wept and would not eat. Elkanah her husband would say to her, "Hannah, why are you weeping? Why don't you eat? Why are you downhearted? Don't I mean more to you than ten sons?" Once when they had finished eating and drinking in Shiloh, Hannah stood up. Now Eli the priest was sitting on a chair by the doorpost of the LORD's temple. In bitterness of soul Hannah wept much and prayed to the LORD. And she made a vow, saying, "O LORD Almighty, if you will only look upon your servant's misery and remember me, and not forget your servant but give her a son, then I will give him to the LORD for all the days of his life, and no razor will ever be used on his head". . . . She said, "May your servant find favor in your eyes". Then she went her way and ate something, and her face was no longer downcast. Early the next morning they arose and worshiped before the LORD and then went back to their home at Ramah. Elkanah lay with Hannah his wife, and the LORD remembered her. So in the course of time Hannah conceived and gave birth to a son. She named him Samuel, saying, "Because I asked the LORD for him" (1 Sam. 1:5-11, 18-20).

Samuel said, "Why do you consult me, now that the LORD has turned away from you and become your enemy? The LORD has done what he predicted through me. The LORD has torn the kingdom out of your hands and given it to one of your neighbors—to David. Because you did not obey the LORD or carry out his fierce wrath against the Amalekites, the LORD has done this to you today. The LORD will hand over both Israel and you to the Philistines, and tomorrow you and your sons will be with me. The LORD will also hand over the army of Israel to the Philistines. Immediately Saul fell full length on the ground, filled with fear because of Samuel's words. His strength was gone, for he had eaten nothing all that day and night (1 Sam. 28:16-20).

Now Ahab told Jezebel everything Elijah had done and how he had killed all the prophets with the sword. So Jezebel sent a messenger to Elijah to say, "May the gods deal with me, be it ever so severely, if by this time tomorrow I do not make your life like that of one of them". Elijah was afraid and ran for his life. When he came to Beersheba in Judah, he left his servant there, while he himself went a day's journey into the wilderness. He came to a broom bush, sat down under it and prayed that he might die. "I have had enough, Lord", he said. "Take my life; I am no better than my ancestors". Then he lay down under the bush and fell asleep. All at once an angel touched him and said, "Get up and eat". He looked around, and there by his head was some bread baked over hot coals, and a jar of water. He ate and drank and then lay down again. The angel of the Lord came back a second time and touched him and said, "Get up and eat, for the journey is too much for you". So he got up and ate and drank. Strengthened by that food, he traveled forty days and forty nights until he reached Horeb, the mountain of God. There he went into a cave and spent the night (1 Kgs. 19:1-9).

Then the king returned to his palace and spent the night without eating and without any entertainment being brought to him. And he could not sleep. At the first light of dawn, the king got up and hurried to the lions' den. When he came near the den, he called to Daniel in an anguished voice, "Daniel, servant of the living God, has your God, whom you serve continually, been able to rescue you from the lions?" Daniel answered, "O king, live forever! My God sent his angel, and he shut the mouths of the lions. They have not hurt me, because I was found innocent in his sight. Nor have I ever done any wrong before you, O king". The king was overjoyed and gave orders to lift Daniel out of the den. And when Daniel was lifted from the den, no wound was found on him, because he had trusted in his God. At the king's command, the men who had falsely accused Daniel were brought in and thrown into the lions' den, along with their wives and children. And before they reached the floor of the den, the lions overpowered them and crushed all their bones (Dan. 6:18-24).

Jesus called his disciples to him and said, "I have compassion for these people; they have already been with me three days and have nothing to eat. I do not want to send them away hungry, or they may collapse on the way" (Mt. 15:32).

We put no stumbling block in anyone's path, so that our ministry will not be discredited. Rather, as servants of God we commend ourselves in every way: in great endurance; in troubles, hardships and distresses; in beatings, imprisonments and riots; in hard work, sleepless nights and hunger; in purity, understanding, patience and kindness; in the Holy Spirit and in sincere love; in truthful speech and in the power of God; with weapons of righteousness in the right hand and in the left; through glory and dishonor, bad report and good report; genuine, yet regarded as impostors; known, yet regarded as unknown; dying, and yet we live on; beaten, and yet not killed; sorrowful, yet always rejoicing; poor, yet making many rich; having nothing, and yet possessing everything (2 Cor. 6:3-10).

I have labored and toiled and have often gone without sleep; I have known hunger and thirst and have often gone without food; I have been cold and naked. Besides everything else, I face daily the pressure of my concern for all the churches (2 Cor. 11:27-28).

1. What lessons can we learn from Fasting Due to Emotional Distress?

____

____

2. Which lesson has had the greatest impact on your life? Explain.

____

____

3. How is Fasting Due to Emotional Distress relevant today?

____

____

4. What is your purpose in Fasting Due to Emotional Distress? Be specific. I am fasting to:

____

____

5. What spiritual power and breakthrough do you desire to unlock through Fasting Due to Emotional Distress?

____

____

6. If you experienced this spiritual breakthrough, how would your life be different? How would your relationships (family, friends, church) be different or affected by this spiritual breakthrough? Be specific.

____

____

7. How can your faith be increased and/or strengthened through Fasting Due to Emotional Distress? How will you be benefited by having your faith increased and/or strengthened?

____

____

8. What other benefits, whether physical, emotional, relational, psychological, and spiritual do you desire to achieve during Fasting Due to Emotional Distress?

____

____

9. What might you discover about yourself during Fasting Due to Emotional Distress?

____

____

____

10. How could Fasting Due to Emotional Distress change your life?

____

____

11. What steps would you take to bring out these changes in your life? Who should be involved and to what extent?

____

____

12. What specific trials and tribulations are you presently facing in life? How can Fasting Due to Emotional Distress help you to experience breakthrough in the midst of your present storm?

____

____

13. Do you sometimes feel that during the difficult times in life that you have no peace and/or that God has become distant? Why? What steps should you take to sense His peace and presence?

____

____

14. What length of time (days) and hours each day will you commit to during Fasting Due to Emotional Distress? When do you plan to begin and end your fast?

____

____

Prayer

Fasting is one of the spiritual disciplines that the Lord has established for you to achieve the spiritual power and breakthrough not only within your life but also in the lives of those whom are close to your heart. I acknowledge that I have become too comfortable in my current state of living and I sense you Holy Spirit calling me to confront the issues that I have been avoiding and find the freedom to live solely for Jesus Christ. Help me through fasting due to emotional distress to break free from the bondages that have been controlling my life for too long. Therefore, prayerfully consider and write a prayer that you will address to the Lord that reflects a new commitment and dedication to Him.

Fasting Due to Emotional Distress Journal

As you progress through this fast, write down any insights the Lord speaks to you, spiritual growth, and personal thoughts to further reflect upon in your walk with the Lord.

Summary Questions to Thematic Fasting

1. What are the primary themes throughout Thematic Fasting? Name them in order of prominence.

2. What does this show you regarding the types of sins that have affected God's people throughout history?

3. To what degree are these sins or wickedness still prevalent within your personal life, family, community, city, and/or nation?

4. What are the primary lessons that we can learn from Thematic Fasting?

5. Which fast was the *most* meaningful to you? Why?

6. Which fast was the *least* meaningful to you? Why?

7. How does your understanding of true fasting, as described in Thematic Fasting, change the way in which you perceive and respond to our community and culture?

____

____

8. What steps do you need to take to live a life of abundance and freedom from the "sin that so easily entangles"?

   Therefore, since we are surrounded by such a great cloud of witnesses, let us throw off everything that hinders and the sin that so easily entangles, and let us run with perseverance the race marked out for us. Let us fix our eyes on Jesus, the author and perfecter of our faith, who for the joy set before him endured the cross, scorning its shame, and sat down at the right hand of the throne of God. Consider him who endured such opposition from sinful men, so that you will not grow weary and lose heart (Heb. 12:1-3).

____

____

The Thematic Fasting Journal

Take some time to reflect on these fasts. What are some of the common themes that were the most relevant to you? How can finding victory in these areas transform your life?

____

____

____

____

____

____

____

____

Chapter 11: The Topical Fasts

The purpose of this chapter is to present numerous examples of topical fasting that can be found in Scripture. The following topical fasts include fasting due to current circumstances, fasting and interceding on behalf of others, fasting to achieve marital harmony, and fasting as the ultimate sustenance for Christians. Each fast concludes by reflecting and responding to questions relevant to each fast.

The Circumstance Fast

Please read the following Scripture reference and then respond to the questions that follow.

> Just before dawn Paul urged them all to eat. "For the last fourteen days", he said, "you have been in constant suspense and have gone without food—you haven't eaten anything. Now I urge you to take some food. You need it to survive. Not one of you will lose a single hair from his head". After he said this, he took some bread and gave thanks to God in front of them all. Then he broke it and began to eat. They were all encouraged and ate some food themselves. Altogether there were 276 of us on board. When they had eaten as much as they wanted, they lightened the ship by throwing the grain into the sea (Acts 27:33-38).

The Circumstance Fast involves an involuntary type of fast since when we are in the midst of the trials and tribulations in life or "constant suspense" do we not often find that we have no hunger and do not sense that we should eat. It also can be said that during times of anxiety, sorrow, worry, mourning, mental distress or anguish that we have no desire for food (Dan. 6:18-24), or there is no food available (Mt. 15:32; 2 Cor. 6:5; 11:27). God in His Word has promised to be faithful to His children in the midst of the storms of life.

We can also rest in the Lord going through these storms and remain cheerful when we realize that if we believe that the Lord is not finished with us yet, no circumstances or storm can hinder what He has for us. As Paul was the spiritual leader on the ship so Christians must be in the world. Likewise, we must remember that when we recognize that Jesus is our spiritual leader we will be victorious in the midst of storms and take on great responsibilities.[79]

The following questions are a guide to help you to sail through the storms of life knowing that the Lord is there beside us and "he who began a good work in you will carry it on to completion until the day of Christ Jesus" (Phil. 1:6). You will find the freedom and joy when you place your life in the hands of the Lord trusting Him to carry you through the storms of life. They will also assist you in applying the Circumstance Fast to your personal life. It is vital that you pray and ask the Holy Spirit to give you the guidance and direction, wisdom, and the best course of action as you complete the Circumstance Fast.

1. What lessons can we learn from the Circumstance Fast?

____

[79] Keith Brooks, *Summarized Bible: Complete Summary of the New Testament* (Bellingham, WA: Logos Bible Software, 2009), 42. <http://www.faithcycleministry.org/Fasting/Fasting4.html>. Accessed on December 10, 2013.

2. Which lesson has had the greatest impact on your life? Explain.

3. How is the Circumstance Fast relevant today?

4. What is your purpose in the Circumstance Fast? Be specific. I am fasting to:

5. What spiritual power and breakthrough do you desire to unlock through the Circumstance Fast?

6. If you experienced this spiritual breakthrough, how would your life be different? How would your relationships (family, friends, church) be different or affected by this spiritual breakthrough? Be specific.

7. How can your faith be increased and/or strengthened through the Circumstance Fast? How will you be benefited by having your faith increased and/or strengthened?

8. What other benefits, whether physical, emotional, relational, psychological, and spiritual do you desire to achieve during the Circumstance Fast?

____

____

9. What might you discover about yourself during the Circumstance Fast?

____

____

10. How could the Circumstance Fast change your life?

____

____

11. What steps would you take to bring out these changes in your life? Who should be involved and to what extent?

____

____

12. What specific trials and tribulations are you presently facing in life? How can the Circumstance Fast help you to experience breakthrough in the midst of your present storm?

____

____

13. Do you sometimes feel that during the difficult times in life that you have no peace and/or that God has become distant? Why? What steps should you take to sense His peace and presence?

____

____

____

14. What length of time (days) and hours each day will you commit to during the Circumstance Fast? When do you plan to begin and end your fast?

____

____

Prayer

Fasting is one of the spiritual disciplines that the Lord has established for you to achieve the spiritual power and breakthrough not only within your life but also in the lives of those whom are close to your heart. I acknowledge that I have become too comfortable in my current state of living and I sense you Holy Spirit calling me to confront the issues that I have been avoiding and find the freedom to live solely for Jesus Christ. Help me through the Circumstance Fast to break free from the bondages that have been controlling my life for too long. Therefore, prayerfully consider and write a prayer that you will address to the Lord that reflects a new commitment and dedication to Him.

____

____

____

____

____

The Circumstance Fast Journal

As you progress through this fast, write down any insights the Lord speaks to you, spiritual growth, and personal thoughts to further reflect upon in your walk with the Lord.

____

____

____

____

____

The Intercessory Fast

Please read the following Scripture references and then respond to the questions that follow.

When I went up on the mountain to receive the tablets of stone, the tablets of the covenant that the LORD had made with you, I stayed on the mountain forty days and forty nights; I ate no bread and drank no water. . . . Then the LORD told me, "Go down from here at once, because your people whom you brought out of Egypt have become corrupt. They have turned away quickly from what I commanded them and have made a cast idol for themselves". And the LORD said to me, "I have seen this people, and they are a stiff-necked people indeed! Let me alone, so that I may destroy them and blot out their name from under heaven. And I will make you into a nation stronger and more numerous than they". So I turned and went down from the mountain while it was ablaze with fire. And the two tablets of the covenant were in my hands. When I looked, I saw that you had sinned against the LORD your God; you had made for yourselves an idol cast in the shape of a calf. You had turned aside quickly from the way that the LORD had commanded you. So I took the two tablets and threw them out of my hands, breaking them to pieces before your eyes. Then once again I fell prostrate before the LORD for forty days and forty nights; I ate no bread and drank no water, because of all the sin you had committed, doing what was evil in the LORD's sight and so provoking him to anger. I feared the anger and wrath of the LORD, for he was angry enough with you to destroy you. But again the LORD listened to me. And the LORD was angry enough with Aaron to destroy him, but at that time I prayed for Aaron too. . . . And when the LORD sent you out from Kadesh Barnea, he said, "Go up and take possession of the land I have given you". But you rebelled against the command of the LORD your God. You did not trust him or obey him. You have been rebellious against the LORD ever since I have known you. I lay prostrate before the LORD those forty days and forty nights because the LORD had said he would destroy you. I prayed to the LORD and said, "O Sovereign LORD, do not destroy your people, your own inheritance that you redeemed by your great power and brought out of Egypt with a mighty hand. Remember your servants Abraham, Isaac and Jacob. Overlook the stubbornness of this people, their wickedness and their sin (Deut. 9:9, 12-20, 23-27).

Then Ezra withdrew from before the house of God and went to the room of Jehohanan son of Eliashib. While he was there, he ate no food and drank no water, because he continued to mourn over the unfaithfulness of the exiles (Ezra 10:6).

In the first year of Darius son of Xerxes (a Mede by descent), who was made ruler over the Babylonian kingdom—in the first year of his reign, I, Daniel, understood from the Scriptures, according to the word of the LORD given to Jeremiah the prophet, that the desolation of Jerusalem would last seventy years. So I turned to the Lord God and pleaded with him in prayer and petition, in fasting, and in sackcloth and ashes (Dan. 9:1-3).

"Even now", declares the LORD, "return to me with all your heart, with fasting and weeping and mourning". Rend your heart and not your garments. Return to the LORD your God, for he is gracious and compassionate, slow to anger and abounding in love, and he relents from sending calamity. Who knows? He may turn and have pity and leave behind a blessing—grain offerings and drink offerings for the LORD your God. Blow the trumpet in Zion, declare a holy fast, call a sacred assembly. Gather the people, consecrate the assembly; bring together the elders, gather the children, those nursing at the breast. Let the bridegroom leave his room and the bride her chamber. Let the priests, who minister before the LORD, weep between the temple porch and the altar. Let them say, "Spare your people, O LORD. Do not make your inheritance an object of

> scorn, a byword among the nations. Why should they say among the peoples, 'Where is their God?'" Then the LORD will be jealous for his land and take pity on his people (Joel 2:12-18).
>
> The Ninevites believed God. They declared a fast, and all of them, from the greatest to the least, put on sackcloth. When the news reached the king of Nineveh, he rose from his throne, took off his royal robes, covered himself with sackcloth and sat down in the dust. Then he issued a proclamation in Nineveh: "By the decree of the king and his nobles: Do not let any man or beast, herd or flock, taste anything; do not let them eat or drink. But let man and beast be covered with sackcloth. Let everyone call urgently on God. Let them give up their evil ways and their violence. Who knows? God may yet relent and with compassion turn from his fierce anger so that we will not perish". When God saw what they did and how they turned from their evil ways, he had compassion and did not bring upon them the destruction he had threatened. But Jonah was greatly displeased and became angry (Jon. 3:5-4:1).

There are various contexts throughout Scripture where men and women of God interceded on behalf of others. In the fasts listed above, we can see a common theme of rebellion, habitual sin, shame and disgrace, confession of sin, consequences, and restoration. We also see the intercession of Moses, Ezra, and prophets as they identified with the Israelites, confessed the sin of the people, which demonstrates their unity with them and the horror at their sin. These Scripture references noted above have already been discussed under, The Moses Fast (Deut. 9:9, 18, 25-29); Ezra Fast (Ezra 8:21-23; 10:6); Daniel Fast (Dan. 9:1-3); Joel Fast (Joel 2:12-18); and The Nineveh Fast (Jon. 3:1-10).

The following questions are a guide to help you to identify and confess the sin on behalf of others, such as: your family, church, community, or nation. You will find the freedom and joy you desire as you seek the Lord to bring transformation to the purpose and focus of the intercession. They will also assist you in applying the Intercessory Fast to your personal life. It is vital that you pray and ask the Holy Spirit to give you the guidance and direction, wisdom, and the best course of action as you complete the Intercessory Fast.

1. What lessons can we learn from the Intercessory Fast?

___

___

2. Which lesson has had the greatest impact on your life? Explain.

___

___

3. How is the Intercessory Fast relevant today?

___

4. What is your purpose in the Intercessory Fast? Be specific. I am fasting to:

5. What spiritual power and breakthrough do you desire to unlock through the Intercessory Fast?

6. If you experienced this spiritual breakthrough, how would your life be different? How would your relationships (family, friends, church) be different or affected by this spiritual breakthrough? Be specific.

7. How can your faith be increased and/or strengthened through the Intercessory Fast? How will you be benefited by having your faith increased and/or strengthened?

8. What other benefits, whether physical, emotional, relational, psychological, and spiritual do you desire to achieve during Intercessory Fast?

9. What might you discover about yourself during the Intercessory Fast?

10. How could the Intercessory Fast change your life?

___

___

11. What steps would you take to bring out these changes in your life? Who should be involved and to what extent?

___

___

12. Do you practice intercessory prayer? If so, how often? Does your church have intercessors?

___

___

13. What are some of the needs within your church, community, and/or nation that could be affected through intercession?

___

___

14. How could intercessory prayer make a difference in your life, your family, church, community, and nation? Make a list of needs and/or issues that a breakthrough is needed and then gather a team of intercessors to fast, pray, and intercede for these needs. Always remember to fast, pray, and intercede for your missionaries.

___

___

15. What length of time (days) and hours each day will you commit to during the Intercessory Fast? When do you plan to begin and end your fast?

___

___

Prayer

Fasting is one of the spiritual disciplines that the Lord has established for you to achieve the spiritual power and breakthrough not only within your life but also in the lives of those whom are close to your heart. I acknowledge that I have become too comfortable in my current state of living and I sense you Holy Spirit calling me to confront the issues that I have been avoiding and find the freedom to live solely for Jesus Christ. Help me through the Intercessory Fast to break free from the bondages that have been controlling my life for too long. Therefore, prayerfully consider and write a prayer that you will address to the Lord that reflects a new commitment and dedication to Him.

____

____

____

____

____

The Intercessory Fast Journal

As you progress through this fast, write down any insights the Lord speaks to you, spiritual growth, and personal thoughts to further reflect upon in your walk with the Lord.

____

____

____

____

____

____

____

____

The Sexual Fast

Please read the following Scripture reference and then respond to the questions that follow.

> The husband should fulfill his marital duty to his wife, and likewise the wife to her husband. The wife's body does not belong to her alone but also to her husband. In the same way, the husband's body does not belong to him alone but also to his wife. Do not deprive each other except by mutual consent and for a time, so that you may devote yourselves to prayer. Then come together again so that Satan will not tempt you because of your lack of self-control. I say this as a concession, not as a command (1 Cor. 7:3-6).

The purpose of the Sexual Fast is for a husband and wife to set aside time for mutual abstinence from sexual intimacy and devotion to fasting and prayer. The Apostle Paul clarifies some misunderstanding concerning marriage and celibacy where some were abstaining from sex and others were divorcing their spouses. Moreover, some were committing acts of sexual immorality (v. 5b; cf. v. 2). Paul in addressing these issues states three conditions where a husband and wife could abstain for sexual relations: (1) abstaining with mutual consent; (2) abstaining with an agreed upon time period; or (3) abstaining to devote themselves to fasting and prayer.[80]

The following questions are a guide to help you and your spouse focus on a specific issue within your marriage. You will find the freedom and joy you desire as you mutually seek the Lord together and allow Him to guide and direct you in every decision in your marital life. They will also assist you in applying the Sexual Fast to your personal life. It is vital that you pray and ask the Holy Spirit to give you the guidance and direction, wisdom, and the best course of action as you complete the Sexual Fast.

1. What lessons can we learn from the Sexual Fast?

___

___

2. Which lesson has had the greatest impact on your life? Explain.

___

___

3. How is the Sexual Fast relevant today?

___

___

[80] Walvoord and Zuck, eds., *The Bible Knowledge Commentary*, Vol. 2, 517. Richards, *The Bible Reader's Companion*, electronic ed., 763. Brooks, *Summarized Bible: New Testament*, 49.

4. What is your purpose in the Sexual Fast? Be specific. I am fasting to:

____

____

5. What spiritual power and breakthrough do you desire to unlock through the Sexual Fast?

____

____

6. If you experienced this spiritual breakthrough, how would your life be different? How would your relationships (family, friends, church) be different or affected by this spiritual breakthrough? Be specific.

____

____

7. How can your faith be increased and/or strengthened through the Sexual Fast? How will you be benefited by having your faith increased and/or strengthened?

____

____

8. What other benefits, whether physical, emotional, relational, psychological, and spiritual do you desire to achieve during Sexual Fast?

____

____

9. What might you discover about yourself during the Sexual Fast?

____

____

10. How could the Sexual Fast change your life?

____

11. What steps would you take to bring out these changes in your life? Who should be involved and to what extent?

12. What are the marital issues that you both presently face and desire to breakthrough to find freedom and joy in your marriage? Make a list and then fast and pray to receive your freedom.

13. What one (1) marital issue do you desire to resolve as you mutually commit yourselves to fasting? Remember to stay focused on only one issue at a time.

14. Are there areas of frustration, resentment, bitterness, anger, shame, humiliation that need healing? Allow your spouse to be open and honest so that the healing can begin. Ask the Lord

15. What length of time (days) and hours each day will you commit to during the Sexual Fast? When do you plan to begin and end your fast?

Prayer

Fasting is one of the spiritual disciplines that the Lord has established for you to achieve the spiritual power and breakthrough not only within your life but also in the lives of those whom are close to your heart. I acknowledge that I have become too comfortable in my current state of living and I sense you Holy Spirit calling me to confront the issues that I have been avoiding and find the freedom to live solely for Jesus Christ. Help me through the Sexual Fast to break free from the bondages that have been controlling my life for too long. Therefore, prayerfully consider and write a prayer that you will address to the Lord that reflects a new commitment and dedication to Him.

____

____

____

____

____

The Sexual Fast Journal

As you progress through this fast, write down any insights the Lord speaks to you, spiritual growth, and personal thoughts to further reflect upon in your walk with the Lord.

____

____

____

____

____

____

____

____

____

The Eucharistic Fast

Please read the following Scripture reference and then respond to the questions that follow.

> For I received from the Lord what I also passed on to you: The Lord Jesus, on the night he was betrayed, took bread, and when he had given thanks, he broke it and said, "This is my body, which is for you; do this in remembrance of me". In the same way, after supper he took the cup, saying, "This cup is the new covenant in my blood; do this, whenever you drink it, in remembrance of me". For whenever you eat this bread and drink this cup, you proclaim the Lord's death until he comes. Therefore, whoever eats the bread or drinks the cup of the Lord in an unworthy manner will be guilty of sinning against the body and blood of the Lord. A man ought to examine himself before he eats of the bread and drinks of the cup. For anyone who eats and drinks without recognizing the body of the Lord eats and drinks judgment on himself. That is why many among you are weak and sick, and a number of you have fallen asleep. But if we judged ourselves, we would not come under judgment. When we are judged by the Lord, we are being disciplined so that we will not be condemned with the world (1 Cor. 11:23-32).

According to Augustine, in his response to the question, why follow the Eucharist Fast, he states that it is the ultimate sustenance for Christians and should be chosen above every other form of nutrition, both physical and spiritual. He further states,

> Through the Eucharistic fast our priorities are demonstrated physically as the Eucharist becomes the first food of the day for us. In Augustine's context of daily Eucharist, then, the practice presented a great symbol to the Church: for the faithful, their "daily bread", the first food that passed their lips each morning, was their spiritually-first and greatest meal, the very bread of angels. The Eucharistic fast, therefore, was a practice that honored the place of the Eucharist in the life of faith and promoted the proper ordering of Christian priorities: the intimate union between Christ and his faithful in the Eucharist should hold pride of place in our hearts and in our days.[81]

The following questions are a guide to help you remember the significance of observing the Eucharist which places as its highest priority the body and blood of the Lord that was shed for your salvation, healing, deliverance, restoration, reconciliation, wholeness. You will find the freedom and joy you desire as you begin each day focusing upon the Lord and then allow the Holy Spirit to guide and direct your path throughout the day. They will also assist you in applying the Eucharist Fast to your personal life. It is vital that you pray and ask the Holy Spirit to give you the guidance and direction, wisdom, and the best course of action as you complete the Eucharist Fast.

1. What lessons can we learn from the Eucharistic Fast?

---

[81] "Letters of St. Augustin", In Philip Schaff, ed., *The Nicene & Post-Nicene Fathers of the Christian Church: First Series*, Vol. 1 (Edinburgh, UK: T. & T. Clark, 1886), WORD*search* CROSS e-book, Second Edition, "Letter 54 - To *Januarius*". "The Eucharistic Fast", <http://www.catholicculture.org/culture/library/dictionary/index.cfm?id=33400>. Accessed on November 4, 2013.

2. Which lesson has had the greatest impact on your life? Explain.

3. How is the Eucharistic Fast relevant today?

4. What is your purpose in the Eucharistic Fast? Be specific. I am fasting to:

5. What spiritual power and breakthrough do you desire to unlock through the Eucharistic Fast?

6. If you experienced this spiritual breakthrough, how would your life be different? How would your relationships (family, friends, church) be different or affected by this spiritual breakthrough? Be specific.

7. How can your faith be increased and/or strengthened through the Eucharistic Fast? How will you be benefited by having your faith increased and/or strengthened?

8. What other benefits, whether physical, emotional, relational, psychological, and spiritual do you desire to achieve during the Eucharistic Fast?

____

____

9. What might you discover about yourself during the Eucharistic Fast?

____

____

10. How could the Eucharistic Fast change your life?

____

____

11. What steps would you take to bring out these changes in your life? Who should be involved and to what extent?

____

____

12. Take a moment to list your daily priorities in the order in which you complete the list. What modifications, based upon the Eucharist Fast, need to be done?

____

____

13. How do these priorities relate to your relationship with the Lord, family, and work?

____

____

14. What length of time (days) and hours each day will you commit to during the Eucharistic Fast? When do you plan to begin and end your fast?

____

Prayer

Fasting is one of the spiritual disciplines that the Lord has established for you to achieve the spiritual power and breakthrough not only within your life but also in the lives of those whom are close to your heart. I acknowledge that I have become too comfortable in my current state of living and I sense you Holy Spirit calling me to confront the issues that I have been avoiding and find the freedom to live solely for Jesus Christ. Help me through the Eucharistic Fast to break free from the bondages that have been controlling my life for too long. Therefore, prayerfully consider and write a prayer that you will address to the Lord that reflects a new commitment and dedication to Him.

The Eucharistic Fast Journal

As you progress through this fast, write down any insights the Lord speaks to you, spiritual growth, and personal thoughts to further reflect upon in your walk with the Lord.

Summary Questions to Topical Fasting

1. What are the primary themes throughout Topical Fasting? Name them in order of prominence.

2. What does this show you regarding the types of sins that have affected God's people throughout history?

3. To what degree are these sins or wickedness still prevalent within your personal life, family, community, city, and/or nation?

4. What are the primary lessons that we can learn from Topical Fasting?

5. Which fast was the *most* meaningful to you? Why?

6. Which fast was the *least* meaningful to you? Why?

7. How does your understanding of true fasting, as described in Topical Fasting, change the way in which you perceive and respond to our community and culture?

____

____

8. What steps do you need to take to live a life of abundance and freedom from the "sin that so easily entangles"?

    Therefore, since we are surrounded by such a great cloud of witnesses, let us throw off everything that hinders and the sin that so easily entangles, and let us run with perseverance the race marked out for us. Let us fix our eyes on Jesus, the author and perfecter of our faith, who for the joy set before him endured the cross, scorning its shame, and sat down at the right hand of the throne of God. Consider him who endured such opposition from sinful men, so that you will not grow weary and lose heart (Heb. 12:1-3).

____

____

The Topical Fasting Journal

Take some time to reflect on these fasts. What are some of the common themes that were the most relevant to you? How can finding victory in these areas transform your life?

____

____

____

____

____

____

____

____

Chapter 12: Warnings and Abuses Concerning Fasting

The purpose of this chapter is to present the numerous warnings and abuses concerning fasting that can be found in Scripture. Each fast concludes by reflecting and responding to questions relevant to each fast.

The abuses concerning fasting are usually seen in the belief that if God's people voluntarily self-inflict suffering upon themselves in an attempt to demonstrate their sincerity with God, then God will quickly respond to their need. However, this cannot be true since if it was true then the prophets of Baal in Elijah's time were correct. They had cried from morning to late afternoon without any response, then they began to "slashed themselves with swords and spears, as was their custom, until their blood flowed" (1 Kgs. 18:28). The prophets of Baal were literally telling God, look at us and our suffering, why do you not pay attention. Simply being uncomfortable with gnawing pangs of hunger or thirst is not advocated in the Scriptures as a way of getting God's attention.

There are a number of ways in which fasting can be abused,

1. Fasting can become a formal practice instead of an internal dedication to the Lord and repentance from sin (Isa. 58:5; Joel 2:13);
2. Fasting can be a religious exercise that disguises the true motives of the hearty which are often sinful or wicked (cf. 1 Kgs. 21:9-13; Isa. 58:41);
3. Fasting can practiced for monetary gain rather than for spiritual or ministerial reasons (Isa. 58:7);
4. Fasting can be practiced for physical appearances without a sincere heart felt worship to God (cf. Mt. 6:16);
5. Fasting can be practiced for penitent purposes like the false teachers obligated the Early Church (1 Tim. 4:3).[82]

The following are some examples of how fasting can be abused[83]:

The Queen Jezebel Fast

Please read the following Scripture reference and then respond to the questions that follow.

So Ahab went home, sullen and angry because Naboth the Jezreelite had said, "I will not give you the inheritance of my fathers". He lay on his bed sulking and refused to eat. His wife Jezebel came in and asked him, "Why are you so sullen? Why won't you eat?" He answered her, "Because I said to Naboth the Jezreelite, 'Sell me your vineyard; or if you prefer, I will give you another vineyard in its place'. But he said, 'I will not give you my vineyard'". Jezebel his wife said, "Is this how you act as king over Israel? Get up and eat! Cheer up. I'll get you the vineyard of Naboth the Jezreelite". So she wrote letters in Ahab's name, placed his seal on them, and sent them to the elders and nobles who lived in Naboth's city with him. In those letters she wrote: "Proclaim a day of fasting and seat Naboth in a prominent place among the people. But seat two scoundrels opposite him and have them testify that he has cursed both God and the king. Then take him out and stone him to death". So the elders and nobles who lived in Naboth's city did as Jezebel directed in the letters she had written to them. They proclaimed a fast and seated Naboth

---

[82] Towns, *Fasting for Spiritual Breakthrough*, 187.

[83] Towns, *Fasting for Spiritual Breakthrough*, 238-39.

> in a prominent place among the people. Then two scoundrels came and sat opposite him and brought charges against Naboth before the people, saying, "Naboth has cursed both God and the king". So they took him outside the city and stoned him to death. Then they sent word to Jezebel: "Naboth has been stoned and is dead". . . . When Ahab heard these words, he tore his clothes, put on sackcloth and fasted. He lay in sackcloth and went around meekly (1 Kgs. 21:4-14, 27).

Each person must choose good or evil and with each decision we will face the consequences, whether positive or negative. When we choose the behaviour, we choose the consequences. Our character is conveyed through our choices. But when we need to choose, we must be guided by the Word of God to make the correct decision (cf. The Saint Paul Fast).[84]

The following questions are a guide to help you to choose between good and evil in everything that you do on a daily basis.

> The good man brings good things out of the good stored up in him, and the evil man brings evil things out of the evil stored up in him. But I tell you that men will have to give account on the day of judgment for every careless word they have spoken. For by your words you will be acquitted, and by your words you will be condemned" (Mt. 12:35-37).

You will find the freedom and joy as you choose behaviours that follow the precepts of the Word of God. They will also assist you in applying the Queen Jezebel Fast to your personal life. It is vital that you pray and ask the Holy Spirit to give you the guidance and direction, wisdom, and the best course of action as you complete the Queen Jezebel Fast.

1. What lessons can we learn from the Queen Jezebel Fast?

____

____

2. Which lesson has had the greatest impact on your life? Explain.

____

____

3. How is the Queen Jezebel Fast relevant today?

____

____

____

[84] Richards, *The Bible Reader's Companion*, electronic ed., 238.

4. What is your purpose in the Queen Jezebel Fast? Be specific. I am fasting to:

5. What spiritual power and breakthrough do you desire to unlock through the Queen Jezebel Fast?

6. If you experienced this spiritual breakthrough, how would your life be different? How would your relationships (family, friends, church) be different or affected by this spiritual breakthrough? Be specific.

7. How can your faith be increased and/or strengthened through the Queen Jezebel Fast? How will you be benefited by having your faith increased and/or strengthened?

8. What other benefits, whether physical, emotional, relational, psychological, and spiritual do you desire to achieve during Queen Jezebel Fast?

9. What might you discover about yourself during the Queen Jezebel Fast?

10. How could the Queen Jezebel Fast change your life?

11. What steps would you take to bring out these changes in your life? Who should be involved and to what extent?

12. State and explain a good decision that you have recently made, the consequences, the effect it had upon another person. What did you learn from this good decision?

13. What steps can you take to ensure that you repeat the same good decision again?

14. State and explain a bad decision that you have recently made, the consequences, the effect it had upon another person, and how you rectified the bad decision. What did you learn from this bad decision?

15. What steps can you take to ensure that you do not repeat the same bad decision again?

16. Have you ever found yourself making the right decision at the wrong time? What happened?

17. What lessons can we learn from King Ahab, Jezebel, Naboth and the "two scoundrels"? Name and explain at least one (1) lesson from each character.

____

____

18. What length of time (days) and hours each day will you commit to during the Queen Jezebel Fast? When do you plan to begin and end your fast?

____

____

Prayer

Fasting is one of the spiritual disciplines that the Lord has established for you to achieve the spiritual power and breakthrough not only within your life but also in the lives of those whom are close to your heart. I acknowledge that I have become too comfortable in my current state of living and I sense you Holy Spirit calling me to confront the issues that I have been avoiding and find the freedom to live solely for Jesus Christ. Help me through the Queen Jezebel Fast to break free from the bondages that have been controlling my life for too long. Therefore, prayerfully consider and write a prayer that you will address to the Lord that reflects a new commitment and dedication to Him.

____

____

____

____

____

The Queen Jezebel Fast Journal

As you progress through this fast, write down any insights the Lord speaks to you, spiritual growth, and personal thoughts to further reflect upon in your walk with the Lord.

____

The Hypocrites Fast

Please read the following Scripture reference and then respond to the questions that follow.

> "Why have we fasted", they say, "and you have not seen it? Why have we humbled ourselves, and you have not noticed?" Yet on the day of your fasting, you do as you please and exploit all your workers. Your fasting ends in quarreling and strife, and in striking each other with wicked fists. You cannot fast as you do today and expect your voice to be heard on high (Isa. 58:3-4).

The Hebrew prophet Isaiah in this context does not condemn all fasting, but he does expose their hypocritical behaviour of displaying a form of fasting—denial of food, covering themselves in sackcloth and ashes, postures of mourning and humiliation, being recognized by God for their alleged suffering—while living a lifestyle of unrighteousness, injustice, selfishness, and neglect of the needs of others.

The following questions are a guide to help you to recognize hypocritical behaviour and an external form of fasting without the internal transformation that comes through the work of the Holy Spirit in our lives.

> But mark this: There will be terrible times in the last days. People will be lovers of themselves, lovers of money, boastful, proud, abusive, disobedient to their parents, ungrateful, unholy, without love, unforgiving, slanderous, without self-control, brutal, not lovers of the good, treacherous, rash, conceited, lovers of pleasure rather than lovers of God—having a form of godliness but denying its power. Have nothing to do with them (2 Tim. 3:1-5).

You will find the freedom and joy as you choose behaviours that follow the precepts of the Word of God. They will also assist you in applying the Hypocrites Fast to your personal life. It is vital that you pray and ask the Holy Spirit to give you the guidance and direction, wisdom, and the best course of action as you complete the Hypocrites Fast.

1. What lessons can we learn from the Hypocrites Fast?

____

____

2. Which lesson has had the greatest impact on your life? Explain.

____

____

3. How is the Hypocrites Fast relevant today?

____

4. What is your purpose in the Hypocrites Fast? Be specific. I am fasting to:

5. What spiritual power and breakthrough do you desire to unlock through the Hypocrites Fast?

6. If you experienced this spiritual breakthrough, how would your life be different? How would your relationships (family, friends, church) be different or affected by this spiritual breakthrough? Be specific.

7. How can your faith be increased and/or strengthened through the Hypocrites Fast? How will you be benefited by having your faith increased and/or strengthened?

8. What other benefits, whether physical, emotional, relational, psychological, and spiritual do you desire to achieve during Hypocrites Fast?

9. What might you discover about yourself during the Hypocrites Fast?

10. How could the Hypocrites Fast change your life?

11. What steps would you take to bring out these changes in your life? Who should be involved and to what extent?

12. Ask the Lord to reveal areas in your life where you have or are presently living a life of hypocrisy. What areas did the Lord reveal to you? How does this make you feel?

13. Do you portray a form of godliness (e.g., legalism), without an internal transformation of character through the power of the Holy Spirit? Explain.

14. What steps can you take while fasting to break away from a lifestyle of hypocrisy?

15. What steps can you take to live a life of holiness?

16. What length of time (days) and hours each day will you commit to during the Hypocrites Fast? When do you plan to begin and end your fast?

Prayer

Fasting is one of the spiritual disciplines that the Lord has established for you to achieve the spiritual power and breakthrough not only within your life but also in the lives of those whom are close to your heart. I acknowledge that I have become too comfortable in my current state of living and I sense you Holy Spirit calling me to confront the issues that I have been avoiding and find the freedom to live solely for Jesus Christ. Help me through the Hypocrites Fast to break free from the bondages that have been controlling my life for too long. Therefore, prayerfully consider and write a prayer that you will address to the Lord that reflects a new commitment and dedication to Him.

The Hypocrites Fast Journal

As you progress through this fast, write down any insights the Lord speaks to you, spiritual growth, and personal thoughts to further reflect upon in your walk with the Lord.

The Pharisees Fast

Please read the following Scripture reference and then respond to the questions that follow.

> The Pharisee stood up and prayed about himself: "God, I thank you that I am not like other men—robbers, evildoers, adulterers—or even like this tax collector. I fast twice a week and give a tenth of all I get" (Lk. 18:11-12).

Stephen R. Covey in his book *The Eighth Habit* speaks of five (5) metastasizing emotional cancerous behaviours that are found in

> people who don't have their own deep internal act together seek their security from sources outside themselves. Because they're codependent with their environment, they engage in these destructive, cancerous behaviours. . . . These five emotional cancers literally metastasize their cancerous cells into relationships, and sometimes through an entire culture.[85]

These cancerous behaviours include: criticizing, complaining, comparing, competing, and contending.[86] In one way or another, the Pharisee demonstrated each of these cancerous behaviours.

The following questions are a guide to help you to recognize destructive and emotional cancerous behaviours and then take the necessary steps to find freedom and joy as you choose behaviours that follow the precepts of the Word of God. They will also assist you in applying the Pharisees Fast to your personal life. It is vital that you pray and ask the Holy Spirit to give you the guidance and direction, wisdom, and the best course of action as you complete the Pharisees Fast.

1. What lessons can we learn from the Pharisees Fast?

____

____

2. Which lesson has had the greatest impact on your life? Explain.

____

____

---

[85] Stephen R. Covey, *The 8th Habit: From Effectiveness to Greatness* (New York: Free Press, 2004), 135.

[86] Covey states, "although competition for a sense of worth within relationships, families, and work teams and cultures is damaging, I believe that it can be very healthy in settings such as athletics and the marketplace. It can stretch and draw out the best in people and organizations. In the marketplace, you can look upon your competitors as your teachers against whom you can benchmark yourselves. While you may be trying to beat out your competitors, what you are really trying to do is win better for your customers and to learn from those who are doing it better and faster than you are. That's the power of the free enterprise system: competition inside the marketplace, cooperation inside the workplace". Stephen R. Covey, *The 8th Habit: From Effectiveness to Greatness* (New York: Free Press, 2004), 136.

3. How is the Pharisees Fast relevant today?

____

____

4. What is your purpose in the Pharisees Fast? Be specific. I am fasting to:

____

____

5. What spiritual power and breakthrough do you desire to unlock through the Pharisees Fast?

____

____

6. If you experienced this spiritual breakthrough, how would your life be different? How would your relationships (family, friends, church) be different or affected by this spiritual breakthrough? Be specific.

____

____

7. How can your faith be increased and/or strengthened through the Pharisees Fast? How will you be benefited by having your faith increased and/or strengthened?

____

____

8. What other benefits, whether physical, emotional, relational, psychological, and spiritual do you desire to achieve during the Pharisees Fast?

____

____

9. What might you discover about yourself during the Pharisees Fast?

____

10. How could the Pharisees Fast change your life?

11. What steps would you take to bring out these changes in your life? Who should be involved and to what extent?

12. Take a moment to do an honest inventory of your life and see if any or all of these cancerous behaviours operate within your life on a continual basis. Ask the Lord to help you break these negative influences in your life. How do think that these cancerous behaviours affect your life and the lives of others?

13. How can the following two (2) verses be used to live victorious over these emotional cancerous behaviours?

    We demolish arguments and every pretension that sets itself up against the knowledge of God, and we take captive every thought to make it obedient to Christ (2 Cor. 10:5).

    Do not conform any longer to the pattern of this world, but be transformed by the renewing of your mind (Rom. 12:2).

14. Do you find yourself criticizing others? In what ways. What does this say about you?

15. Do you find yourself complaining about things often? In what ways. What does this say about you?

16. Do you find yourself competing against others in an unhealthy and/or dysfunctional way? In what ways. What does this say about you?

17. Do you find yourself contending with others? In what ways. What does this say about you?

18. Do you find yourself comparing yourself to others? In what ways. What does this say about you?

19. What does the Word of God say about you in relation to comparing yourself to others?

20. How might comparing yourself with others affect your relationship with them?

21. What steps can you take while fasting to break away from a judgmental behaviour?

22. What length of time (days) and hours each day will you commit to during the Pharisees Fast? When do you plan to begin and end your fast?

____

____

Prayer

Fasting is one of the spiritual disciplines that the Lord has established for you to achieve the spiritual power and breakthrough not only within your life but also in the lives of those whom are close to your heart. I acknowledge that I have become too comfortable in my current state of living and I sense you Holy Spirit calling me to confront the issues that I have been avoiding and find the freedom to live solely for Jesus Christ. Help me through the Pharisees Fast to break free from the bondages that have been controlling my life for too long. Therefore, prayerfully consider and write a prayer that you will address to the Lord that reflects a new commitment and dedication to Him.

____

____

____

____

____

The Pharisees Fast Journal

As you progress through this fast, write down any insights the Lord speaks to you, spiritual growth, and personal thoughts to further reflect upon in your walk with the Lord.

____

____

____

____

____

The Conspiracy Fast

Please read the following Scripture reference and then respond to the questions that follow.

> The next morning the Jews formed a conspiracy and bound themselves with an oath not to eat or drink until they had killed Paul. More than forty men were involved in this plot (Acts 23:12-13).

Throughout Scripture, the thought of doing harm to another is contrary to the two great commands spoken by Jesus,

> "Love the Lord your God with all your heart and with all your soul and with all your mind". This is the first and greatest commandment. And the second is like it: "Love your neighbor as yourself". All the Law and the Prophets hang on these two commandments (Mt. 22:37-40)

Jesus, in this context, follows a "Jewish interpretive technique" which in Jewish culture stressed together "love the Lord your God . . ." and "love your neighbor as yourself". These two commands are inseparable and the foundation to the Christian life.[87]

> Hear, O Israel: The Lord our God, the Lord is one. Love the Lord your God with all your heart and with all your soul and with all your strength. These commandments that I give you today are to be upon your hearts. Impress them on your children. Talk about them when you sit at home and when you walk along the road, when you lie down and when you get up. Tie them as symbols on your hands and bind them on your foreheads. Write them on the doorframes of your houses and on your gates (Deut. 6:4-9).

> Do not seek revenge or bear a grudge against one of your people, but love your neighbor as yourself. I am the Lord (Lev. 19:18).

The following questions are a guide to help you to recognize destructive thoughts and behaviours that have the possibility of committing harm against another person. You will find the freedom and joy as you choose behaviours that follow the precepts of the Word of God. They will also assist you in applying the Conspiracy Fast to your personal life. It is vital that you pray and ask the Holy Spirit to give you the guidance and direction, wisdom, and the best course of action as you complete the Conspiracy Fast.

1. What lessons can we learn from the Conspiracy Fast?

____

____

2. Which lesson has had the greatest impact on your life? Explain.

____

[87] "Matthew 22:34-40", In Craig S. Keener, *The IVP Bible Background Commentary, New Testament* (Downers Grove, IL: InterVarsity Press, 1993), WORD*search* CROSS e-book.

3. How is the Conspiracy Fast relevant today?

4. What is your purpose in the Conspiracy Fast? Be specific. I am fasting to:

5. What spiritual power and breakthrough do you desire to unlock through the Conspiracy Fast?

6. If you experienced this spiritual breakthrough, how would your life be different? How would your relationships (family, friends, church) be different or affected by this spiritual breakthrough? Be specific.

7. How can your faith be increased and/or strengthened through the Conspiracy Fast? How will you be benefited by having your faith increased and/or strengthened?

8. What other benefits, whether physical, emotional, relational, psychological, and spiritual do you desire to achieve during the Conspiracy Fast?

9. What might you discover about yourself during the Conspiracy Fast?

____

____

10. How could the Conspiracy Fast change your life?

____

____

11. What steps would you take to bring out these changes in your life? Who should be involved and to what extent?

____

____

12. Explain why the Jews formed a conspiracy to kill Paul. What kind of threat was Paul to the Judaic ideology? Why was he a threat?

____

____

13. Have you ever conspired to harm someone such as your spouse, neighbour, co-worker, or anyone? This may include even the thought to carry out harm against someone, without taking any action. Briefly describe.

____

____

14. Describe your emotional state surrounding the thought and/or action to harm someone.

____

____

15. If you carried out this scheme, what did you learn?

____

16. What steps should you take to restore the relationship that has been damaged by your actions? If this harm was carried, briefly state the steps that you would take to restore the relationship. If it was only a thought without any action, briefly state the steps that would you take to guard against these thoughts recurring?

17. What does the Word of God say about doing harm against another person or thing? This could include property, an animal, or simply carrying out an act that inflicts physical, emotional, psychological pain, suffering, or loss upon someone or something.

18. What length of time (days) and hours each day will you commit to during the Conspiracy Fast? When do you plan to begin and end your fast?

Prayer

Fasting is one of the spiritual disciplines that the Lord has established for you to achieve the spiritual power and breakthrough not only within your life but also in the lives of those whom are close to your heart. I acknowledge that I have become too comfortable in my current state of living and I sense you Holy Spirit calling me to confront the issues that I have been avoiding and find the freedom to live solely for Jesus Christ. Help me through the Conspiracy Fast to break free from the bondages that have been controlling my life for too long. Therefore, prayerfully consider and write a prayer that you will address to the Lord that reflects a new commitment and dedication to Him.

The Conspiracy Fast Journal

As you progress through this fast, write down any insights the Lord speaks to you, spiritual growth, and personal thoughts to further reflect upon in your walk with the Lord.

The False Teacher's Fast

Please read the following Scripture reference and then respond to the questions that follow.

> The Spirit clearly says that in later times some will abandon the faith and follow deceiving spirits and things taught by demons. Such teachings come through hypocritical liars, whose consciences have been seared as with a hot iron. They forbid people to marry and order them to abstain from certain foods, which God created to be received with thanksgiving by those who believe and who know the truth (1 Tim. 4:1-3).

The following questions are a guide to help you to recognize false teachers and their morally corrupt teachings. You will find freedom and joy as you commit yourself to the Lord, the Word of God, and allow the Holy Spirit who is the Spirit of truth to guide and direct you into all truth. They will also assist you in applying the False Teacher's Fast to your personal life. It is vital that you pray and ask the Holy Spirit to give you the guidance and direction, wisdom, and the best course of action as you complete the False Teacher's Fast.

> But when he, the Spirit of truth, comes, he will guide you into all truth. He will not speak on his own; he will speak only what he hears, and he will tell you what is yet to come. He will bring glory to me by taking from what is mine and making it known to you (Jn. 16:13-14).

> We are from God, and whoever knows God listens to us; but whoever is not from God does not listen to us. This is how we recognize the Spirit of truth and the spirit of falsehood (1 Jn. 4:6).

1. What lessons can we learn from the False Teacher's Fast?

____

____

2. Which lesson has had the greatest impact on your life? Explain.

____

____

3. How is the False Teacher's Fast relevant today?

____

____

4. What is your purpose in the False Teacher's Fast? Be specific. I am fasting to:

____

5. What spiritual power and breakthrough do you desire to unlock through the False Teacher's Fast?

6. If you experienced this spiritual breakthrough, how would your life be different? How would your relationships (family, friends, church) be different or affected by this spiritual breakthrough? Be specific.

7. How can your faith be increased and/or strengthened through the False Teacher's Fast? How will you be benefited by having your faith increased and/or strengthened?

8. What other benefits, whether physical, emotional, relational, psychological, and spiritual do you desire to achieve during the False Teacher's Fast?

9. What might you discover about yourself during the False Teacher's Fast?

10. How could the False Teacher's Fast change your life?

11. What steps would you take to bring out these changes in your life? Who should be involved and to what extent?

____

____

12. Take a moment to reflect on your relationship with the Lord. Do you find that your faith in God is not as strong as you thought? What could you do to strengthen your relationship with the Lord?

____

____

13. Take an inventory of the theology that you have listened to or been exposed to lately and evaluate it against the Word of God like the Bereans in the Book of Acts (17:11). Ask the Holy Spirit who is the Spirit of truth to reveal areas or error. On a separate piece of paper write these down on one side of the paper and then on the other side write the truth from the Word of God.

    Now the Bereans were of more noble character than the Thessalonians, for they received the message with great eagerness and examined the Scriptures every day to see if what Paul said was true (Acts 17:11).

____

____

14. Make a list of the characteristics of false teachers. What can you learn from this list? How can this list better prepare you to understand and confront these types of teachings?

____

____

15. Define apostasy. What does Scripture say about apostasy in the end times? How can we guard ourselves from falling away from the Lord?

____

____

16. How can we set an example as Paul instructed Timothy? What is its relevance in the ends times?

17. How can fasting and prayer help the Christian to live like Jesus Christ and remain strong in faith and finish the race strong like Paul in the end times?

18. Based upon the False Teacher's Fast, to what extent should fasting be a part of the Christian life in the end times?

19. What length of time (days) and hours each day will you commit to during the False Teacher's Fast? When do you plan to begin and end your fast?

Prayer

Fasting is one of the spiritual disciplines that the Lord has established for you to achieve the spiritual power and breakthrough not only within your life but also in the lives of those whom are close to your heart. I acknowledge that I have become too comfortable in my current state of living and I sense you Holy Spirit calling me to confront the issues that I have been avoiding and find the freedom to live solely for Jesus Christ. Help me through the False Teacher's Fast to break free from the bondages that have been controlling my life for too long. Therefore, prayerfully consider and write a prayer that you will address to the Lord that reflects a new commitment and dedication to Him.

The False Teacher's Fast Journal

As you progress through this fast, write down any insights the Lord speaks to you, spiritual growth, and personal thoughts to further reflect upon in your walk with the Lord.

Summary Questions to the Warnings and Abuses Concerning Fasting

1. What are the primary themes throughout the Warnings and Abuses Concerning Fasting? Name them in order of prominence.

____

____

2. What does this show you regarding the types of sins that have affected God's people throughout history?

____

____

3. To what degree are these sins or wickedness still prevalent within your personal life, family, community, city, and/or nation?

____

____

4. What are the primary lessons that we can learn from the Warnings and Abuses Concerning Fasting?

____

____

5. Which fast was the *most* meaningful to you? Why?

____

____

6. Which fast was the *least* meaningful to you? Why?

____

____

____

7. How does your understanding of true fasting, as described in the Warnings and Abuses Concerning Fasting, change the way in which you perceive and respond to our community and culture?

____

____

8. What steps do you need to take to live a life of abundance and freedom from the "sin that so easily entangles"?

   Therefore, since we are surrounded by such a great cloud of witnesses, let us throw off everything that hinders and the sin that so easily entangles, and let us run with perseverance the race marked out for us. Let us fix our eyes on Jesus, the author and perfecter of our faith, who for the joy set before him endured the cross, scorning its shame, and sat down at the right hand of the throne of God. Consider him who endured such opposition from sinful men, so that you will not grow weary and lose heart (Heb. 12:1-3).

____

____

The Warnings and Abuses Concerning Fasting Journal

Take some time to reflect on these fasts. What are some of the common themes that were the most relevant to you? How can finding victory in these areas transform your life?

____

____

____

____

____

____

____

____

Subject Index

Scripture Index

Old Testament

Hebrew and Greek Indexes

Hebrew Index

Greek Index

Author and Person Index

References Cited

Barnes, Albert. *Albert Barnes' Notes on the Bible.* In Rick Meyers, e-Sword, Version 10.2.1, 2000-2012. <http://www.e-sword.net>, n.d.

Barry, John D. and Lazarus Wentz, eds. *The Lexham Bible Dictionary.* Bellingham, WA: Logos Bible Software, 2012.

Brand, Chad, Charles Draper, Archie England et al. *Holman Illustrated Bible Dictionary.* Nashville, TN: Holman Bible Publishers, 2003.

Brooks, Keith. *Summarized Bible: Complete Summary of the New Testament.* Bellingham, WA: Logos Bible Software, 2009.

________. *Summarized Bible: Complete Summary of the Old Testament.* Bellingham, WA: Logos Bible Software, 2009.

Covey, Stephen R. *The 8th Habit: From Effectiveness to Greatness.* New York: Free Press, 2004.

Dockery, David S., ed. *Holman Concise Bible Commentary: Simple, Straightforward Commentary on Every Book of the Bible.* Nashville, TN: Broadman & Holman Publishers, 1998.

Freedman, David Noel, ed. *The Anchor Yale Bible Dictionary.* 6 vols. New York: Doubleday, 1992.

Gaebelein, Frank E., ed. *The Expositor's Bible Commentary, Volume 3: Deuteronomy, Joshua, Judges, Ruth, 1 & 2 Samuel.* Grand Rapids, MI: Zondervan Publishing House. Database © 2010 WORDsearch CROSS e-book, 1992.

________. *The Expositor's Bible Commentary, Volume 6: Isaiah, Jeremiah, Lamentations, Ezekiel.* Grand Rapids, MI: Zondervan Publishing House. Database © 2010 WORDsearch CROSS e-book, 1986.

Gilbrant, Thoralf, ed. *The Complete Biblical Library, Hebrews-Jude.* Springfield, IL: World Library Press, Inc., WORDsearch CROSS e-book, 1989.

________. *The Complete Biblical Library, Matthew.* Springfield, IL: World Library Press, Inc., WORDsearch CROSS e-book, 1988.

________. *The Complete Biblical Library Greek-English Dictionary, Alpha-Gamma.* Springfield, MO: Complete Biblical Library, WORDsearch CROSS e-book, 1991.

________. *The Complete Biblical Library Greek-English Dictionary, Delta-Epsilon.* Springfield, MO: Complete Biblical Library, WORDsearch CROSS e-book, 1991.

________. *The Complete Biblical Library Hebrew-English Dictionary, Gimel-Zayin.* Springfield, IL: World Library Press, Inc., WORDsearch CROSS e-book, 1998.

________. *The Complete Biblical Library Hebrew-English Dictionary, Heth-Yodh.* Springfield, IL: World Library Press, Inc., WORDsearch CROSS e-book, 1998.

________. *The Complete Biblical Library Hebrew-English Dictionary, Kaph-Mem.* Springfield, IL: World Library Press, Inc., WORDsearch CROSS e-book, 1998.

________. *The Complete Biblical Library Hebrew-English Dictionary, Nun-Ayin.* Springfield, IL: World Library Press, Inc., WORDsearch CROSS e-book, 1998.

________. *The Complete Biblical Library Hebrew-English Dictionary, Pe-Resh.* Springfield, IL: World Library Press, Inc., WORDsearch CROSS e-book, 1998.

________. *The Complete Biblical Library Hebrew-English Dictionary, Sin-Taw.* Springfield, IL: World Library Press, Inc., WORDsearch CROSS e-book, 1998.

Hagee, John, *Life's Challenges, Your Opportunities*. Lake Mary, FL: Charisma House, 2009.

Harris, R. Laird, Gleason L. Archer, Jr. and Bruce K. Waltke, eds. *Theological Wordbook of the Old Testament.* electronic ed. Chicago, IL: Moody Press, 1999.

Hastings, James, ed., *Dictionary of the Apostolic Church.* New York: Charles Scribner's Sons, 1918.

Henry, Matthew. *Matthew Henry's Commentary on the Whole Bible: Complete and Unabridged in One Volume.* Peabody, MA: Hendrickson Publishers, 1994.

Keener, Craig S. *The IVP Bible Background Commentary - New Testament.* Downers Grove, IL: InterVarsity Press, WORDsearch CROSS e-book, 1993.

Kittel, Gerhard, Geoffrey W. Bromiley and Gerhard Friedrich, eds. *Theological Dictionary of the New Testament.* electronic ed. 10 vols. Grand Rapids , MI: William B. Eerdmans Publishing Company, 1964.

Kittel, Gerhard, Gerhard Friedrich and Geoffrey W. Bromiley, eds. *Theological Dictionary of the New Testament: Abridged in One Volume.* Grand Rapids, MI: William B. Eerdmans Publishing Company, 1985.

Mays, James Luther, ed. *Harper's Bible Commentary.* San Francisco, CA: Harper & Row, 1988.

Mish, Frederick C. *Merriam-Webster's Collegiate Dictionary.* Springfield, MA: Merriam-Webster, Inc., 2003.

Paschall, Franklin H. and Herschel H. Hobbs, eds. *The Teacher's Bible Commentary: A Concise, Thorough Interpretation of the Entire Bible Designed Especially for Sunday School Teachers.* Nashville, TN: Broadman and Holman Publishers, 1972.

Pink, A. W. *An Exposition of the Sermon on the Mount.* Rick Meyers, e-Sword, Version 10.2.1, 2000-2012, <http://www.e-sword.net>, n.d.

Piper, John. *A Hunger for God: Desiring God Through Fasting and Prayer.* Wheaton, IL: Crossway Books, 1997.

Richards, Lawrence O. *The Bible Readers Companion.* electronic ed. Wheaton, IL: Victor Books, 1991.

Schaff, Philip, ed. *The Nicene & Post-Nicene Fathers of the Christian Church: First Series.* Vol. 1. Edinburgh, UK: T. & T. Clark, WORDsearch CROSS e-book, 1886.

Schultz, Samuel J. and Gary V. Smith, *Exploring the Old Testament*. Wheaton, IL: Crossway Books, 2001).

Towns, Elmer L. *A Journey Through The Old Testament: The Story of how God Developed His People in the Old Testament.* Fort Worth, TX: Harcourt Brace Custom Publishers, 1989.

________. *Fasting for Spiritual Breakthrough.* Ventura, CA: Regal Books, 1996.

Tylor, Edward Burnett. *Primitive Culture.* Vol. 2. Boston, MA: Estes and Lauriat, 1871.

Wallis, Arthur. *God's Chosen Fast: A Spiritual and Practical Guide to Fasting.* Fort Washington, PA: CLC Publications, 1968.

Walvoord, John F. and Roy B. Zuck, eds. *The Bible Knowledge Commentary: An Exposition of the Scriptures.* Vol. 1. Wheaton, IL: Victor Books, 1985.

________. *The Bible Knowledge Commentary: An Exposition of the Scriptures.* Vol. 2. Wheaton, IL: Victor Books, 1985.

Wiersbe, Warren W. *The Bible Exposition Commentary.* Vol. 2. Wheaton, IL: Victor Books, 1996.

Williams, Keith, ed. *Chronological Life Application Study Bible*. Carol Stream, IL: Tyndale House Publishers, Inc., 2012.

Wood, D. R. W., I. Howard Marshall, A. R. Millard et al., eds. *New Bible Dictionary.* 3rd edition. Downers Grove, IL: InterVarsity Press, 1996.

Internet Resources

Bright, Bill. <http://www.unityinchrist.com/prayer/ fasting.htm>. Accessed on November 15, 2013.

________. "Why Should Christians Fast?" <http://www.cru.org/training-and-growth/devotional-life/personal-guide-to-fasting/02-why-you-should-fast.htm>. Accessed on November 15, 2013.

Cove, Gordon. *Revival Now! Through Prayer and Fasting.* <http://rockofroseville.com/files/ 2009/09/Fasting.pdf>. Accessed on November 15, 2013.

Should Christians "Fast" Today? <http://www.bible.ca/d-fasting.htm>. Accessed on November 15, 2013.

"The Eucharistic Fast". <http://www.catholicculture.org/culture/library/dictionary/index.cfm?id= 33400>. Accessed on November 4, 2013.

Towns, Elmer L. *Fasting for Spiritual Breakthrough Study Guide.* <http://digitalcommons.liberty.edu/cgi/viewcontent.cgi?article=1016&context=towns_books>. Accessed on November 15, 2013.

<http://www.enterthebible.org/resourcelink. aspx?rid=343>. Accessed on December 10, 2013.
<http://www.faithcycleministry.org/Fasting/Fasting4.html>. Accessed on December 10, 2013.
<http://www.faithcycleministry.org/content/fasting-9>. Accessed on December 10, 2013.
<http://www.faithcycleministry.org/content/fasting-10>. Accessed on December 10, 2013.

Sheldon Juell is available for speaking engagements and public appearances.
For more information contact:

Sheldon Juell
C/O Advantage Books
P. O. Box 160847
Altamonte Springs, FL 32716

sheldonjuell@yahoo.com

To purchase additional copies of this book or other books published by Advantage Books call our order number at

407-788-3110 (Book Orders Only)

Or visit our bookstore website at:
www.advbookstore.com

Advantage BOOKS

Longwood, Florida, USA
"we bring dreams to life"™
www.advbookstore.com

CPSIA information can be obtained
at www.ICGtesting.com
Printed in the USA
LVOW04s0541250717
542509LV00004B/4/P

9 781597 553872